EDITED BY TED J. PHILLIPS,
DEBORAH MOORE CLARK, AND SUSAN R. FURR

PUB THEOLOGY & BEYOND

NEW OPTIONS FOR RELIGIOUS DISCOURSE

To
James and Kasey

May your futures be as bright as our roaring bonfires.
May your dreams blossom like the flowers in our gardens.
and
May your lives be filled with joy, wonder, and adventure.

Susan and Ted

Advance Praise for *Pub Theology & Beyond*

The vibrant chorus of voices that fill *Pub Theology: New Options for Religious Discourse* injected my spirit with fierce, renewed energy. This collection challenges, educates, and offers abundant inspiration for all who seek deeper meaning and wholeness in a weary world that can so often feel meaningless and broken. I finished every entry giddily desperate to discuss its contents with anyone I could find, which seems not only the point but a sure sign of this book's possibility-packed potential.

—Micah Bucey
Author of The Book of Tiny Prayer:
Daily Meditations from the Plague Year

Church is people, not a building. We meet people where they are, just like Jesus did, with the good news that God loves them. *Pub Theology* gives excellent conversations about how to meet people where they are with conversations that can be healing and powerful. We need fresh expressions like these to be the Body of Christ in our culture.

—Ken Kessler
BGAV, Empower Coaching Director

If you've ever enjoyed a pint or two with good friends at the pub, you know how good it is that the rule barring religion and politics is thrown right out. The pub is the place where real life is talked about, and real theology is done. Deep, broad, and provocative, this book is just what I was looking for to add to the conversation. I welcome its wise and gritty authors to have a seat and give us something of substance to talk about.

—Rev. Ryon Price
Senior Pastor, Broadway Baptist Church
Fort Worth, Texas

One of the most difficult aspects of being a Baptist shaman is we too often practice our craft in isolation. This lovely collection is just the restorative we need post covid to combat our deadening isolation. Like sharing a cold adult beverage poolside with some of our brightest friends and colleagues, these thoughtful considerations can invigorate our theological discussions. The fresh wind of the divine spirit gusts through these pages, occasionally blowing us away.

—*The Rev. Dr. Michael S. Usey*
Lead pastor, College Park: An American Baptist Church
Greensboro, North Carolina

Smyth & Helwys Publishing, Inc.
6316 Peake Road
Macon, Georgia 31210-3960
1-800-747-3016
©2022 by Ted J. Philips, Deborah Moore Clark, and Susan R. Furr
All rights reserved.

Library of Congress Cataloging-in-Publication Data

Names: Phillips, Ted James, editor. | Clarke, Deborah Moore, editor. |
  Furr, Susan R., editor.
Title: Pub theology and beyond : new options for religious discourse /
  edited by Ted James Phillips, Deborah Moore Clarke, and Susan Renee
  Furr.
Description: First. | Macon, GA : Smyth & Helwys Publishing, 2022. |
  Includes bibliographical references.
Identifiers: LCCN 2022007361 | ISBN 9781641733663 (paperback)
Subjects: LCSH: Conversation--Religious aspects--Christianity--Miscellanea.
  | Oral communication--Religious aspects--Christianity--Miscellanea. |
  Witness bearing (Christianity)--Miscellanea. | Theology,
  Doctrinal--Miscellanea.
Classification: LCC BV4597.53.C64 P83 2022 | DDC
  241/.672--dc23/eng/20220412
LC record available at https://lccn.loc.gov/2022007361

Disclaimer of Liability: With respect to statements of opinion or fact available in this work of nonfiction, Smyth & Helwys Publishing Inc. nor any of its employees, makes any warranty, express or implied, or assumes any legal liability or responsibility for the accuracy or completeness of any information disclosed, or represents that its use would not infringe privately-owned rights.

ACKNOWLEDGMENTS

My spiritual journey has been significantly enhanced since I started working on this book. The collective effort was influenced by a wide range of individuals, and I want to thank them for their contributions.

A few years ago, the Reverend Ms. Chrissy Tatum Williamson suggested that I should write a book about pub theology. She is now the senior minister at Greystone Baptist Church in Raleigh, North Carolina.

The Reverend J. Andrew Daugherty started the pub theology group that I have led for seven years. He is now the senior minister at Pine Street Church in Boulder, Colorado. When Andrew departed as the faith formation minister at Myers Park Baptist Church in Charlotte, North Carolina, he asked if he could pass the baton on to me.

Over the years, there has been a natural inflow and outflow of participants in our pub theology group. I want to recognize the longtime, core members of the group: Cynthia Adcock, John Bambach, Jane Brock, Angelina Corbet, Nancy Culp, Alice Hoogenakker, Barbara Lucas, Thomas Lucas, Patterson McCoy, Elaine Price-Hudson, Chaz Seale, Peggy Seale, and Mickey Sigmon. In memoriam: Dottie Burnside and Jerry Hoogenakker.

When I was a psychology and religion major at Carson-Newman University in Jefferson City, Tennessee, the religion professors were helpful with personal guidance and progressive thinking. During the early 1970s, these progressive professors were ahead of their time, and their assistance and leadership cannot be overestimated.

The Reverend Ms. Robin Coira is a retired minister who has given permission to reproduce her Words of Institution that she used when leading and serving Holy Communion at Myers Park Baptist Church.

I am thankful to all the contributors who made this book a reality. They are as follows: Cynthia F. Adcock, W. Benjamin Boswell, Deborah Moore Clark, Nancy E. Culp, J. Andrew Daugherty, Susan R. Furr, Everett C. Goodwin, Bill J. Leonard, Barbara B. Lucas, Mia M. McClain, Cody J. Sanders, John E. Saunders Jr., H. Stephen Shoemaker, Chaz Seale, Peggy Seale, and Oliver M. Thomas.

When I met with the Reverend Ms. Mia McClain in spring 2019 to review our pub theology group, she suggested that I consider contemporary issues as part of our individual meetings. As a result of this discussion, the second half of this book focuses on contemporary topics. She is the current associate minister for faith formation and outreach at Myers Park Baptist Church.

My deepest appreciation and most sincere gratitude go to the Reverend Ms. Deborah Moore Clark, a co-editor, for editing and proofreading most of the chapters. She is the author of *O Come, Let Us Bow Down and Worship*. Additionally, Dr. Susan R. Furr edited four chapters. Susan, a co-editor, is a professor in the counseling department at the University of North Carolina at Charlotte.

I also want to thank my favorite preacher and theologian, the Reverend Dr. Bill J. Leonard, dean emeritus of the Divinity School at Wake Forest University. Dr. Leonard was the founding dean of the Divinity School, and he is the James and Marilyn Dunn professor of Baptist Studies and professor of church history. Bill has published numerous books and articles, and I thank him for providing insightful guidance and direction throughout the entire undertaking.

I also wish to express my sincere appreciation to Leslie Andres for her outstanding editing and assistance with the book. Additionally, my thanks to Holly Bean for her support and responsiveness and to Keith Gammons of Smyth & Helwys. Keith has provided invaluable guidance and leadership during the publishing process.

The last person I am thankful for is my wife, Dr. Susan Furr, who also is a writer, co-editor, and proofreader of this book. She is my lifelong soulmate and closest friend. In our thirty-five-plus years of marriage, she has always supported and loved me. Our journey together has included many incredible travel experiences, and they have been priceless. My life would not be the same without her.

—Ted J. Phillips

CONTENTS

Introduction
WHY PUB THEOLOGY?
Ted J. Phillips
1

Primer
GROUP LEADERSHIP
Susan R. Furr
11

Meeting 1
HOLY COMMUNION: SACRAMENT OF BREAD AND WINE
Ted J. Phillips
25

Meeting 2
CHRISTIAN BAPTISM
John E. Saunders Jr.
39

Meeting 3
THE HIDDEN TREASURE OF SABBATH
H. Stephen Shoemaker
55

Meeting 4
LIFE AS THE WORK OF FAITH
Everett C. Goodwin
65

Meeting 5
A THEOLOGY OF WORSHIP
Deborah Moore Clark
73

Meeting 6
CHURCH AS COMMUNITY
J. Andrew Daugherty
85

Meeting 7
CHURCH AND THE FUTURE
Cody J. Sanders
95

Meeting 8
SPIRITUAL PRACTICES
Ted J. Phillips
105

Meeting 9
THE LORD'S PRAYER . . . THE PERFECT PRAYER?
Chaz Seale and Peggy Seale
127

Meeting 10
A HISTORICAL AND THEOLOGICAL RESPONSE TO SYSTEMIC RACISM: A PROCESS OF LIBERATION
Oliver M. Thomas
139

Meeting 11
SALVATION AND LIBERATION: A RADICAL FAITH
Bill J. Leonard
153

Meeting 12
QUEER THEOLOGY
Nancy E. Culp
163

Meeting 13
WHITENESS
W. Benjamin Boswell
173

Meeting 14
STOLEN COOKIES: A TAKE ON BLACK LIVES MATTERING
Mia M. McClain
183

Meeting 15
THE STRANGER: IMMIGRATION AND SOCIAL JUSTICE
Cynthia F. Adcock
199

Meeting 16
MARGINALIZED PEOPLE
Barbara B. Lucas
211

ABOUT THE CONTRIBUTORS
221

INTRODUCTION

WHY PUB THEOLOGY?
TED J. PHILLIPS

Matthew 18:20 says, "For where two or three are gathered in my name, I am there among them" (NRSV).

INTRODUCTION

The idea for this book started when our family visited one of the most famous pubs in the world, The Eagle. Located in Cambridge, England, The Eagle is like most other English pubs where friends gather to relax, have a pint, have some fun, and discuss whatever comes up. Conversations range from politics and the state of the commonwealth to family, religion, and international issues. However, The Eagle is one of a kind. This is where, on February 28, 1953, Francis Click and James Watson announced the discovery of DNA. On the ceiling in one room is a colored painting of the double helix. Many call this room "Eagle DNA."

Another important room in the rear of The Eagle is referred to as the "RAF bar." This is like no other room we had ever visited before. On the walls and on the ceiling, both British and American pilots of WWII wrote notes to their wives, lovers, and families. They wrote these messages on the walls and ceiling because there was no guarantee that they would return the next day from flying missions over the English Channel into France and Belgium. Their words are still visible today, and they are both fascinating and solemn to read and experience.

Throughout English history, pubs have been places where people of all classes and education discussed all manner of issues. Pubs are leveling spaces where people are viewed as individuals. They certainly do not always agree with one another, but they listen to what each other says, and everyone's opinion and point of view matters. On any given afternoon or evening, there are multiple conversations going on. An idea struck me.

INITIAL QUESTIONS TO CONSIDER

- Are you interested in robust and stimulating discussions on different topics in theology and how they might impact contemporary issues?
- Are you looking to grow or restart your spiritual journey?
- Do you view yourself as spiritually minded?
- Are you an individual who values discussing highly relevant issues in today's world?
- Do you have questions that you are uncomfortable or unwilling to ask at your church or place of worship?

If you answer yes to any of these questions, then *Pub Theology and Beyond: New Options for Religious Discourse* might be the book for you.

During my visit to The Eagle, I discovered for myself the significance and potential of pub theology, where small groups can focus on theology, the study of God, and on contemporary social issues. Pub theology can also offer a space where people engage in *active listening* to others before they contribute their own thoughts. It can be a setting where people ask and share thoughts and feelings they might not share at their church or regular place of worship. As a result, pub theology groups provide leveling spaces where members can truly be themselves.

Pub theology also creates an environment of spirituality and awareness. In *Everything Belongs*, Richard Rohr shares, "Spirituality is about seeing. It's not about earning or achieving. It's about relationship rather than results or requirements."[1] Genuine relationships and effective group process and leadership are critical to the growth of a pub theology group. (Group process and leadership guidelines are presented in the primer chapter, "Group Leadership.")

In addition, this special environment allows all members to be on their respective journeys of faith. They come to rest, relax, be challenged, have fun, learn, and grow. Pub theology provides a setting where the group can discuss a broad range of theological issues and contemporary topics. All people are accepted, and differences of opinion and thought are desired and respected. Over time, more questions than answers are discovered among the respective group members. Ultimately, the experience can have an amazing impact on each person as everyone becomes stronger in thought and action.

---

1. Rohr, *Everything Belongs*, 33.

PUB THEOLOGY: A LOOK BACK

I want to take a look back and provide important background regarding our pub theology group and its impact on me, our members, and Myers Park Baptist Church in Charlotte, North Carolina. Our specific group consists of fourteen long-term core members. In addition, we have had a natural inflow and outflow of other members during the seven years we have met. The group normally averages twelve to eighteen members each time we meet. Over time, we have become a strong interpersonal group with solid relationships, a significantly high level of trust, and an ongoing desire and expectation that we respect and trust one another. For the core members to stay together seven years is a clear testament to what we mean to one another, both individually and collectively. We support one another in times of need and commit ourselves to the goals of the group. Members come prepared, and our discussions are robust, fun, insightful, and spirited.

Our pub theology group was originally started by the Reverend J. Andrew Daugherty, who was the faith formation minister at Myers Park Baptist Church. When he departed, he asked me to take over the leadership and facilitation of the group. In the past seven years, I have led approximately 100 individual pub theology sessions. Topics have included some of the following: Holy Spirit; Is There a Heaven?; Mary Magdalene; Forgiveness and Reconciliation; Capital Punishment; Judas Iscariot: Villain or Hero?; Faith and Works; The Trinity; Theories of Atonement; and Kolberg's Theory of Moral Development.

We typically discuss spiritual topics, but this book has provided the opportunity to broaden our conceptual view to include significant contemporary topics. This is an important additional strength of the book. The contemporary sessions are designed for someone who is just being introduced to a specific topic and also for someone who is searching for more complex questions and answers.

One of the foundational pieces of most churches involves fostering a sense of fellowship and community among its membership. Myers Park Baptist created in their faith formation division a "Connections" framework. This focus provided a variety of experiences that were offered to promote engagement, a stronger sense of community, and deeper and richer interpersonal relationships. Usually, these offerings were a onetime event, or they might last a month or so. Our pub theology group was the exception because we just finished our seventh year. We have taken a sabbatical from our group meetings during the preparation of this book since six core members were assisting with the writing. When all the production requirements have been submitted, we will resume meeting together.

This experience of leading and facilitating our pub theology group has been the most significant part of my spiritual journey in the back half of my life. In leading this type of experience, I have been immersed in the preparation and facilitation of each subject. This has helped me to grow spiritually regarding these various spiritual topics. Additionally, I have become more confident in my skills of listening, facilitating, interacting, reflecting, and summarizing. I have grown in my willingness and dedication to prepare, facilitate, and lead each time the group meets.

WHAT IS PUB THEOLOGY?

Pub theology happens in a space where individuals gather to discuss and explore a variety of issues and topics in a relaxed, supportive, and nonjudgmental environment. It is a leveling space where all are welcome. Therefore, there are no barriers like one's theological understanding or background, socioeconomic or education levels, gender, race, sexual orientation, faith traditions, or age. One person asked if our group was a bunch of men sitting back in their chairs with their arms crossed, smoking cigars. The opposite is true: in our experience, women outnumber the men two to one.

The best approach is to explore one theological topic or a contemporary issue each time the group meets. If you need another meeting to finish your discussion, you certainly have that flexibility. We have discovered that the leader and group members should remain fluid and be responsive to the natural flow of the conversation. However, if the discussion veers off for too long, members have the responsibility to steer the group back to the designated topic.

Regular attendance provides significant benefits for each member and enhances the sense of community for the entire group. The camaraderie and support develop over time, and as a result, members need to make a commitment to be present at every meeting unless otherwise engaged. Only when trust has developed will members begin to open up and take higher levels of risk. Here are some additional factors to consider as you build a pub theology group.

SET A MEETING TIME

Our group meets for ninety minutes, normally from 6:00 to 7:30 p.m. We have learned over time that ninety minutes is well suited to discuss the topic and to take a deeper dive. But you could meet any time during the day or over lunch. The information for the upcoming meeting is emailed out on the preceding Saturday, which gives members the opportunity to read, study, and reflect ahead of time. We have set an expectation that members arrive and be seated by 5:45 p.m. if it is an evening meeting. Some come even earlier to beat the traffic.

START WITH PATIENCE

Patience is needed at the beginning. Try to start with at least nine participants. Group leadership will be discussed in the next chapter, but this core group needs to be highly committed to attending and participating. Commitment is important because trust, respect, and vulnerability will take time to develop. Over time, pub theology members can share the benefits of the experience with others.

ESTABLISH SOME NORMS

Merriam-Webster's Collegiate Dictionary defines a *norm* as a "principle of right action binding upon the members of a group and serving to guide, control, or regulate proper and acceptable behavior." Pub theology norms are a set of guidelines that group members agree to adhere to. I recommend that you review them at the beginning of the fall, spring, and summer.

Below are a set of norms that you can adjust to your own group. These norms are based on ones that originated with Myers Park Baptist Church, but they have been modified to meet our specific needs.

1. Respect each other's points of view. Respect is the essential foundation for a pub theology group. If members cannot accept and respect one another, the group will not function effectively, and the potential for individual and group growth will be lost. Everyone comes from a distinct set of religious traditions and spiritual experiences. One's uniqueness and influential experiences are the springboard for learning and spiritual growth.

2. Maintain an enriching, supportive, and nonjudgmental experience. To maximize the enriching benefits of participation in a pub theology group, each member needs to be supportive of every other member of the group. Differences are appreciated, but it is important that members do not feel or think that they are being judged. If they do, they will not open up and share their amazing and remarkable stories, questions, or ideas. This is a space where members can share questions and concerns that they might not share on their church campuses.

3. *Engage in focused listening.* Another basic expectation is focused listening. This means active and attentive listening where everyone truly listens to what others say rather than thinking about what to share next. The goal is to listen first and contribute second. This condition makes the experience much richer and helps each member to hear what someone is sharing, both verbally and nonverbally.

4. *Try to stick with the guided discussion.* Pub theology involves a guided discussion, although some fluidity can occur. A guided discussion means having a regular process for discussing one specific topic each time you meet. The process includes the following elements:
• a suggested reading to complete in advance,
• a specific focus for the discussion,
• a set of questions as jumping-off points, and
• a limited amount of fluidity.

5. *Establish an environment of confidentiality.* Because we are not in a pure counseling environment, we cannot totally guarantee confidentiality. But all group members agree that "what is said in a pub theology group stays in a pub theology group." This expectation of confidentiality is an ongoing condition within the group. We can expect trust to grow and flourish if this understanding is present each time we meet.

6. *Ensure that the group is open to all and closed to none.* I added this norm a few years ago for a couple of reasons. First, there was a misconception that men dominated in numbers and in participation. The opposite is true, as women in our group outnumber men two to one. Second, as Jesus taught, all are welcome regardless of gender, income, race, sexual orientation, or religious affiliation. Our group primarily comes from a Christian tradition, but we also come from a variety of religious backgrounds.

7. *Encourage each other to get back on topic if you stray too far from the subject.* The leader has primary responsibility for this norm. As mentioned, some fluidity is allowed, but going off on a related issue is only permitted for a limited amount of time. All group members are expected to address the issue if the tangent goes on for too long. Placing full responsibility only on the leader inhibits the discussion and the flow of the topic.

8. *Note that all participants are both learners and teachers.* This norm is a simple reminder that everyone in the group has these two roles. We

share our own truths and also receive help from the contributions of each member. We all grow in this experience in heart, mind, and spirit.

POSSIBLE TIMELINE FOR THE FIRST YEAR

These suggestions can help you plan the first year of your pub theology group.

June and July
- Gain approval for the pub theology group (if needed).
- Find a location and work out the details with the pub manager (if applicable).
- Meetings might be more social in the summer.
- Refer to the end of this introduction for details if you plan to meet in a pub or bar.

August
- Distribute initial publicity materials.
- Approach potential members individually to explain the program and assess their interest and commitment level.

September
- Continue publicity and gain final commitments.
- Develop an email list of participants.
- Two weeks in advance, send an email reminding everyone that the first meeting is the last Tuesday in September.

October
- Consider meeting every other Tuesday. Weekly is too much, and once a month is not enough. Meetings two and three occur in October.
- Remember to send a group email on the preceding Saturday before each meeting.

November
- Meetings four and five occur this month. Avoid the Tuesday before Thanksgiving.

December
- Meetings six and seven occur this month, but be respectful of holiday commitments.
- Lock in spring dates for meetings.
- Consider having a holiday party in a location different from where you normally meet. You might have dinner and play games afterwards.
- Request feedback from participants.

January
- Take the month off.
- Publicize the group and ask group members for their help.

February
- First and second meetings of spring occur this month.

March
- Third and fourth meetings occur this month.
- Avoid St. Patrick's Day, especially if you meet at a pub or bar.

April
- Fifth and sixth meetings occur this month.
- Ask for feedback during the sixth meeting and discuss plans for summer.

May
- Take the month off.
- Prepare for June, July, and August.

June, July, and August
- Meet only once a month to give core members and the leader a break.
- Meetings might be more social in the summer, such as backyard barbecues or pool parties.

August
- Start the process for a new year of the pub theology group.

IF MEETING IN A PUB OR BAR . . .

Find a space with a private meeting room that can comfortably hold nine to fifteen members. The location of the room should be separate from the other part of the establishment. You will not obtain the essential benefits of a pub theology group unless you find a space that meets these criteria:

- Be sure no cover charge is required. This is important because members should feel no pressure to order a certain amount of food and drink. (Many of our members order only water or tea.)
- Meet on Tuesday evenings to avoid conflicts with Monday night or Thursday night NFL football. Tuesdays are traditionally slower evenings for food and drink sales. If you can find the right location, the pub manager will appreciate the business and free publicity.
- Avoid music or television in the room where you meet. You need a space where everyone can hear one another.
- Have the early arrivals sit farthest away from the entrance. When a member arrives late, this helps the server minimize the disruption of taking and delivering their food and drink orders.
- Configure the tables so everyone can see and hear each other. This can be a challenge, but both verbal and nonverbal communication is important in a pub theology group. We connect the tables to make one large table so we can see each other.
- Be mindful of the parking regulations around the pub. Illegal parking is not recommended.
- Discuss expectations with the primary server as soon as the group leader arrives. It's best for the server to take drink and food orders ahead of the discussion. The benefit is that the server delivers orders with little disruption to the conversation.
- Be cautious about alcohol consumption. In our group, members who do drink have only one or two beers or glasses of wine during the ninety-minute meeting. Participants often order something to eat, and this is important too. Sharing a meal is part of our connecting process.

CONCLUSION

Pub theology needs an environment where discussions are centered on theology and current issues and how they relate to our lives today. The overriding principle and purpose of the group is to explore a topic of theology or a contemporary issue. This book is designed to supply everything you need for the first year. In the following chapters, you will see a variety of topics—some expected and some unexpected. We do not discuss our respective churches at pub theology group meetings. We are centered solely on the topic before us. Normally, we recommend some type of reading in advance, whether it is provided by the leader or members find it themselves. In addition, we encourage information from various sources and usually create some "deep dive" questions as "jumping-off" points for the discussion.

Pub theology should promote a safe and open environment for robust and enlightening discussions. The benefits of this type of group range from spiritual growth and understanding to asking questions that might not normally be asked on a church campus. Members actively listen before they speak, and growth occurs both individually and collectively. In addition, there are norms for the group to follow. Discussions focus on a variety of spiritual topics and contemporary issues that are affecting individuals and communities today.

BIBLIOGRAPHY

Attridge, Harold W. *The HarperCollins Study Bible*. San Francisco: HarperOne, 2006.

Rohr, Richard. *Everything Belongs*. New York: Crossroad Publishing, 2003.

GROUP LEADERSHIP

SUSAN R. FURR

The key to developing a successful pub theology group is effective leadership. Without a leader who is skilled in facilitation, active listening, questioning, reflecting, modeling, and even confronting, the group can devolve into a forum for arguing personal opinions as opposed to stimulating deeper exploration. A successful group becomes more than just a collection of individuals.[1] These individuals have a shared purpose and focus with a commitment to work together to achieve mutual goals.[2] It is the job of the leader to create a safe and supportive environment for this type of process to develop. While the leader wants to foster connections among members, it is also important to define the group in such a way that it does not become a therapy or personal support group where members address underlying personal issues. Walking a line between being supportive but not delving into individual mental health issues can present a challenge to the leader. Being prepared to address these issues if they arise is important for keeping the group on track to meet its primary purpose. In this primer, we will address how to initially set up a group, the stages of group development, and essential leadership skills.

ESTABLISHING THE GROUP

While pub theology groups often originate within a church setting, group membership is generally open to anyone who is interested in participating. Inclusiveness is an important value, but it is essential that those who are interested in joining have a clear understanding of the purpose of the group, the way the group will operate, and the commitment expected when joining. One of the most effective ways to reduce possible problem

---

1. Conyne, *Group Work Leadership*, 8.
2. Conyne, Crowell, and Newmeyer, *Group Techniques*, 6.

behavior is for people to be informed about the expectations before joining. For example, some members may recall college days when deep, late-night discussions were accompanied by drinking and occasionally evolved into spirited arguments. They may long for this type of open forum and the chance to challenge the beliefs of others. A diversity of viewpoints definitely facilitates growth among members but also needs to occur in a way that does not threaten other members. By understanding the goals and purpose of the group, those who choose to participate will value the importance of healthy group dynamics.

ADVERTISING THE GROUP

In many religious organizations, a menu of different groups and activities is offered yearly, and these groups are well publicized. It is the leader's responsibility to create a description of the group that establishes a "clarity of purpose" statement that defines the purpose of the group; without such clarity, the group is likely to fail.[3] Having a lay member review this statement can be useful in getting a sense of how well potential members will understand the purpose and nature of the group.

As part of setting up the group, finding an appropriate space may be one of the biggest challenges. Finding a pub setting that (1) has a private space for a small group and (2) provides seating arrangements that allow for everyone to have a place around the table can be difficult. A private room is essential if members are to feel safe enough to share and explore new ideas. Sitting in some type of circular arrangement is necessary for members to become actively engaged.[4] This type of seating arrangement conveys equality and gives all members a chance to be equally involved. To accomplish this arrangement, a room with movable tables that can be pushed together where all members can see each other is preferable. Although tables might be viewed as creating a barrier in situations where self-disclosure is expected, this type of group may benefit from having space to share a meal or to organize materials such as handouts or questionnaires to stimulate discussion. Given these constraints, it is important that the number of members be limited to a maximum of fifteen or twenty people. Although members do not have to attend each session, which may occur biweekly, it is important for them to attend regularly in order for group dynamics to develop. Connections between members only develop if

---

3. Gladding, *Groups*, 34.
4. Ibid., 36.

people see each other regularly. Group size needs to ensure that the ideal ten to twelve members are present each meeting. If too many people attend, there is not enough space for everyone to participate; if too few are present, the power of the group is diminished. When the group becomes too large, the meeting will turn into a symposium with the leader becoming the focus of the group. Enough members need to be present each week for the discussion to be lively with varying perspectives. Group dynamics often work best with ten to twelve members. Given that not everyone will be able to attend each meeting, it is important to have a larger pool to draw from so the group can accommodate absences. Having a clear purpose for the group along with specific and practical procedures will contribute to the success of the group.[5] Information such as a definitive starting date and ending date will allow members to make a clear commitment to the group. In our experience, a member committed for the fall meetings could decide to continue meeting in the spring.

GROUP RULES AND GENERAL EXPECTATIONS

For many people, pub theology will be a new experience, creating some anxiety or apprehension in the members as well as the leader.[6] Even experienced leaders may feel some anxiety upon starting a new group. Will members become engaged in the group? Will conflicts emerge because of differing views? In continuing groups, adding new members will affect previous dynamics in the interactions. It is important to see this anxiety as normal in the beginning stages of a group and address it by establishing clear rules and expectations.

One place to begin addressing any concerns is through a review of the advertised group goals. Members need to be aligned with the common purpose of the group. The leader can accomplish this by reviewing the purpose of the group and having members share their reasons for joining or continuing when a new series is begun. As members share, the leader can point out similarities among members, which will help build group cohesion. When differences arise in some members' purpose for joining, the leader needs to be astute about how to respond. Welcoming differences may help the group gain a broader perspective. But if the reason the member is joining appears contrary to the purpose of the group, it will be important to acknowledge that the group may not meet that particular

---

5. Jacobs, Masson, Harvill, and Schimmel, *Group Counseling*, 47.
6. Gladding, *Groups*, 39.

goal.[7] If there is a great discrepancy between the purpose of the group and what a member expects from the group, a private conversation after the meeting may be needed to prevent future disruption. Not every group can meet every person's goals.

Once members have defined and agreed on the group's purpose, leaders must establish guidelines to manage how the group is facilitated. Both the leader and members need to know how to be accountable for their own behaviors. This process can occur in two ways: leaders may initiate a general rule, and members may add and refine this rule.[8] One way to begin the group is to introduce the topic of group rules or guidelines for the purpose of helping members function to their maximum potential. Ask members what they believe would make the group a safe and stimulating experience. Through this sharing process, the leader can begin summarizing what is important to members in terms of the behavior of the participants. Before beginning the group, it is helpful for the leader to identify key rules the leader believes are necessary for the group to function well. When possible, state rules in a positive way such as "members will listen to each other respectfully" as opposed to "no interrupting." The leader can bring up these suggestions if the group does not identify them.

One key problem that has been identified in group interactions is related to time management and not allowing one member to dominate the meeting.[9] The leader can set criteria for how much time is allotted to an activity or how much time everyone has when sharing during a group round. Some groups have a "time keeper" for each meeting who will remind everyone when it is time to shift to a new topic. While rules such as respecting each other are an important foundation for the group, it can be helpful to operationalize this type of guideline by adding some behavioral descriptors such as "members will demonstrate respect for each other by sharing their thoughts using 'I' messages" or "members will allow other members to complete their ideas without interrupting."

Because this is not a counseling group, the issue of confidentiality may not seem relevant. Yet because members may want to explore ideas that do not always align with church doctrine, members need to have a sense of safety to share formative thoughts and question traditions without

---

7. Bridbord, DeLucia-Waack, Jones, and Gerrity, "The nonsignificant impact of an agenda setting treatment for groups," 302.

8. Gladding, *Groups*, 91.

9. Jacobs et al., *Group Counseling*, 398.

worrying that they will be reported back to church staff. Members may agree to the concept of confidentiality yet may find it difficult to enforce. Confidentiality has been viewed as an important component of building group trust and cohesion even in groups that are not counseling oriented.[10] The leader may want to give examples of ways that confidentiality may be violated, such as members sharing thoughts expressed by specific group members to people outside of the group. Members are always free to share any of their own thoughts with others but do need to respect the privacy of other group members.

GROUP STAGES AND DYNAMICS

BEGINNING STAGE

Group leaders must understand that groups evolve over time. As mentioned previously, apprehension is common in early meetings and will dissipate once members develop an understanding of how the group will operate. In these opening stages, members may benefit from having structure that gives direction for what is expected from them.[11] Initially, leaders may focus on giving the power of the group to the members and might open the meeting by asking for their thoughts—only to be met by silence. When leaders add structure at the beginning, however, members will be more inclined to connect with others in the group. For example, going over the purpose of the group and the format for each session may facilitate the members gaining an understanding that they are in the group for a common purpose. This presentation should probably take no more than a few minutes. Then the leader can move to some type of introductory exercise.

One way of building early cohesion is to have members pair with someone they do not know well and share information about any past history related to joining the group. By providing members with possible questions to answer, the leader can lay the foundation for finding commonalities among members. After interacting for the designated amount of time (the leader always needs to let members know time limits), the pairs can regroup and introduce their partners. This activity can also take place with just "going around the circle" and having members share the same information with the entire group. As the members share, the leader is listening

---

10. Corey, Williams, and Moline, "Ethical and legal issues in group counseling," doi.org/10.1207/s15327019eb0502_4.

11. Jacobs et al., *Group Counseling*, 76.

carefully and looking for either similarities among members or unique qualities a member is bringing to the group. Keep in mind that involving group members in these early meetings is crucial to building a strong foundation for the success of the pub theology group but will not result in immediate connections. These beginning meetings are about stimulating interest and building a safe environment for exploration where members begin forming a common identity. If all voices are heard and respected, members will begin to develop an attachment to the group that makes it a vital part of their personal exploration and growth. One powerful force that is seen in early meetings is a sense of universality or the concept that members share a common thread. In pub theology, that thread is the openness to exploring religious beliefs, traditions, and doctrines in a nonjudgmental atmosphere. Members will need to "test" that this atmosphere is genuine before being willing to dive deeply into complex ideas.

Closing any group session takes more than announcing "our time is up." It is recommended that leaders allot at least ten minutes at the end for summarizing and addressing any "loose ends."[12] The leader can facilitate this process by asking open-ended questions such as "What is one idea from today's meeting that you will reflect on this week?" or "What surprised you the most about our discussion tonight?" It may also be important to check on any strong emotions that were triggered by the discussion and assess how the members will deal with these feelings in the coming week. Ideas that emerge from group discussions may challenge long-held beliefs and be distressing for participants. Because of these emotions, members often need time to reflect on what was shared or new questions that have arisen. Some may also want to express personal reactions to the discussions that occurred. This can also be a time for the leader to "plant seeds" about the next meeting. The leader may want to stay around for a few minutes after the meeting to address individual questions but needs to be cautious about getting into an extensive discussion with individuals, as this may be viewed as favoring some members over others. Discussions about the group and how it is operating need to take place within the group.

MIDDLE STAGE

In counseling groups, there is often a period of group transition as the members move from getting to know one another to testing the limits of the group. Members may form alliances with others whom they believe

---

12. Ibid., 177.

share similar beliefs and may even challenge those whom they perceive as different from them. They may try to get the leader to join their side as a way of validating their values. Some group theorists have labeled this stage as "storming," where members may have competing ideas. Although many groups have little difficulty with this stage, the leader needs to be aware of conflicts that evolve and are either avoided, leading to shutting down group discussion, or dwelled on, making the group get stuck on a single issue. One sign that there may be underlying conflict is a drop in attendance in the group. Another indicator of issues may be demonstrated by a decrease in energy over several meetings. The leader may want to observe if the loss of interest is from a few individuals or the group as a whole. A good practice is to check in periodically to see if the group is still addressing members' needs or if a change of direction is needed. If there is concern that the group will hesitate to give constructive feedback for fear of hurting the leader, then some type of anonymous feedback system can be developed. Groups do run a natural course where the need has been fulfilled and the group is no longer helpful. This issue can be addressed by the group as a whole or by approaching the individuals who seem to have lost interest. After several weeks, members should have developed a comfortable working relationship with the leader and other members. There is even the possibility that new topics for discussion will emerge from members, with the members willing to assume the role of facilitator for these topics. If this happens, the presence of the leader is still beneficial in keeping the group focused and providing skills to address any conflicts.

A number of issues can arise during the middle stage.[13] While the earlier meetings need structure to reduce anxiety, less structure is needed as trust builds among members. Members still may like some predictability in format but often are ready to take on more responsibility for the group discussion. Leaders may continue to over-lead the group and not give space for the members' contributions. As the group forms stronger relationships, it is also easy to let the beginning of the group focus on updates from each member, leaving little time for the topic at hand. Over time, the leader may need to assess if the group has become more of a social group than a group that fosters exploration. One indicator of this change is when the focus of the group shifts frequently from the original topic. Such shifting will prevent the group from gaining a deeper understanding of the topic.

---

13. Ibid.

As the group progresses, members may begin to settle into roles where a few of them dominate the discussion, resulting in some members feeling devalued or ignored. It is up to the leader to shift the focus to include other members and to redirect discussions in ways that involve everyone. At times, it might be necessary to revisit the guidelines and remind members of keeping the group open to all. During this working phase of the group, the leader must often balance how much material to introduce (group content) and how much time to allow for discussion and reflection (group process). The content is the foundation of fostering discussion, so it needs to be selected carefully to provide direction for the group. Although material can be sent in advance of the meeting, keep in mind that most members live busy lives and may not have time to read in advance. Be mindful not to base the group on work done during personal time, or you might have members at two different levels of understanding. The activities will be more effective if they are not dependent on outside work. While covering the content is important, it is also critical to allot time for processing the material. Meaning is derived through reflection on new ideas. Members need to be challenged with ideas that stretch their conceptions and perhaps even make them uncomfortable. It is through increasing their cognitive complexity that deeper meaning is derived and a stronger belief system emerges. The leader cannot teach this meaning—it has to be derived by the members through reflection and contemplation. And the leader has to be open to the idea that individuals will arrive at different meaning-making systems that enrich their own spiritual experiences.

CLOSING STAGE

Finally, the group will enter the closing stage. Not only is a closing needed for each session, but members need to be aware of the ending date and be reminded of it in advance. Typically, the final session is focused on synthesizing the significant ideas that emerged from the group. It is a time for summarizing the experience of being in pub theology and reviewing personal gains of members. This can also be a good time to have members reflect on how they will use this experience to foster their own spiritual growth and perhaps commit to making certain changes in their lives. Members need a chance as well to express appreciation to fellow members and hopes they may have for them. If there were topics that were not addressed but are still lingering, these can be identified and used as information for future groups. Often, groups like these resume when a new church calendar is created. There may be a core group of members who want to continue as new members also join. Some of the same procedures need to be followed to ensure that the new group becomes cohesive and productive.

GROUP FACILITATION SKILLS

Facilitating a pub theology group may be quite different from teaching a Sunday school class or leading a committee meeting. Although there will be some preparation of content to present to the group and some design of activities to stimulate discussion, the leader will be charged with encouraging member involvement, maintaining the focus of the group, and intervening when members engage in distracting behaviors. E. E. Jacobs and others have identified a number of helpful strategies and skills needed by group leaders.[14]

STRATEGIES FOR INVOLVING MEMBERS

One way to engage members is to use group *rounds* in which the leader asks everyone around the circle to respond to a question or prompt. This activity both creates the expectation that everyone will be involved in the group and also sets the focus of the group. In early stages, rounds are a good way to begin meetings and can serve as a way of getting everyone to reintroduce themselves in a group where few know each other. Rounds can also be helpful for ending a meeting by having everyone share something they can take away from that experience. A simple closing may include sharing one thing that stood out to each person in a short phrase or word.

Another way to make sure members are involved is to allow pairs of members to discuss an idea and then come back and share in the larger group. For members who may be hesitant to speak in front of others, pairs provide the opportunity to test an idea before taking a risk with the larger group. It can be helpful to make sure people pair up with someone other than the person they have chosen to sit next to, particularly if friends or partners are attending the group together. This is a great strategy to build group cohesion among those who might not know each other well.

Finally, the leader can engage in *linking* members by pointing out similarities that connect different members. This is a way of helping members feel more connected in their journeys by pointing out that they are not alone. Often just a simple statement, such as "That is similar to the

---

14. Ibid., 129–67.

question Anne has been struggling with," can help build cohesion among the members. This skill is particularly useful in the early stages of the group.

FOCUSING THE GROUP

A challenge for group leaders can be how long to stay on a topic and when to shift the focus. If the focus is held too long, members may lose interest, yet allowing the group to shift focus frequently or rapidly will not encourage in-depth discussion. A guideline for holding the focus is based on whether the discussion is still relevant to the topic of the meeting and whether members are still interested in the topic. One way to judge the importance of the current focus is to consider what the leader provided in advance of that day's meeting. For example, if the leader gave a four-point outline to cover, and only one point has been addressed halfway through the meeting, then it might be important to shift to the next topic. The leader can simply indicate a need to move forward based on the agenda. If interest in the topic has decreased, then the leader needs to note that and see if the group is ready to shift to the next topic.

There also may be times when the leader needs to hold the focus, such as when one member brings up a new topic that distracts from the current discussion. It is important for the leader to act quickly to redirect the group back to the current topic, perhaps by asking the member if the topic can be put on hold until the group finishes discussing the current topic. Then it is important for the leader to return later to the topic that has been put on hold to see if it is still relevant to the group. The primary purpose of pub theology is to facilitate members gaining a deeper understanding of conventional religious and spiritual tenets and their beliefs around these topics. Delving deeper into different theological perspectives can be challenging for members and will require both time and a supportive environment. Shifting topics too quickly can derail this process.

However, there are instances when a topic is exhausted and the discussion becomes repetitive. The leader is faced with two choices—shift to a new topic or find a way to deepen the focus. To maintain energy, the leader can acknowledge that the group seems finished with this topic and then introduce the next topic on the agenda. But if a deeper focus is desired, the leader needs to be able to ask thought-provoking questions that can challenge members to consider other points of view. The leader may even consider creating these probing questions in advance in order to be prepared for moving the group to a more insightful level of discussion.

Typically, moving to a deeper level should occur only after the group has developed trust, which happens during the middle stage of the group. It is also important to make sure there is enough time left in the meeting to adequately process these deeper reflections. Because moving to a deeper level often involves sharing more personal information and reactions, the leader needs to be sure the members are prepared to handle it. Perhaps a member had a crisis of faith related to rejection because of sexual orientation. The leader needs to be aware of the level of support that is available within the group before encouraging more personal disclosure. At times, keeping the focus on an issue (in this example, the church's view on sexual orientation) rather than on the member's personal experience might prevent the group from becoming a therapy group, which is not its purpose.

FACILITATING SKILLS

Two key skills in facilitating a group are cutting off and drawing out members. While drawing out a member seems socially appropriate, cutting off a member may be contrary to how we normally communicate.[15] Consider addressing these processes during the rule-setting portion of the first meeting. Members need to understand the importance of keeping the group focused, so one of the leader's responsibilities is to interject when comments evolve into storytelling that moves the group away from the topic. Additionally, when comments become harmful to other members, the leader needs to intervene. The crucial issue for the leader is how to cut off comments in a respectful but clear way so members understand why they are being cut off. For example, a member may begin expressing anger at a previous religious affiliation and describing how this group was harmful. As this expression evolves into a personal tirade, the leader observes other members becoming uncomfortable and intervenes by saying to the member, "This seems like an important issue for you. How can the group help you with this?" Or perhaps a member begins focusing on issues that are not congruent with the group's purpose. During times of intense political discussion, a group member may try to engage other members in political debates to see where they stand. The leader can redirect the discussion by asking how this focus fits with the purpose of the group and what the other members want to focus on. Any type of strong, personal value statement that places judgments on others needs to be blocked by the leader so that discussion returns to the whole group. Group members

---

15. Ibid., 168.

will feel a sense of safety when they recognize that the leader will not allow another member to engage in inappropriate behaviors.

Drawing out members is often easier for the leader. This skill begins with observing members and paying attention to those who have not shared. Sometimes just using eye contact with a quiet member will invite the person to participate. Other times, acknowledging that the group has not heard from some members but would value what they have to say will be an encouragement. Keep in mind that more introverted members may need time to think about what they want to say, so allow them a few moments to think about a question before asking for input. Be sure to acknowledge responses from all members—appreciation for sharing is an encouragement for everyone.

ACTIVE LISTENING SKILLS

One way to help members feel heard is by using active listening skills. Although these skills appear to be simple, they have to be consciously practiced. *Restating* is one such skill that involves repeating what was just said but using slightly different language to let members know they are heard. A similar skill is *summarizing*, where the leader pulls together important elements from a discussion to help organize several perspectives. *Questioning* should follow the Socratic approach of asking open-ended questions that lead to deeper exploration and include the use of "what" and "how." This type of questioning encourages further exploration and stimulates the group's thinking. Allowing *silence* can be productive for the group, allowing members time to reflect and integrate ideas. It can be tempting to jump in and rescue members who begin feeling uncomfortable with silence, but let the pressure work for the group. Members often begin to bring up their own ideas that would have stayed hidden otherwise.

CONCLUSION

The freedom to explore ideas and values within the format of a pub theology group provides a welcomed opportunity for members who want more active involvement in their spiritual journeys. The group leader provides a structure to allow this process to evolve in a safe and meaningful environment. The advantage of using a group process is that the leader does not have to provide answers for the members but only organizes the vehicle for their journey. The only way to learn to facilitate a group effectively is to join in this process and learn from your experiences. As long as members feel accepted and respected, they will grow and benefit from this experience.

BIBLIOGRAPHY

Bridbord, K., J. DeLucia-Waack, E. Jones, and D. Gerrity. "The nonsignificant impact of an agenda setting treatment for groups: Implications for future research and practice." *Journal for Specialists in Group Work* 29/3 (2004). doi.org/10.1080/01933920490477129.

Conyne, R. K. *Group Work Leadership: An Introduction for Helpers*. Thousand Oaks, CA: Sage, 2014.

Conyne, R. K, J. L. Crowell, and M. D. Newmeyer. *Group Techniques: How to Use Them Purposefully*. Upper Saddle River, NJ: Pearson, 2008.

Corey, G., G. Williams, and M. Moline. "Ethical and legal issues in group counseling." *Ethics & Behavior* 5/2 (1995). doi.org/10.1207/s15327019eb0502_4.

Gladding, S. T. *Groups: A Counseling Specialty*. Boston: Pearson, 2016.

Jacobs, E. E., R. L. Masson, R. L. Harvill, and C. J. Schimmel. *Group Counseling: Strategies and Skills*. Belmont, CA: Brooks/Cole, 2012.

MEETING 1

HOLY COMMUNION: SACRAMENT OF BREAD AND WINE

TED J. PHILLIPS

Each of the meeting chapters from this point forward covers either a spiritual topic or a contemporary issue. I've suggested Holy Communion as the topic for your pub theology group's first meeting because most people will have some familiarity with it. There is no set order to the chapter topics, but some are more complicated than others. You might want to consider less controversial topics for the first couple of months as your group forms and builds trust.

Each session follows this general outline:

- Welcome by the leader
- Refreshments as the meeting begins
- Short icebreaker
- Quick reminder of the pub theology guidelines or expectations
- Facilitator's introduction of the meeting's topic
- Discussion of the subject and movement to the jumping-off points in which the facilitator and other members will encourage an engaging, honest, and robust conversation
- Closing remarks by the leader or facilitator

GETTING TO KNOW EACH OTHER

Group members are asked to introduce themselves in no specific order. The leader may want to model the introduction by indicating that they will go first. Provide the introductory information in advance so everyone will be prepared.

Group members are to share
- Name
- Faith tradition
- Hopes and expectations for the pub theology group
- Something about themselves that no one in the group knows

Since introductions take place during this first meeting, the topic on Holy Communion may extend into the second meeting. Each meeting also provides icebreakers at the end of each reading, prior to the Jumping-Off Points, and they provide a casual way to offer participants another way to get to know one another.

REVIEWING PUB THEOLOGY NORMS

Refer to the introduction (page 1) for the descriptions of these norms. Review all of them during the first meeting. After the norms are discussed, ask group members if they agree with the norms. If disagreements emerge, discuss the norms further. Once these expectations are established, begin the topic discussion. We've included information below on the topic of Holy Communion. Leaders can research the topic and decide how to guide the conversation.

OVERVIEW

Holy Communion, the sacrament of bread and wine, is one of the most important sacraments in Christianity. There are two primary elements: The first is the significance of the bread and wine. Bread was the primary daily staple in the time of Jesus and the early church. Wine was shared at meals, with guests, at dinners, at weddings, and at other special events. Both were vital components when individuals and groups met together. The second element is the "sacrament" itself. A sacrament is a religious ceremony where an individual or a group has a special kind of grace conveyed to them. For Christians, the sacrament of bread and wine is a foundational experience where Christians encounter and remember Jesus, his life, and his ministry.

THE BREAD AND WINE

The sharing of food around a table is central to the biblical narrative. Bread and wine are significant in both the Old and New Testaments. During the time of Moses, the chosen people of God traveled through the wilderness for many years. Within this Bible story, the chosen people stated that they were hungry. As a result, they remarked that they were better off when they were slaves back in Egypt. The story continues with God hearing their concerns and providing manna for them to eat. God continued to supply this manna daily. (See Exodus 16.)

Earlier in the Old Testament, while they were slaves in Egypt, an angel warned God's chosen people of a terrible pending event. They were to mark their entrance doors with the blood of a lamb. If the doorway was marked with blood, the "death angel" would "pass over" that home, and no harm would come to the firstborn son. What do you think about the "death angel"? Have you ever imagined what it was like that horrific night? The "passing over" event has been remembered and celebrated through the centuries by the Jewish people. The event is called the "Passover" celebration, and it continues even today. In 2022, the Jewish Passover was from Friday, April 15, to Saturday, April 23. The Passover meal involves a shared family meal in one's own home. It is not experienced through collective worship like the Christian celebration of Easter, which in 2022 occurred during the Passover celebration. During the Passover meal, unleavened bread and wine are used; all leavened bread and grain must be removed from the home. In general, the Passover season parallels Christianity's Easter season. As an example, Jesus' last meal with his disciples was celebrating their Passover meal together. This meal in Christianity became Holy Communion or the Last Supper.

During the time of Jesus, when individuals, families, and guests ate together, it was one of their most important social activities. They considered bread a necessity of life. When people ate together, it signaled a bond of acceptance and openness. When you invite special people in your life to dine within your home, what is important about this event? What does it mean to you?

In the New Testament, the presence of bread and wine was an important part of everyone's daily life, and this included special events. In John 2:3-8, Jesus is attending a wedding when something interesting happens.

> When the wine gave out, the mother of Jesus said to him, "They have no wine." And Jesus said to her, "Woman, what concern is that to you and to me? My hour has not yet come." His mother said to the servants, "Do whatever he tells you." Now standing there were six stone water jars for the Jewish rights of purification, each holding twenty or thirty gallons. Jesus said to them, "Fill the jars with water." And they filled them up to the brim. He said to them, "Now draw some out, and take it to the chief steward." So they took it.[1]

The story goes on to say that normally the best wine was served first, and when that was gone, inferior wine was brought out to drink. Here, the best wine was served last, and this caused the wine steward to be confused. The story continues to say that Jesus' disciples believed in him and stayed with him. Imagine that you are attending this wedding. Describe your reaction when you observe that Jesus has turned vats of water into wine.

When individuals sit down to eat with one another, special things can happen. James K. A. Smith in *You Are What You Love* says, "There is a social, even political, reality enacted here; there are no box seats at this table, no reservations for VIPs, no filet mignon for those who can afford it while the rest eat breadcrumbs from the table."[2] Eating with Jesus was a leveling experience. In *The Wisdom Jesus*, Cynthia Bourgeault remarks about Jesus, "His two great requests were that we 'love one another as I have loved you' and that we share bread and wine together as an open channel of that interabiding love."[3] People usually do not sit down with one another unless they share a basic amount of acceptance and trust. As time passes, their bonds grow stronger. What have you witnessed when people who do not know each other well eat together?

Learning, building trust, and sharing community are all potential benefits when eating a meal with others. Sharing a meal can lead to discussions of issues of faith, observations of systemic concerns of inequity, and, most importantly, better understandings of one another. Differences of opinion and perspective do exist, but any differences should be treated with respect. Deeper levels of growth and understanding can emerge from these conversations. Trust, acceptance, and care make the fellowship stronger. This evolution means even more risk-taking and transparency as the group gets closer and closer. This process also gives individuals a better sense of

---

1. Attridge, *HarperCollins Study Bible*, 1818.
2. Smith, *You Are What You Love*, 98.
3. Bourgeault, *Wisdom Jesus*, 188.

empathy—the willingness to "walk in another person's shoes," to imagine their perspectives and feelings. How do you feel when you find yourself in a similar situation?

Jesus continuously demonstrated empathy. His empathy extended to his willingness to have meals with the less fortunate, the poor, and the oppressed. Jesus sat and ate with tax collectors, women, and other marginalized individuals. He was criticized for his actions, but his ministry focused on these individuals and groups of people. If Jesus were here today, who would he be eating with?

Now let's look at the concept of the bread and wine from a different point of view. How important are the bread and wine to you? Enlarge this idea to your use of all food and drink. Is your need being met? Each of us has our own lenses that affect how we perceive and view the world. These lenses help form our thoughts, habits, and behaviors. Think about where you were born, where you grew up, how often you went to your family's place of worship, and where you went to school. All these experiences affected who you are now. Were you born in the Midwest, Northeast, West, South, or in another country? Each of these geographic areas also affects our perceptions of the world.

I have been fortunate that my wife showed me the benefits of traveling outside of the United States. My view of the world and people in it changed the first time we went to Europe. I truly wish that more Americans had the opportunity to visit other countries. Traveling to other countries means seeing how people belonging to other cultures live; it means sitting down, eating, and talking with people who are different from us. This is where real learning and understanding start to happen. As a result, we begin to view others through a different set of thoughts, feelings, and assumptions. Traveling can be life changing.

Since we have discussed the bread and wine from a variety of stories, we will now examine the sacrament of Holy Communion. Jesus' last meal with his disciples may have become the initial practice that many Christians call "Holy Communion," the Lord's Supper, and the Eucharist.

HOLY COMMUNION

The practice of Holy Communion has grown over the centuries, and many Christians believe that it is the most important sacrament. Holy Communion was instituted by Jesus during the last meal before his arrest and crucifixion. A sacrament might be described as the intersection of God and individuals. The sacrament of Holy Communion focuses on *what it becomes* or *what it symbolizes*. It is practiced by Roman Catholicism, Eastern Orthodox, and Protestant denominations. *Harper's Bible Dictionary* defines sacraments as "religious ceremonies in which visible means are used in the belief that a special divine grace is, or may be, thereby conveyed to the subject. The Bible does not use the term, though the meaning is biblical."[4] A sacrament is a rite that symbolizes an aspect of faith.

Holy Communion creates a special environment of remembrance and celebration. It helps us remember that God was in Christ. Marcus J. Borg, in *Speaking Christian*, writes that "Gathering at a table for bread and wine has been an essential practice in Christianity from its beginning and continues to be celebrated as the 'primary Christian sacrament.'"[5] Holy Communion symbolizes a new covenant. Therefore, it can be viewed as a primary portal for our interactions with Jesus, God, and the Holy Spirit. Holy Communion is also a unique reminder that Jesus is always central to our worship. It is conducted as a communal activity, and the atmosphere is attuned to the quiet work of the Holy Spirit. What does the practice of Holy Communion mean to you? How does your church perform this sacrament?

Roman Catholics, Greek Orthodox, and certain Protestants including Lutherans and members of the Anglican communion participate in the Eucharist each time they gather for worship. The Greek word for Eucharist is from *eucharistos*, and it means grateful and thankful.[6] Gratitude is viewed as a foundational component of the experience. Borg shares that "The Eucharist is about food, shared food, and inclusivity; it is about becoming one with Christ and one in Christ; it is about spiritual food for the journey; and it is about participating in Jesus' passion for a different kind of world."[7] Other Protestant denominations do Holy Communion periodically, which might be quarterly or on special days like Easter and Christmas Eve.

Smith states, "The Lord's Supper isn't just a way to remember something that was accomplished in the past; it is a feast that nourishes our hearts. Here is an existential meal that retrains our deepest, most human hungers."[8] Over and over in his book, Smith advocates that worship is an

---

4. Miller and Miller, *Harper's Bible Dictionary*, 633.
5. Borg, *Speaking Christian*, 217.
6. *Merriam-Webster's Collegiate Dictionary*, 430.
7. Borg, *Speaking Christian*, 222.
8. Smith, *You Are What You Love*, 98.

environment where we can reform our minds, bodies, and spirits.[9] The practice of Holy Communion is an important occasion to truly sense one's nearness to Jesus and God. It is important to be cognizant that group members may come from a variety of faith traditions. Even if all participants have the same faith tradition, each one will view Holy Communion from their respective beliefs and faith. Any differences are to be appreciated.

There is a significant difference between what Roman Catholics and Protestants believe transpires during Holy Communion.

CATHOLIC/EASTERN ORTHODOX— TRANSUBSTANTIATION

In Roman Catholicism, "we believe that at every Mass, bread and wine become Jesus—his body, blood, soul and divinity—even though we can't fully understand how it happens. The miracle of the Eucharist is a mystery, something that human reason and intelligence can never fully grasp."[10] *Transubstantiation* is the belief that the bread and wine are transformed in some form to the body and blood of Christ. It "is a scholastic term that attempts to explain how bread and wine can become the body and blood of the Lord without losing their exterior appearance."[11] Roman Catholics believe this miracle of transubstantiation flows through the authority of Jesus Christ during consecration of the elements, an authority that is given to the priest when the words of institution are used and the chalice is raised: "This is my body, this is my blood." In essence, they believe that Jesus' body and blood are fully present during the sacrament.

LUTHERAN—REAL PRESENCE

Lutherans do not accept the concept of transubstantiation, but they believe in "real presence." Real presence means that the substance of the bread and wine coexists with the presence of the body and spirit of Jesus Christ. According to Trevin Wax, Martin Luther, a German priest and theologian, was bothered with the Roman Catholic view on two fronts:

---

9. Ibid., 77.

10. Christiansen, "How can I explain transubstantiation?" nwcatholic.org/voices/cal-christiansen/how-can-i-explain-transubstantiation.

11. Ibid.

First, he disagreed sharply with the practice of withholding the cup from the laity. Second, Luther believed that the Roman Catholic understanding of the sacrament as a "good work and sacrifice" was the "most wicked abuse of all." Luther argued forcefully that the mass must be seen as a testament—something to receive, not a good work to perform. . . . The center of Luther's theology of the Lord's Supper is the idea of "sacramental union." At the Lord's Table, in this sacred moment in which the elements of bread and wine are sacramentally united to the body and blood of Christ, God simultaneously reveals and hides himself.[12]

In *The Homebrewed Christianity Guide to Church History*, Bill Leonard indicates that "this idea of 'real presence' separated Luther from other Reformers as evident at the Marburg Colloquy in 1529."[13] Lutherans also believe that Communion is the gift of Jesus Christ.

CALVIN/REFORMED—SPIRITUAL PRESENCE

Within the Reformed tradition, Calvinists believe that the spirit of Jesus Christ is present during Communion but that Christ remains in heaven: "The Holy Spirit is the bond of the believer's union with Christ. Therefore, that which the minister does on the earthly plane, the Holy Spirit accomplishes on the spiritual plane."[14] They emphasize mutual love among believers. The Calvinists believe Communion is to inspire thanksgiving and gratitude among all believers.

John Calvin, Reformation leader in Geneva, Switzerland, insisted that while believers do not receive Christ's physical presence with the bread and the cup, they do experience his spiritual presence when they come to the Lord's Table. In his classic work, *The Institutes of Christian Religion*, Calvin wrote, "It is enough for us that Christ, from the substance of his flesh, breathes life into our souls. He defuses his own life into us, though the real flesh of Christ does not enter us."[15]

---

12. Wax, "Luther vs Zwingli 2: Luther on the Lord's Supper," thegospelcoalition.org/blogs/trevin-wax/luther-vs-zwingli-2-luther-on-the-lords-supper.

13. Leonard, *The Homebrewed Christianity Guide to Church History*, 128.

14. Mathison, "Calvin's Doctrine of the Lord's Supper," ligonier.org/learn/articles/calvins-doctrine-lords-supper.

15. Calvin, *Institutes of Christian Religion*, 271.

ZWINGIAN/REFORMED—MEMORIAL REMEMBRANCE

Keith Mathison says that "Ulrich Zwingi [Reformation leader in Switzerland] argued that Christ's words 'This is my body' should be read, 'This signifies my body' . . . [and] claimed that the Lord's Supper is a symbolic memorial, an initiatory ceremony in which the believer pledges that he is a Christian and proclaims that he has been reconciled to God through Christ's shed blood."[16] Zwingi believed that Jesus Christ is not present in the elements at Communion. Rather, Jesus is present in the faith of those gathered at the table who remember his death and resurrection together.

SOCIETY OF FRIENDS (QUAKERS)—GATHERED MEETING

The members of the Society of Friends (Quakers) do not use the physical elements at all. "The Quaker movement was founded on the conviction that the whole of life is sacramental. . . . No rite or ritual is necessary. The Quaker ideal is to make every meal at every table a Lord's Supper."[17] They favor the inner light of Christ, which they focus on spiritually. Quakers suggest that the members of the gathered meeting feed on Christ in their hearts without the need for external signs.

OBSERVING COMMUNION

As you can see, there is a variety of belief and practice regarding Communion among the Protestant denominations and Roman Catholicism. Each has its own approach to the belief, but all have their focus on Jesus Christ. Where have you experienced Holy Communion in a special way that was meaningful to you?

The celebration and observance of the Communion experience can extend to environments outside a church campus. A retreat setting can be an excellent venue where Holy Communion can take on special significance. There should be a facilitator, but the retreat participants can facilitate the sharing of the bread and wine. This type of unique atmosphere can make Communion highly personal—what some might describe as a "mountaintop" experience.

---

16. Mathison, "Calvin's Doctrine of the Lord's Supper."

17. "The Sacraments: Aspects of the Quaker Vision," firstfriendswhittier.org/welcome/sacraments.html.

Holy Communion is also an event that can be shared by Christians all around the world. World Communion Sunday, observed the first Sunday of every October, began in 1933 to promote Christian unity and ecumenical cooperation by focusing on observance of the Eucharist. This practice is to recognize that all Christian traditions have a common bond in the celebration of Jesus and the grace that he brings to all who call themselves Christians or followers of Jesus. How can you observe World Communion Sunday?

POSSIBLE WORDS FOR COMMUNION

Rev. Robin P. Coira, who is now retired, used the following words when she served Communion at Myers Park Baptist Church:

> On the night that he was arrested, Jesus took the bread, and when he had given thanks, he blessed it, broke it, and gave it to his disciples saying, "This is my body, which is given for you, eat in remembrance of me."
>
> In the same way, after supper, he took a cup. And after giving thanks, he gave it to them saying, "This is the cup of the new covenant, given for you. When you drink it, drink in remembrance of me."

What words or phrases have created meaning for you in the observance of Communion?

CONCLUSION

Most Christians view Holy Communion as the most important sacrament. Communion focuses our attention on Jesus and reminds us to follow in his commitment to assist the poor, the marginalized, and the oppressed. The practice of Holy Communion demonstrates the importance of the bread and wine during the time of Jesus. When people sit together to partake in a meal, many benefits are possible, including understanding, respect, and acceptance. In addition, we use all our senses in the Communion experience. While there are differences in belief regarding exactly what happens during Communion, all who participate are focused on Jesus and God. Some participate in Holy Communion each time they meet for worship, while others observe it periodically throughout the year. The Holy Communion experience is a leveling space where all can sense God's wonder and Jesus' ministry.

PUB THEOLOGY

INTRODUCTION: COMMUNION—SACRAMENT OF BREAD AND WINE

Marcus J. Borg in *Speaking Christian* shares that "Gathering at a table for bread and wine has been an essential practice in Christianity from its beginning and continues to be celebrated as the primary Christian sacrament."[18] When individuals sit down to eat with one another, special things can happen. James A. K. Smith in *You Are What You Love* shares that "The Lord's Supper isn't just a way to remember something that was accomplished in the past, it is a feast that nourishes our hearts. Here is an existential meal that retrains our deepest, most human hungers."[19]

ICEBREAKER

This is a way for group members to get to know each other and welcome any new group members. This activity will help with listening skills and to get people comfortable with sharing within the group.

Ask each member to consider the questions below and have them answer only one question and share with one other person. The next step is to have each person share with the group their partner's answer.

- What is your favorite childhood memory or story?
- What's the kindest act you have ever seen someone do?
- What is a hobby that you have and how did you get started doing it?
- Who was your favorite teacher and why?
- Who is your spiritual mentor?
- Name a spiritual turning point in your life that makes you smile/cry.

JUMPING-OFF POINTS

- Marcus J. Borg asks this question in *Speaking Christian*: "What did this meal of bread and wine really mean in its first-century historical context?"[20] With whom did Jesus eat, and why is this important?

---

18. Borg, *Speaking Christian*, 217.
19. Smith, *You Are What You Love*, 98.
20. Borg, *Speaking Christian*, 219.

- During Communion when you eat the bread and drink the wine, how does this benefit you in your spiritual journey?
- What questions and insights do you have during your participation in Communion?
- Since some churches now include members who have various Protestants and Roman Catholic backgrounds, how might Communion best be handled to accommodate both their similarities and differences?
- During Communion, what parts of your faith tradition are not considered or included at your place of worship? How does this affect your personal experience?
- What is specifically relevant to you during Communion?
- Is there anything in the sacrament of Communion that does not make sense to you? How could you learn more?

BIBLIOGRAPHY

Attridge, Harold W. *The HarperCollins Study Bible*. New York: HarperCollins, 2006.

Borg, Marcus J. *Speaking Christian*. New York: HarperCollins, 2012.

Bourgeault, Cynthia. *The Wisdom Jesus*. Boston: Shambhala, 2008.

Calvin, John. *The Institutes of Christian Religion*. Edited by Tony Lane and Hillary Osborne. Grand Rapids: Baker Academic, 1987.

Christiansen, Cal. "How can I explain transubstantiation?" *Northwest Catholic*. October 2016. nwcatholic.org/voices/cal-christiansen/how-can-i-explain-transubstantiation.

Leonard, Bill. *The Homebrewed Christianity Guide to Church History*. Minneapolis: Fortress, 2017.

Mathison, Keith A. "Calvin's Doctrine of the Lord's Supper." *Tabletalk Magazine*. November 1, 2006. ligonier.org/learn/articles/calvins-doctrine-lords-supper.

McLaren, Brian. *A New Kind of Christianity*. New York: HarperCollins, 2010.

Miller, Madeleine S., and J. Lane Miller. *Harper's Bible Dictionary*. New York: Harper and Row, 1961.

Smith, James K. A. *You Are What You Love*. Grand Rapids: Brazos, 2016.

"The Sacraments: Aspects of the Quaker Vision." Whittier First Friends Church. firstfriendswhittier.org/welcome/sacraments.html.

Wax, Trevin. "Luther vs Zwingli 2: Luther on the Lord's Supper." *The Gospel Coalition*. February 11, 2008. thegospelcoalition.org/blogs/trevin-wax/luther-vs-zwingli-2-luther-on-the-lords-supper.

MEETING 2

CHRISTIAN BAPTISM
JOHN E. SAUNDERS JR.

INTRODUCTION

Water baptism has been a foundational practice in the Christian church since Jesus was baptized by John the Baptist as recorded in the Gospels. The baptism of Jesus demonstrated the importance of baptism to the Christian faith. In Matthew 3:15, John questioned why Jesus should be baptized. Jesus replied, "for in this way it is fitting for us to fulfill all righteousness" (NASB). In trying to understand this statement, Roy Edgemon offers four ways that this baptism fulfilled all righteousness: "First, Jesus was baptized to identify with sinful humanity. Second, he set an example. Early followers took the example seriously. Third, Jesus was announcing the beginning of his ministry. Fourth, Jesus was identifying his ministry with John's."[1] The baptism of Jesus made it clear that Jesus was the one whom John was proclaiming to be the Messiah.

Matthew concludes his Gospel with these words of Jesus: "All authority has been given to Me in heaven and on earth. Go therefore and make disciples of all the nations, baptizing them in the name of the Father and the Son and the Holy Spirit, teaching them to observe all that I commanded you; and lo, I am with you always, even to the end of the age" (Matt 28:18-20, NASB). These verses give instructions concerning those who come to faith in Jesus. A first step in a person's faith relationship with Jesus is baptism. "It is evident from these verses that baptism," Boice writes, "is an initiatory sacrament belonging to the task of making disciples; the text speaks of the authority or lordship of Christ and of the baptized person as one who recognizes and professes."[2] However, major issues arise out of this

---

1. Edgemon, *Doctrines Baptists Believe*, 117.
2. Boice, *Foundations of the Christian Faith*, 597.

subject of baptism, and two of the most contentious are the meaning and the mode of baptism. Through the centuries, various Christian groups have adopted differences in these areas.

Baptism is "a rite using water as a symbol of religious purification."[3] There are closely related words for baptism in the New Testament. One is a verb and the other is a noun. The verb is *baptizō*. It was a common word found in many Greek writings of the first century. It means to immerse, submerge, dip, or soak. This word can also occur with a variety of other meanings. "In the English Bible *baptizō* has generally been transliterated to give us the word *baptize*," Boice writes. "When a word is transliterated into English from another language, it is quite often an indication of a multiplicity of meanings. If *baptizō* had meant only 'immerse,' then 'immerse' would be the word used."[4]

The Greeks used the word *baptizō* to mean a change has taken place, such as a change of identity.[5] "Thus, to give a few examples, it can refer to a change having taken place by immersing an object in a liquid, as in dyeing cloth, by drinking too much wine and thus getting drunk, by over exertion, and by other causes."[6] Other uses in classical Greek include dipping animals or the sinking of a ship.[7] It was also used for washing things by dipping them and for cleaning the body by bathing.[8] One of the nouns used for baptism in the New Testament was *baptismos*. It means to wash or purify by washing. This word was used for washing dishes, for the Jewish ceremonial washings, and for Christian baptism.[9] The early church practiced the immersion of individuals in water as a symbol of faith in Jesus and of "initiation into the Christian community."[10]

PRE-CHRISTIAN BAPTISM

Many Christian practices and beliefs have a background in the Jewish community. The practice of baptism also comes from a Jewish practice. Johnnie Godwin, writing in the *Holman Dictionary of the Bible*, states that

---

3. Ibid., 615.
4. Boice, *Foundations of the Christian Faith*, 598.
5. Ibid.
6. Ibid.
7. Hobbs, *Baptist Faith and Message*, 84.
8. Schoenheit, *Baptism*, 212.
9. Ibid.
10. Buttrick, "Baptism," 348.

in the Septuagint, "The Greek word *baptizō*, 'immerse, dip, submerge' is used metaphorically in Isaiah 21:4 to mean, 'go down, perish,' and in 2 Kings 5:14 for Naaman's dipping in the Jordan River seven times for cleansing from his skin disease."[11]

Other groups used the water-cleansing ritual prior to the Jewish and Christian traditions. Even though baptism is usually thought of as a Jewish or Christian rite, "ablution or bathing was common in ancient nations as a preparation for prayers and sacrifice, or as expiatory of sin."[12]

Just like other religions at the time, the Jews used water for religious purification purposes. The tabernacle during the time of Moses had a basin for ritual washing. In the Old Testament, there are requirements for priests to be cleansed in order to carry out their duties (Exod 30:17; 40:12; Num 8:6, 7).

Baptism was also used for those who converted to the Jewish faith.[13] The rite is not found in the Old Testament; however, there are references in the writings of Epictetus, the Sibylline Oracles, and the Mishnah that allow us to date the practice to the early first century.[14] Godwin continues, "At some point close to the time of Jesus, Judaism began a heavy emphasis on ritual washings to cleanse from impurity. This goes back to priestly baths required prior to offering sacrifices (see Lev 16:4, 24). Probably shortly prior to the time of Jesus, or contemporary with him, Jews began baptizing Gentile converts, but circumcision of males still remained the primary entrance rite into Judaism."[15] Also in the region was the Jewish Essene Qumran community located south of Jericho near the Dead Sea. This community practiced the ritual of cleansing by immersion in water.[16]

The first-century Christians were not the only ones who baptized their adherents. During this time, several different groups used some form of baptism in their religious rites. The purpose was to remove guilt, to symbolize moral cleansing, and to indicate a new start in life. The mystery religions would use forms of immersion as an initiation into their religious communities.[17]

---

11. "Baptism," in Butler, ed., *Holman Dictionary of the Bible*, 148–49.
12. "Baptism," in *Dr. William Smith's Dictionary of the Bible*, 233.
13. Buttrick, "Baptism," 348.
14. Ibid.
15. "Baptism," in Butler, ed., *Holman Dictionary of the Bible*, 150.
16. Ibid., 159.
17. Polcyn and Verbrugge, "Baptism," 681.

BAPTISM IN THE NEW TESTAMENT

When John the Baptist emerged from the wilderness baptizing in the Jordan River, the Jews would have been familiar with the act. Even though John's baptism may have been a form of proselyte baptism, it was significantly different. In John 1:6, 11, John the Baptist immersed those who were repenting of their sins, having a change of heart and mind. It was not a way of joining any religious group at that time. He administered the rite of baptism to Jews and to Gentiles, which was a significant difference from proselyte baptism. "Further, for John the ethical significance of the rite became prominent," Buttrick writes. "He implored the Pharisees and Sadducees 'bear fruit that befits repentance.'"[18]

John also linked this baptism of repentance with the kingdom of God and the coming Messiah. "The most striking association of John's baptism is eschatological—he links the rite with his proclamation of the coming kingdom of God."[19] In Matthew 3:2, John proclaims, "Repent, for the kingdom of God is at hand" (NASB). There is a distinct moral component to the baptism of John. It is not just accepting an idea or a religious ideal. It is a radical change of one's life in order to prepare the people for the coming of God's kingdom. John acknowledges that one is coming who is greater than he, and John is not worthy to untie his sandals. This other person will baptize with "the Holy Spirit and fire" (Matt 3:11). George Buttrick writes about baptism in *The New Interpreter's Dictionary of the Bible*,

> Fresh light has been thrown on the meaning of John's baptism by a comparison with the symbolic actions of the Old Testament prophets. It has been suggested that these actions be understood not only as a vivid means of expressing the will of God, but also in some degree as helping to bring about its fulfillment. Seen in this light, John's baptism prepared those who submitted to it to face the coming Day of the Lord, confident that those who repented would be forgiven and granted a place in the future messianic community.[20]

It was John who had baptized Jesus. This created some confusion on John's part because John saw Jesus as the Messiah, who did not need to be baptized. John could not understand why Jesus wanted to be baptized.

---

18. Buttrick, "Baptism," 349.
19. Ibid., 349.
20. Ibid.

Through his baptism, Jesus acknowledged the standard to which John was calling all believers. He demonstrated that the life of repentance demanded by John was right for Jesus and those who would follow him and was "able to identify with sinful mankind and be a model for others to follow."[21]

John's baptism then prepared repentant sinners for receiving the baptism of the Holy Spirit and fire that he spoke about: "When Jesus comes into a life, the Holy Spirit comes with His saturating presence and purifies. He empowers and cleanses the believer in a spiritual baptism."[22] In the New Testament, "the rite of baptism with water as the symbol of entry into the Christian Community was practiced from the day of Pentecost onward" (see Acts 2:38, 41).[23] Baptism was the immersion of a believer in water, by the church, upon profession of faith in Jesus. "That this was the use of Baptism is evident from the practice of Apostolic Christians. The baptized had received his word. This followed repentance and preceded baptism."[24]

In the New Testament, there are many occasions when individuals are baptized upon hearing and then believing the gospel message. This demonstrates a believer's baptism, or one who is baptized because they have believed and repented of their sin. We see this on several occasions in the book of Acts. In Acts 8:26-40, Stephen leads an Ethiopian eunuch to understand that Isaiah 53:7, where the prophet writes about the lamb to be slaughtered, is referring to Jesus. After the eunuch declares his belief in Jesus as the Son of God, Philip baptizes him. In Acts 10, Peter encounters the centurion Cornelius and shares with him about Jesus. The Holy Spirit descends upon all who are present, and Paul declares in verses 47-48, "'Surely no one can refuse the water for these to be baptized who have received the holy spirit just as we did, can he?' And he ordered them to be baptized in the name of Jesus Christ" (NASB). In Acts 16, when Paul goes to Macedonia, he meets Lydia; she is baptized after "the Lord opened her heart to respond to the things spoken by Paul." Later in Acts 16:33, the Philippian jailer and his household are baptized. In each of these instances, baptism follows belief in Jesus.

Throughout the New Testament, baptism is also used metaphorically or symbolically. It was a Christian's testimony of their death to the old self and the emergence of a new creation, and it "symbolizes the death, burial,

---

21. "Baptism," in Butler, ed., *Holman Dictionary of the Bible*, 150.
22. Ibid., 151.
23. Buttrick, "Baptism," 349.
24. Boyce, *Abstract of Systematic Theology*, 378.

and resurrection of Jesus."[25] This implies a new way of living or walking in newness of life in Christ (Rom 6:4). Baptism can also mean to clothe oneself with Christ (Gal 3:27). Christian baptism is a sharing of the death and resurrection and all that brought Christ to those events (Rom 6:1-7; Col 2:12).

Baptism is also a symbol of a person's union with Jesus. "Paul's basic understanding of baptism was that the believer is baptized 'unto Christ.' Baptism serves to illustrate the union Christ brought about through faith" (see Gal 3:26-27).[26] Baptism in the New Testament is vital to the life of a believer, with significant symbolism for a life with Jesus.

Baptism is not considered necessary for salvation, but it is the first step in discipleship and the first evidence of obedience to following Jesus.[27] In Acts 2:38, Peter states, "Repent and each of you be baptized in the name of Jesus for the forgiveness of sins." Baptism pictures an individual coming to know Jesus as Savior and Lord; that lordship implies obedience to Jesus' teachings and his example for living.

Baptism in the New Testament took place wherever there was water and someone to do the baptizing. This is seen in Scriptures such as Acts 8:36, when Philip baptizes the Ethiopian eunuch; when Ananias baptizes Saul in 9:18; and in 10:47-48 as Paul tells others to baptize Cornelius and his household. There does not seem to be a requirement for any designated church pastor to carry out the baptism.

THE PRACTICE OF BAPTISM IN THE EARLY CHURCH

As the early church moved into the second and third centuries, there was much discussion around theological issues and the different teachings of various church leaders. When it came to baptism, it was no different. As each group sought to understand the New Testament teaching for baptism, they could not agree about its practice. "The church has attempted to build its practice upon that of the New Testament, but has not agreement always, as to what the practice was."[28]

---

25. Hobbs, *What Baptists Believe*, 83.
26. Polcyn and Verbrugge, "Baptism," 681.
27. "Baptism," in Butler, ed., *Holman Dictionary of the Bible*, 151.
28. Ibid., 151.

One of the big issues following the deaths of the apostles and the growth of the faith involved heresies. The problem was that a heresy to one group might be considered a doctrine for another. Early on, there was not a consistent New Testament Scripture to give guidance. So, to combat these heresies, attempts were made to gather together writings to form sacred literature for Christians. Another part of the attempt to combat the heresies was the development of the Apostles' Creed by the church in Rome. The creed was to be a symbol of the faith or a means of recognizing those who were true followers of Jesus. Baptism was a significant part of the creed. Justo González explains the symbolism of the creed:

> One of the main uses of this "symbol" was baptism, where it was presented to the candidate in the form of three questions: 1. Do you believe in God the Father almighty? 2. Do you believe in Christ Jesus, the Son of God, who was born of the Holy Ghost and of Mary the virgin, who was crucified under Pontius Pilate, and died and rose again on the third day, living among the dead, and ascended unto heaven and sat at the right hand of the Father, and will come again to judge the quick and the dead? 3. Do you believe in the Holy Ghost, the holy church, and the resurrection of the dead?[29]

These three questions are built around the pattern of Matthew 28:19: "baptizing them in the name of the Father, the Son, and the Holy Spirit." This was the beginning of the Christian church sorting out the meaning of baptism. The more universal Nicene Creed affirms baptism when it states, "We acknowledge one baptism unto the remission of sins."[30]

As early Christian groups grew and developed, they instituted worship around Scripture reading, prayers, singing of hymns, and Communion. One characteristic of the Communion services was that only those who had been baptized could attend.[31] Baptism was also a part of the worship service of the early church. It was the custom to baptize converts as soon as they were converted. However, as the church reached and converted many more Gentiles, some changes had to be made to the immediacy of baptizing the converts. A period of preparation, trial, and instruction was required before baptism occurred. This idea of catechumenate could last as long as three years. The candidates had to give evidence in their daily lives that they had

---

29. González, *Story of Christianity*, 64.
30. Moody, *Word of Truth*, 8.
31. González, *Story of Christianity*, 1:94.

been converted. After this they could be added to the list to be baptized. It is clear that baptism was a serious matter for the early church.

Justo González describes the baptism process in this way: Usually baptism was administered once a year on Easter Sunday.[32] Early in the third century, it was customary for those about to be baptized to fast on Friday and Saturday and then to be baptized early Sunday morning, which was the time of the resurrection of Jesus. On emerging from the waters, the neophytes were given white robes as a sign of their new life in Christ. They were also given water to drink as a sign that they were thoroughly cleansed, both outside and inside. Then they were anointed, thus making them part of the royal priesthood; and they were given milk and honey, as a sign of the promised land into which they were entering.[33]

Baptism was not something that was done in private. It was a celebration within the community of faith and the community at large. Robert Wilken summarizes the baptismal experience in the early church:

> Everyone had a role, the bishop and other clergy, neighbors, friends, and family. Its recurrence each year in late winter and spring, the gravity of the interrogation, the rigor of fasting, the sonorous phrases of the reed, the drama of the exorcisms, the immersion in water—all heightened the experience. Baptism was a great Christian spectacle, and the excitement of seeing neighbors and friends step forward one by one to go down under the waters riveted the attention of the Christian community.[34]

Later church leaders began to differ on the meaning of baptism and how it was to be administered. In the first three centuries, baptism was usually by immersion. According to González, "The *Teaching of the Twelve Apostles*, a document of uncertain date, prefers that it be done in 'living'—that is running water. But where water was scarce it could be administered by pouring water three times over the head, in the name of the Father, the Son, and the Holy Spirit."[35]

Constantine changed the whole landscape for worship and baptism. After his conversion, Christian worship radically changed from a simple gathering with little fanfare to a service influenced by "imperial protocol."[36]

---

32. Ibid., 1:96.
33. Ibid.
34. Wilken, *Spirit of Christian Thought*, 39.
35. González, *Story of Christianity*, 1:97.
36. Ibid.

A basilica was built by Constantine in Constantinople called the Church of Saint Irene. Other buildings of similar design were built in other places. Near the basilica were additional buildings, including a baptistery. In these buildings, baptism was celebrated usually by immersion or pouring.[37]

The developing Christian communities varied in their approach to the meaning and mode of baptism. Robert Wilken notes, "In spite of the growing body of evidence that water is only symbolic, no doubt there was a diversity of opinion among the early Christians about the relation between water baptism and salvation."[38] Baptism was a washing in water. The preferred method of baptism in the early church was by immersion.[39]

Questions arose: Is baptism necessary for salvation, or is it only symbolic of a new life in Christ? Is baptism to be administered by immersion only, or are pouring (affusion) and sprinkling (aspersion) acceptable? Christian leaders and scholars have been divided over these issues for years. There are many differences of opinion. Some Christian denominations teach that water baptism is necessary for salvation, and some teach that it is not necessary for salvation but is symbolic in nature. Many Christian groups require immersion baptism for becoming a member of their church.

The debates about the correct way to baptize individuals into the Christian faith, either by immersion, affusion, or aspersion, have been argued for centuries. Schoenheit describes the conflict between groups over mode and meaning of baptism when he writes, "From Paul to the Reformation, baptism rituals once again became obsessive and divisive. Baptism in water was declared a sacrament in the Church, and Christians even killed each other over how to do it correctly."[40]

Understanding the meaning of baptism is crucial to understanding the mode of baptism. Many use the terms "sacrament" and "ordinance" interchangeably. Wayne Grudem writes in his book *Systematic Theology*, "If we are willing to explain clearly what we mean, it does not seem to make any difference whether we use the word sacrament or not."[41] In the *Holman Bible Dictionary*, Wayne Ward defines a sacrament as "an outward sign of an inward and spiritual grace. It usually refers to a religious ritual which

---

37. Schoenheit, *Baptism*, 629.
38. Wilken, *Spirit of Christian Thought*, 40.
39. Ibid.
40. Schoenheit, *Baptism*, 914.
41. Grudem, *Systematic Theology*, 966–67.

is believed to carry a special healing or saving power."[42] Alister McGrath says that the term sacrament "is widely used within Christianity to refer to certain rites or church ceremonies which are understood to possess a special spiritual significance. At its heart, a sacrament is an outward and visible sign of an inward and spiritual grace."[43] Baptism is considered to be one of the sacraments. The Roman Catholic Church and the Eastern Orthodox Church have seven sacraments. Protestants only recognize the Lord's Supper and baptism as sacraments.

Many Protestant groups, and especially Baptists, do not use the word "sacrament." They prefer the term "ordinance." Ordinance means something that was ordained by Jesus. "The word Baptists prefer is the term ordinance instead of sacrament to describe baptism," writes Roy Edgemon. "An ordinance is that which is ordained or commanded by Jesus. Ordinance, then, means that which is ordered, set out, decided, marked off, or put in place. An ordinance is a command that has purpose and meaning."[44] In this view, baptism does not convey any grace or salvation upon the individual who is being baptized. Salvation comes by faith, and baptism is symbolic of the death, burial, and resurrection of Jesus. Baptism with water in any way is symbolic. In both the Old Testament and the New Testament, using water to baptize does not confer spiritual grace or salvation.[45]

Early church leaders had diverse opinions about whether baptism conferred salvation:

> Some Christians believed the water was only symbolic and it was the faith in Christ that really got a person saved, while others thought that the water somehow consummated the person's faith and the salvation. In fact, that difference of opinion has always been part of the Christian faith, and today, 2,000 years after Christ, some Christians believe a person must be water baptized to be saved, while others do not.[46]

The early church in Rome began to promote the idea that the sacrament of baptism bestowed grace upon those being baptized. Hobbs writes,

---

42. "Sacrament," in *Holman Dictionary of the Bible*, 1217.
43. McGrath, *Theology*, 170.
44. Edgemon, *Doctrines Baptist Believe*, 117.
45. Schoenheit, *Baptism*, 310.
46. Ibid., 646.

The idea of baptismal regeneration did not appear in Christian teachings until late in the second and early third centuries. Baptismal regeneration came to be accepted by the group which later evolved into the Roman Catholic Church. Today the idea of sacramental baptism persists in Catholicism and to a degree most branches of Protestantism.[47]

During the Reformation, Protestantism was divided over the issue of what the sacraments achieved in a believer's life. McGrath quotes Martin Luther's *Small Catechisms* of 1529 about the signification and causation of divine forgiveness, saying that baptism brings about "forgiveness of sins, saves us from death and the devil, and grants eternal blessedness to all who believe, as the Word and promise of God declare."[48]

Another change was the movement toward sprinkling as the mode for baptism. It is not clear when this change took place. "No usage has been found where *baptizō* means either pouring or sprinkling. The practice of sprinkling for baptism gradually replaced immersion in the Catholic Church, and when it divided into the Roman and Greek branches, the latter retained immersion. The change in mode came after the change in meaning."[49]

A turning point in recovering the New Testament meaning of baptism took place in 1525 in Zurich, Switzerland. Followers of Ulrich Zwingli, George Blaurock, and Conrad Grebel believed that a new church was needed. It was a reaction to those who called themselves Christians simply because they lived in a Christian country and were baptized as infants. In a fountain in the square in Zurich, Grebel baptized Blaurock. Blaurock then baptized others who had professed their faith in Jesus Christ. They did not baptize by immersion because they were more concerned for the meaning of the baptism than the mode. They were soon being called "anabaptists," which means re-baptizers.[50] They really did not re-baptize anyone. They did proclaim that "infant baptism was not valid, and therefore the first real baptism takes place when one receives the rite after having made a public profession of faith."[51]

However, many groups did not hold with the doctrine that baptism brought about the forgiveness of sin. One church in particular was the

---

47. Hobbs, *Baptist Faith and Message*, 85.
48. McGrath, *Theology*, 175.
49. Hobbs, *Baptist Faith and Message*, 86–87.
50. González, *Story of Christianity*, 2:54–55.
51. Ibid., 2:55.

Broadmead Church in Bristol, England. They moved away from the concept of infant baptism in favor of believer's baptism, and eventually going the next step to immersion.[52]

BELIEVER'S BAPTISM AND IMMERSION

Many Christian groups in Europe began to narrowly define the mode of baptism for those who professed their faith or belief in Jesus as Savior and Lord. Leon McBeth writes *The Baptist Heritage*, "Influenced by the Reformation theology of Ulrich Zwingli and John Calvin, the English Bible, and a deep desire for spiritual reform, some of these Separatists adopted baptism for believers only."[53] Eventually the baptism was by total immersion. This movement had a lot of opposition from the Catholic Church and from other Protestants. Because of the way they practiced baptism, they were nicknamed "Baptists."[54]

Many of the groups, even though they practiced believer's baptism, baptized by sprinkling instead of immersion. In the early 1600s, some English Baptist groups began to practice what they considered to be biblical baptism. They did this in two ways. First, they noted that baptism was for those who professed their faith in Jesus and that it was not for infants. Second, it was to be baptism by immersion.[55] Several different church groups were formed as a result of this separation. As Christian denominations developed in the eighteenth and nineteenth centuries, many of them practiced believer's baptism either by immersion or sprinkling.

These faith groups discussed, argued, and divided over how to administer the rite of baptism. For much of the early seventeenth century, some leaders such as Leonard Busher, Henry Jacob, and John Spilsbury were beginning to advocate for believer's baptism by immersion only. In the First London Confession of 1644, it was specified that baptism would be by immersion only.

Even into the nineteenth century, there were many debates and discussions about the proper method of baptism. "Baptist apologists frequently

---

52. Cited in McBeth, *Sourcebook for Baptist Heritage*, 30.

53. McBeth, *The Baptist Heritage*, 21. During the Reformation, different church groups were formed and called Separatists. They were groups of the English Protestants in the sixteenth and seventeenth centuries who separated themselves from what they perceived as corruption in the Church of England.

54. Ibid.

55. Ibid., 44–45.

engage their Methodist counterparts on this issue since the followers of John Wesley were wont to allow their converts to choose whichever mode of baptism they preferred."[56] Contributing to this debate, C. A. Stakely writes in his essay, "Why Immersion and Not Sprinkling or Pouring," "Both in its nature and in its purpose, baptism is an acting out of certain truths or principles, and the more impressive it is made in the mode of its administration, the truer it is to its own genius and the greater influence it exerts over the mind of candidate and observer."[57] James Pettigrew Boyce in *Catechism of Bible Doctrine* concurs with Stakely: "What is Baptism? It is the immersion of the body in water, in the name of the Father, the Son and the Holy Ghost."[58]

INFANT BAPTISM

Christian groups vary in their understanding and practice of infant baptism. Those who disagree with this practice do so because of their belief in believer's baptism. Infants cannot make a decision to follow Christ, therefore they are not baptized. Those who believe baptism is a sign of the new covenant will baptize the infants of believers. Denominations such as Catholicism baptize infants because they believe baptism is a conferring of God's grace and salvation; United Methodists believe baptism is a gift of God's grace that initiates infants (or people of any age) into the faith community and into a covenant relationship with God and God's people. This doctrinal view holds that baptism is valuable and is needed for salvation. If this is true, then even infants must be baptized to be saved. According to Norman Geisler, Augustine was the first to teach the damnation of all unbaptized infants—that essentially the wrath of God "abides on" them.[59]

The New Testament does not directly address infant baptism and therefore neither forbids it nor demands it. So it is difficult to determine when Christians started baptizing infants. McGrath suggests the second or third centuries.[60] When using Scripture as a basis for infant baptism, there are still various interpretations of even the same passages. One example is the Philippian jailer in Acts 16. When he comes to faith in Jesus, he and

---

56. George and George, *Baptist Why and Why Not*, 6.

57. C. A. Stakely, "Why Immersion and Not Sprinkling or Pouring," in George and George, *Baptist Why and Why Not*, 43.

58. Boyce, *Brief Catechism of Bible of Bible Doctrine*. xxii.

59. Geisler, *Systematic Theology*, 3:436.

60. McGrath, *Theology*, 181.

his household are baptized. Presumably, this baptism may or may not have included infants.

Infant baptism is also compared to infant circumcision in the Old Testament as a covenant rite. Those in favor of infant baptism state the following reasons: (1) household baptisms included infants; (2) Jesus' welcome and blessing of children is a mandate so as not to hinder the little children; (3) circumcision included children, and (4) Old Testament children were included in ceremonies of covenant renewal. Those against infant baptism use these reasons: (1) the New Testament requires faith; (2) baptism is based on faith; (3) household baptisms did not necessarily include infants; (4) Jesus' blessing of the children shows his love for them and that they are an example to the disciples, and (5) circumcision is not a good analogy since only males participated.[61]

PUB THEOLOGY

INTRODUCTION

In 1982, the Faith and Order Commission of the Protestant World Council of Churches published a theological document called "Baptism, Eucharist, and Ministry." The statement on baptism seeks to lay out the understanding of baptism within Protestantism. Here is that statement:

> Baptism is the sign of new life through Jesus Christ. It unites the one baptized with Christ and with his people. The New Testament scriptures and the liturgy of the Church unfold the meaning of baptism in various images which express the riches of Christ and the gifts of his salvation. These images are sometimes linked with the symbolic uses of water in the Old Testament. Baptism is participation in Christ's death and resurrection (Romans 6:3-5; Colossians 2:12); a washing away of sin (I Corinthians 6:11); a new birth (John 3:5); an enlightenment by Christ (Ephesians 5:14); a reclothing in Christ (Galatians 3:27); a renewal by the Spirit (Titus 3:5); the experience of salvation from the flood (I Peter 3:20-21); an exodus from bondage (I Corinthians 10:1-2) and a liberation into a new humanity in which barriers of division, whether of sex or race or social status, are transcended (Galatians 3:27-28; I Corinthians 12:13). The images are many but the reality is one.

---

61. "Infant baptism," in Butler, ed., *Holman Dictionary of the Bible*, 695.

ICEBREAKER

In a minute or less, describe an early childhood memory.

JUMPING-OFF POINTS

- Many Scriptures are referenced in the Faith and Order Commission statement. Discuss the major themes that are emphasized and their connection to your understanding of baptism. With which dimensions and levels of meaning do you agree or disagree?
- If you have been baptized as a believer in Jesus, what was the significance of baptism for you and your life? What does it mean to you now?
- If you were baptized as an infant, what was the significance of baptism for you and your life? What does it mean to you now?
- Which of the different symbols of baptism would you like for your church to emphasize more?
- Discuss ways to help believers overcome the differences among Christian groups regarding their views on baptism.

BIBLIOGRAPHY

Boice, James Montgomery. *Foundations of the Christian Faith*. Downers Grove: InterVarsity, 1986.

Boyce, James Pettigrew. *Abstract of Systematic Theology*. Escondido, CA: Den Dulk Christian Foundation, 1887.

Butler, Trent, editor. *Holman Dictionary of the Bible*. Nashville, Broadman, 1991.

Buttrick, George A. *The Interpreter's Dictionary of the Bible A-D*. Nashville: Abingdon, 1962.

Edgemon, Roy T. *The Doctrines Baptist Believe*. Nashville: Convention Press, 1988.

Geisler, Norman. *Systematic Theology*, volume 3. Bloomington, MN: Bethany House, 2004.

George, Timothy, and Denise George, editors. *Baptist Why and Why Not*. Nashville: Broadman and Holman, 1996.

González, Justo. *The Story of Christianity: Complete in One Volume*. Peabody, MA: Hendrickson, 2001.

Grudem, Wayne. *Systematic Theology*. Grand Rapids: Zondervan, 1994.

Hackett, H. B., editor. *Dr. William Smith's Dictionary of the Bible*. 1896. Grand Rapids: Baker Books, 1981.

Hobbs, Herschel. *The Baptist Faith and Message*. Nashville: Convention Press, 1971.

———. *What Baptists Believe*. Nashville: Convention Press, 1964.

McBeth, Leon. *The Baptist Heritage*. Nashville: Broadman, 1987.

———. *A Sourcebook for Baptist Heritage*. Nashville: Broadman, 1990.

McGrath, Alister E. *Theology: The Basics*. Oxford: John Wiley and Sons, 2018.

Moody, Dale. *The Word of Truth*. Grand Rapids: Eerdmans, 1981.

Polcyn, Richard, and Verlyn D. Verbrugge. *The Expositor's Bible Commentary, NIV edition,* vol. 2: New Testament. Grand Rapids: Zondervan, 1994.

Schoenheit, John W. *Baptism: The History and Doctrine of Christian Baptism*. E-book, 2nd ed. Martinsville, IN: Spirit and Truth Fellowship International, 2013.

Wilken, Robert Louis. *The Spirit of Early Christian Thought*. New Haven: Yale University, 2003.

THE HIDDEN TREASURE OF SABBATH

H. STEPHEN SHOEMAKER

The Sabbath is a hidden treasure for many Christians, and in my case it's one late discovered. Growing up in the 1950s as a Baptist boy, my first awareness of Sabbath keeping other than weekly worship was the number of "blue laws" that shut down certain businesses on Sunday and the religious prohibition against enjoying certain forms of secular entertainment such as going to the movies.

Later, as the son of a minister of music, I found that Sunday was the busiest day of the week: morning Sunday school and at least one of two worship services, afternoon Bible training (first Memory Work and then Sword Drill), followed by Training Union and evening worship.

As a pastor, I was once caught mowing my lawn on Sunday afternoon by a neighbor who expressed his shock to a church member. He did not know that mowing the grass was a welcome form of relaxation for me and a resting of my overtaxed mind.

I have come to love the deepest meaning of Sabbath. In this session, I will explore the (1) biblical/historical/theological dimensions of Sabbath and Sabbath keeping, (2) the spiritual meaning of Sabbath and Sabbath keeping, and finally (3) the spiritual practice of Sabbath keeping.

Sabbath keeping is the spiritual practice where we honor the needs of the body, mind, and spirit for rest and where we put into practice our trust in God to provide. If this were easy, there would be no need for the fourth of the Ten Commandments: "Remember the sabbath day, and keep it holy" (Exod 20:8). The Sabbath was the holy gift of God, and keeping it holy meant, first, to stop our work. In the Hebrew language, "sabbath" means "cease."

To the Hebrew people, the Sabbath was founded on two great events: the creation and the exodus. The explanation of the commandment in Exodus connects its meaning to creation: "For in six days the LORD made heaven and earth, the sea, and all that is in them, but rested the seventh day; therefore the LORD blessed the sabbath day and consecrated it" (Exod 20:11). We honor the Sabbath by remembering God the creator. Remembering unites the past with the present. The Sabbath helps us enter time as "holy time," befriending time rather than making it our enemy. God rested on the seventh day and established a holy rhythm of work and rest. We are to do the same.

Walter Brueggemann writes that before the Sabbath was a day of worship, it was a day of rest, "a complete and comprehensive work stoppage."[1] When I traveled to Israel, I entered a stationery store and looked at the calendars. To my surprise, there were no Saturdays in the calendars! No appointments on the Sabbath? If you shop for a stove today, you discover that many stoves have a Sabbath mode so that Orthodox Jews don't have to interact with their appliances from sundown Friday to sundown Saturday. The Hebrew people really mean it when they keep the Sabbath!

Brueggemann goes on to expand the theological meaning of Sabbath: "Israel rests because God rests. This God is not a workaholic. . . . It is ordained in the fabric of creation that the world is not a place of endless productivity, ambition, or anxiety."[2] Too many Christians work on Sunday afternoons or evenings to get ahead on the work that should begin the next day. Endless productivity, ambition, anxiety.

Sabbath keeping demonstrates our trust in God to provide. Jesus spoke of such trust when he said, "Do not worry about your life, what you will eat or what you will drink . . . ." Then he pointed to the lilies of the field and the birds of the air (Matt 6:25-34). I have in my home a beautifully framed piece of calligraphy that depicts in the Japanese language "the lilies of the field" and "the birds of the air." It is a daily reminder to trust in the provision of God and to loosen my anxiety.

First, the Sabbath is rooted in the creation and the gracious rhythm of work and rest. Then, second and just as important, the Sabbath is rooted in the exodus, the deliverance of God's people from slavery. In Deuteronomy, everyone in the household is to rest, the servants and the animals too! Sabbath is a gift for everyone and every creature. And why do we and

---

1. Brueggemann, "Exodus," 1:845.
2. Ibid.

the household rest? Deuteronomy links it to the exodus: "Remember that you were a slave in the land of Egypt, and the LORD your God brought you out from there with a mighty hand and an outstretched arm; therefore the LORD your God commanded you to keep the sabbath day" (Deut 5:15).

On the Sabbath, past and present are united. In slavery, the people worked seven days a week in forced labor. The Sabbath is the mark of their freedom; in their honor, now we rest one day a week. Brueggemann says that Sabbath is a "withdrawal from the anxiety system of Pharaoh, . . . the refusal to let one's life be defined by production and consumption."[3] Moses said to Pharaoh, "Let my people go!" Sometimes it's hard to let *Pharaoh* go. Deuteronomy's form of the commandment urges, "Live now as a free person" (5:15). Paul wrote to the Galatians: "For freedom Christ has set us free. Stand firm, therefore, and do not submit again to a yoke of slavery" (Gal 5:1).

How easily American Christians slip back into the yoke of slavery from which God has delivered us. Noted pastoral theologian Wayne E. Oates coined the phrase "workaholic" in *Confessions of a Workaholic*. Workaholism is dependency, like other addictions; this addiction is to "overwork."[4] It can destroy our health, body, mind, and spirit, as well was our closest relationships. The Sabbath is a way of releasing ourselves from the bondage of overwork. It is a way for us to remember that God is our provider and deliverer.

Now we turn to the spiritual dimension of the Sabbath. Again, our Jewish friends are our teachers. In the great rabbi Abraham Joshua Heschel's collection of sayings, *I Asked for Wonder*, a whole section is devoted to Sabbath. It begins,

> He who wants to enter the holiness of the day must first lay down the profanity of clattering commerce, of being yoked to toil. He must go away from the screech of dissonant days, from the nervousness and fury of acquisitiveness and in embezzling one's own life.[5]

"Embezzling one's own life": this is what addiction to overwork and lack of Sabbath does to us. As Wordsworth wrote,

---

3. Ibid.
4. Oates, *Confessions of a Workaholic*, 4.
5. Heschel, *I Asked for Wonder*, 34.

> The world is too much with us; late and soon
> Getting and spending, we lay waste our powers:
> Little we can see in nature that is ours;
> We have given our hearts away, a sordid boon.[6]

Heschel goes on to say, "Six days we wrestle with the world, wringing profit from the earth; on the Sabbath we especially care for the seed of eternity planted in the soil."[7] Sabbath, he says, is a "palace in time" we build. We can choose to inhabit it or not. Sabbath is a way of acknowledging that we have enough. The poet Wendell Berry spends his sabbaths walking his fields and writing "Sabbath poems." His poem "The Wild Geese" describes the sufficiency of God's provision:

> Horseback on Sunday morning
> harvest over, we taste persimmon
> and wild grape, sharp sweet
> of summer's end . . . .
> We open
> a persimmon to find the tree
> that stands in promise,
> pale, in the seed's marrow.
> Geese appear high over us,
> pass, and sky closes. Abandon,
> as in love and sleep, holds
> them to their way, clear
> in the ancient faith: what we need
> is here. And we pray, not
> for new earth or heaven, but to be
> quiet in heart, and in eye
> clear. What we need is here.[8]

To slow to read this poem is Sabbath.

Third, how do we make Sabbath keeping a spiritual practice? For Jewish people, the Sabbath has not only been a day of cessation from work but also a day of joy and wonder over the goodness of God's world. God rested and took pleasure in what God has made. So can we.

---

6. Wordsworth, "The world is too much with us," 507.
7. Heschel, *I Asked for Wonder*, 34.
8. Berry, "The Wild Geese," 155–56.

The Sabbath is a festive time. One of the most beautiful dimensions of Sabbath in Jewish practice is how it begins—that is, on the evening before, as for Jews every day begins at sunset the night before (following the creation story in Genesis 1). On Friday evening, Sabbath begins with a Shabbat meal where the family joins at the table, sometimes with friends. The mother lights the candle of Sabbath, and all welcome it with joy. Then on to the synagogue for the Shabbat service.

At the beginning of the Christian movement, Jesus' followers would worship as Jews in the synagogue on the Jewish Sabbath. Then they would meet on Sunday evening for worship around the table of the Lord. By the second century, the early Christians had established Sunday as their Sabbath. Just as the Jewish Sabbath was rooted in creation and exodus, the Christian Sabbath was rooted in two events. Jesus' followers worshiped on Sunday, the first day of the week, because on the first day God created the world. And they worshiped on Sunday because that is the day when God raised Jesus from the dead.[9] So for Christians, Sunday became a "day of rest and gladness" and a day of worship, praise and thanksgiving, and remembering who we are as people of God. The goal of Sabbath, however, is not mere "churchgoing"; the goal is God.[10] Sabbath moves us God-ward.

The worship of God can happen in places other than a church building. The enjoyment of God's creation is a form of loving God. In the movie *A River Runs Through It*, the Presbyterian minister takes his boys trout fishing on Sunday afternoons after church. Wendell Berry spent Sunday morning on walks through the woods and fields, and from this Sabbath observance came his "Sabbath poems."[11] And Emily Dickinson found New England worship tedious and wrote this poem:

> Some keep the Sabbath going to church—
> I keep it, staying at Home—
> with a Bobolink for a Chorister—
> And an Orchard, for a Dome—[12]

---

9. See *First Apology of Justin Martyr*, in *The Ante-Nicene Fathers*, 1:186.
10. Bass, "Keeping Sabbath," 85ff.
11. See Berry, *Timbered Choir*, and *Sabbaths* (New York: North Point Press, 1987).
12. Emily Dickinson, poem 324, in *Complete Poems of Emily Dickinson*, 153.

She also wrote to a friend, "The only commandment I ever obeyed—'Consider the Lilies.'"[13] She remembered the Sabbath and kept it holy.

I have found that, in preparing for the Christian Sabbath on Sunday, it has been helpful to have a restful evening the night before. Such "Sabbath welcome" helps me enter more fully into the "Lord's Day" on Sunday, which provides us with a day of rest and worship, indoors and out. It can also provide a leisurely time to enjoy family and friends. But we must be careful lest our Sabbath get over-scheduled with leisure activities and create busyness.

What about those who must work every Sunday? Can Sabbath be a movable feast? Certainly. We can designate another day of the week as our Sabbath, a day of rest and joy. We can build our own "palace in time." Eugene Peterson, the noted Presbyterian minister and writer and translator of Scripture, designated Monday as his Sabbath. After the busiest day of the week on Sunday, he and his wife spent Monday together taking drives, hiking, picnicking, and resting, and on Monday evenings they would share a quiet evening together.[14] Part of what makes the day a Sabbath is its *difference* from every other day of the week; the difference itself is a way of restoring the mind, body, and soul.

At the Passover meal the child asks, "Why is this night different from every other night?" We could ask this question every Sunday (or whatever day is our Sabbath): "Why is this day different from any other day?" Then we could say around the table, "Because on this day God made the world, and on this day God raised Jesus from the dead!"

We can experience Sabbath in other ways. We can establish one hour every day as a Sabbath hour and assist others in the family to help them have such an hour. We can establish a Sabbath day every week and a Sabbath *weekend* every three months—time that offers sanctuary and rest from our frazzled lives.

This leads me to the last dimension of Sabbath the Hebrew people observed. The Hebrew people also observed a Sabbath *year* every seventh year. Things were different that year. The fields laid fallow so the land could heal. The families ate the food stored up from the previous years. It was a kindness to the land, just as Sabbath is a kindness we give ourselves—a time of restoration and rest.

---

13. Emily Dickinson to Alice Tuckerman, June 1884, in *Letters of Emily Dickinson*, L904.

14. Bass, "Keeping Sabbath," 85.

The academic world establishes sabbaticals, sabbatic years every seven years, for faculty to be away for rest, refreshment, research, and writing. That is not available to most of us, but we can establish some consecutive weeks from time to time to provide us a deeper rest than we ordinarily get. I have been blessed that most of my churches have given me a three-month sabbatical every fourth year. As a person who is not good at weekly and daily Sabbath keeping, these times have been essential for my well-being and for the ongoing practice of my ministry.

Time away, of whatever length, can be a Sabbath when we rest and remember who God is and who we are. Gordon Cosby would say at the Church of the Savior in Washington, D.C., "we are human *beings*, not human *doings*!"

I once went for a week's respite at the "Quiet House" at a Texas retreat center called Laity Lodge. The Quiet House is a tiny one-room structure where one can go and be totally alone and rest. On one wall was a framed cross-stitched piece of these words from Psalm 46:

> Be still and know that I am God
> Be still and know that I am
> Be still and know
> Be still

I know no better way to express the meaning of the Sabbath.

PUB THEOLOGY

INTRODUCTION

This session explores the meaning of sabbath and the meaning of rest in our lives today.

ICEBREAKER

When have you experienced deep rest?

JUMPING-OFF POINTS

- What are your earliest impressions of Sabbath and Sabbath keeping?
- As an adult, how do you observe the Sabbath? Is your practice one that you would call restful?

- The author observes that the Jewish Sabbath finds its origins in the stories of the creation and the exodus, and the Christian Sabbath has origins in the creation and the resurrection. How do the origins of Sabbath shape your thoughts about Sabbath keeping?
- Think about a time when you were exhausted. What was happening in your life that brought you to that point, and what happened as a result?
- The author quotes Abraham Heschel, who suggested that by neglecting to keep the Sabbath, we embezzle from our own lives. How have you seen this idea at work in your life or the lives of others?
- Think about a time when you knew yourself to be deeply rested. What did you have to do to achieve that deep rest? How long did your unburdened feeling last?
- The author notes that Wendell Berry and Emily Dickinson both kept Sabbath without attending regular church services. How necessary are church services to keeping the Sabbath holy?
- What are some ways you have found to build a healthy rhythm of work and rest into your life?
- What are some ways you have found to develop an awareness of rest time as holy time?

BIBLIOGRAPHY

Bass, Dorothy. *Practicing Our Faith*. San Francisco: Jossey-Bass, 1977.

Berry, Wendell. "The Wild Geese." In *Collected Poems*. San Francisco: Counterpoint Press, 1984. Poem reprinted by permission of the publisher.

Brueggemann, Walter. "Exodus." In *The New Interpreter's Bible*, vol. 1. Nashville: Abingdon, 1994.

Davidman, Joy. *Smoke on the Mountain, An Interpretation of the Ten Commandments*. Philadelphia: Westminster, 1954.

Dickinson, Emily. *The Complete Poems of Emily Dickinson*. Boston: Little, Brown & Co., 1960.

———. *Letters of Emily Dickinson*. Edited by Thomas H. Johnson and Theodora Ward. 3 vols. Cambridge: Harvard University Press, 1958.

Heschel, Abraham Joshua. *I Asked for Wonder: A Spiritual Anthology*. Edited by Samuel H. Dresner. New York: Crossroad, 1983.

Martyr, Justin. *The First Apology of Justin Martyr*. In The Ante-Nicene Fathers, vol. 1.

Oates, Wayne E. *Confessions of a Workaholic*. New York: World Publishing, 1971.

Wordsworth, William. "The world is too much with us." In *The New Oxford Book of English Verse 1250–1950*. New York: Oxford University Press, 1972.

MEETING 4

LIFE AS THE WORK OF FAITH

EVERETT C. GOODWIN

At an early age, I became aware of the high standards expected of me. Not least were the expectations levied on my role as a preacher's kid. Thus, faith came early and easily. But evidence of faith in behavior and ambition came slower and later. That was not unusual. It is a familiar pattern.

From their earlier vantage point, the Jews gave Christians the notion that "the Word was from God, was in God, and the Word was itself the same as God." So living life from a spiritual perspective became, first, a matter of interpretation of the Word. Living a worthwhile life was a matter of interpretation of many words, dependent most of all on where and when one began to make sense of things—"first principles," so to speak.

According to the ancient texts, God established a strong standard for faithful, obedient human behavior soon after the creation. In the beginning, as the ancient Scriptures record it, God gave the earliest humans one simple rule for life in the Garden of Eden: "of the tree of the knowledge of good and evil you shall not eat, for in the day that you eat of it you shall die" (Gen 2:17). Both the man and the woman succumbed to temptation and violated the rule (Gen 3). Cain and Abel, the progeny resulting from God's first couple in creation, fought each other, and Cain killed Abel over a dispute about whose work was more pleasing to God (Gen 4). That act of violence began a mortal tension between God and God's creation that inevitably seemed to imply immortal consequences.

Later, early Christians continued to experience a tension between the sacred and the profane. Pagan and mystical practices and beliefs clouded their theological formation. The fibers of that tension were frequently stretched and held taut between an active faith and a life focused on righteous work. Faith was most often evaluated by the evidence of obedience to holy ritual; worthy work was judged by standards related to responses to the perceived demands of God for justice and mercy, especially for the poor and the isolated. But frequently those standards were confused with social norms and priorities and thus changed and warped. Ever since then, humans have struggled to provide for their life necessities and to live lives worthy of a holy purpose, however that was defined. The questions "What is the meaning of my life?" and "What does work have to do with it?" have followed rather distantly behind questions like "What will I eat for supper?" or "How can I get rich?"

For some, a life of good and worthy works means a life in harmony with God's commandments that earns them a ticket into Paradise. For others, a life of simple faith is the sole requirement. Such a life is often defined by faithfulness to beliefs and rituals that are assumed to be of God. But for everyone, life has all too often seemed vexed, troubled, and possibly cursed. For those who desire to live in harmony with God, a worthy life seems to require activities that reflect godly presence and purpose. When worthy work is absent, life might be perceived to be pointless.

Jesus spoke often on the priority of life focused on worthy work. As an example, when he called for the disciples to follow him, many were doing their daily work. Jesus called them to stop their fishing and follow him to "fish for people" (Mark 1:17). Similarly, when another of them wished to take time to bury his father before committing to the work ahead, Jesus' response was "Follow me, and let the dead bury their own dead" (Matt 8:22). In a later, more complete encounter with the Pharisee Nicodemus, Jesus expands his meaning. By definition, a Pharisee was a person committed to the ritual work of holiness and perfection. But Jesus asked Nicodemus to reorder both his work and spiritual priorities. The man had asked how to achieve eternal life. Jesus concluded his reply by saying, ". . . those who do what is true come to the light, so that it may be clearly seen that their deeds have been done in God" (John 3:21). If faith is by nature passive and reflective, work is dynamic and revealing. But Jesus said that faith and work need to be intertwined. A faithful life is a work of faith.

The early church was composed of isolated small communities of faith that struggled to discover God's will for them and how to achieve it. It was an age that raised many questions of faith. In seeking to order their common life, early Christians ultimately developed a well-defined hierarchy of ecclesiastical authority that defined matters of faith for them. That authority became the keeper of the keys for the pathway to salvation and created definitions to measure achievement. Claiming authority by God's revelation and will, the early medieval church continued to develop its faith definition and expression through presumably divine decisions sponsored first by individual authority and later by occasional authoritative councils.

Fortunately for the church's long-term spiritual health, it was sometimes guided by wise people. Among them, in the church's earliest years of formation, were Augustine of Hippo (354–430) and, nearly 900 years later, Thomas Aquinas (1225–1274). Augustine's major work was largely personal and aptly titled *Confessions*. Aquinas, more a scholar, sought to define the range of human faith experience in his *Summa Theologica*. Both were foundational writings, and the relationship between faith, works, and salvation was central to both.

Despite the extraordinary intellect of these and others, people in that time were mostly illiterate and unschooled. Their faith was simple, and it was informed and guided by visual illustrations. Examples of these illustrated aids to worship in early church art can still be seen in the interior decoration of churches, surrounding worshipers with reminders of the keys to behavior that lead to eternal life. Many of these depict lives of saints. Their simple and sometimes miraculous examples of charity, love, justice, healing, and obedience were intended to reinforce the characteristics of Christian faith and life. For the few literate people, who mostly labored in monastic communities, handwritten treatises focused on Mary and Jesus, especially his suffering, death, and miraculous healings. Ordinary believers were encouraged to emulate saintly behavior, especially by doing good works that often focused on the poor and orphans and on the needs of strangers and outcasts.

When issues of belief seemed uncertain, formal disputation became an organized process by which remaining doubts were explored and sometimes resolved. The goals of the process were elusive, so debate and disputation moved divergent actions and threatening conflicts toward compromise or to a tapestry of authoritative exceptions. In the medieval church's considerations, God's truth was thus always made clear, even when it was not.

Especially since Augustine, theological issues in disputation have often been framed as dualities: God or humanity, faith or belief, salvation or damnation, faith or works. That is, the fundamentals of faith were positioned as "either/or," never "both/and." Affirmation of the truth of any one assertion of God's will often relied on effective scholarly arguments presented in such disputations. The medieval era encouraged disputations in order to achieve unity, and, failing agreement, people relied on authority. All truth was considered to be universal; any truth must reveal the nature of God. The church subsequently defined the spiritual particularities of proper human behavior. Deviation was condemned as heresy and punishment was brutal, often lethal. Worthy living depended on faithful adherence to authorized belief, and truth was equated with loyalty to the church that upheld it. Faith was rule-based, and the rules were warped by the benefits and prerogatives that favored the church. During its first thousand years, the church was thus both dynamic and obsessed with and increasingly focused on an ordered harmony that strengthened the influence and wealth of the church.

The duality of "faith or works" first developed as a matter of sequential consequences: one believed in God, obeyed the dictates of God's church, and thereby hoped to achieve entry into heaven. Debate over which came first, faith in God or good works approved by God, has been central to theological discourse throughout the history of Christian faith conversations. Whether faith or a worthy life should have priority in achieving God's favor and salvation has frequently been the subject of binary disputation.

As Christian faith developed, different paths to salvation emerged. One powerful example was a life arranged to avoid overt sin. This was the path followed by early hermits and later monastic orders. Some of these sought to build holy life patterns by means of community discipline, and they dedicated themselves to communal living under strict rules of obedience or submission to a life in service to the poor, the sick, or the shunned. Others chose a strict life of prayer and service. Still others involved extreme forms of self-denial; Augustine's self-mutilation to prevent sexual sins was one extreme example. Others included lives dedicated to poverty or to physical or mental hardship. Avoidance of social temptation often resulted in personal and social isolation. Some especially devout supplicants spent lives in radical isolation, living in caves, in deserts, or in other challenging circumstances and always in deprivation. In theory at least, such paths were chosen in the hope of finding the balance between a worthy life of holy work and an earned salvation that secured them a place in the realm of God.

In such a theological system, it made sense to respond to natural disasters as if they were God's judgments on a disobedient or unworthy people. As sad and painful examples, the many plagues that routinely diminished Europe's populations were perceived as divine visitations on unworthy people. Monuments in cities and towns were erected as memorials to times of unspeakable tragedy but also as visible confessionals in desperate response to presumed sins and as reminders to the living of the need for doing God's holy work.

Ultimately, medieval Christians established expectations about what constituted godly living. Most often these included individual submission to scriptural principles, confessions of faith, and obedience to the authoritative community or organization that represented God. To encourage or enforce godly assumptions, certain individuals were perceived to be authorized to have the power to judge the lives and deeds of others. Special powers and responsibilities were attributed to "godly rulers." Human nature being what it is, the expectations often unraveled, and those who were intended to perform them overlooked them. There have been numerous efforts to reform and rejuvenate faith and to shape lives for godly work. At the heart of such reforms is the connection between faith and the work of life.

In the past, the pathways to salvation (or spiritual approval) were narrow and ultimately rested on individual submission to established orthodoxy or hierarchical approval. Violations often led to conviction as a heretic and, frequently, to severe punishment or monetary penalty. Major or minor reforms were occasionally attempted or proposed, but it was not until Martin Luther's assertions of theological error and ecclesiastical corruption in the early sixteenth century that wider dialogue became possible. Luther's simple invitation to debate and disputation on matters of theological importance led to his persecution, but it also led to a lengthy period of reform and division in the church and its organized structures. It also made it possible to reimagine the nature of Christian worship, godly work, and the meaning of salvation. Over several hundred years, these arguments stimulated many wars when verbal disputes contributed to regional or national aspirations. But the Reformation also enabled the Enlightenment, aspects of the Renaissance, and a variety of "isms" that continue until now, most notably pietism and rationalism.

Pietism encouraged outward disciplines or personal habits suggestive of inner obedience or holiness. Its roots may lie early in the reverential worship of saints, but pietism was brought to full flower following the Reformation. It was especially prevalent among European rural communities but was also received into the newly developing gentry class in preindustrial Britain and its parallels in Europe.

Rationalism was first an intellectual movement of the seventeenth and eighteenth centuries. In politics, rationalism sought to understand human nature and behavior in rational terms, rejecting superstition and mystical causes. In religion, it sought to bridge the growing gulf between faith and observed science. It was most popular, then, among educated classes of people, but it spread more widely because of its influence among religious leaders and educators.

On the other hand, Pietism eventually was the majority companion of the emerging value systems in Europe and the New World and was especially a guiding force in the establishment of the American colonies and in the mission fields of Africa, Asia, and other places that the explorers and entrepreneurs traveled and missionaries worked from the seventeenth into the twentieth centuries.

In the mid-nineteenth century, a revolution in the approach to biblical, theological, and historical academic disciplines was interpreted as an attack on the truth of the Bible and on values and traditions held by many people of faith. It introduced historical-critical approaches to original faith documents and later developed demythologizing approaches to sacred traditions that often divided faith communities.

But nineteenth-century academic revolutions in historical and biblical interpretation likewise created the opportunity for a fusion of strictly religious thought with emerging approaches to fields of psychology, sociology, and history. Among religiously oriented folk, these advances also enabled "spirituality" as a newly understood potential of behavior and focus, especially among those who were uncertain about faith built on creeds or rituals predicated on ancient documents. One lasting result has been a new understanding of the older duality of "faith and works." Ironically, it has led to a new, or perhaps renewed, understanding of "life as the work of faith."

In that context, the social gospel movement of the late nineteenth and early twentieth centuries might be seen as a bridge to or a fusion with present-day social justice and reform movements in Western cultures, as just one example. Despite being criticized as a tool of the modernist camp or as a thinly disguised tool of "theological liberalism" or "secular humanism," the social gospel was rooted in pietism. Its primary role was to encourage biblical, even creedal, belief systems but at the same time to encourage those who advocated such belief to "do something about it" by their actions.

The Baptist pastor and seminary professor Walter Rauschenbusch was an early and formative advocate of social gospel action, partly due to his background in German pietism and partly due to his role as pastor of a church in New York's infamous Hell's Kitchen district. In dealing with the spiritual as well as the physical needs of his parish, he discovered in his pietistic tradition the tools to approach them. Later, after he achieved fame as a bit of a revolutionary and advocate of justice for the poor, he became a professor at the Rochester Theological School, later Colgate Rochester. Toward the end of his career, visitors to campus who came to interview him frequently observed that he maintained a daily discipline of Bible study and personal prayer. He believed what he had always believed in theological terms. But his life experience had shown him the implications of those beliefs and how to apply them.

As a child, I understood early that faith was important. My theological awareness was formed by annual family trips to the Village of Mammoth Lakes in California's Sierra Nevada mountains. On a tiny island in the middle of one of the Twin Lakes in Mammoth sits a small, rustic outdoor chapel that, as a result of earthquakes and volcanic activity, is set against the backdrop of a 1,500-foot cliff. For twenty years, my parents and then our family spent several weeks each summer in our nearby cabin. We rarely missed a Sunday service when we were there. Some Sundays, my father was the morning preacher. I spent a lot of time sitting on a log with my attention drawn not to the service but up to that magnificent cliff soaring above. Over the pulpit hung a sign carved into a slab of native redwood bark. It said, "Unto these hills I lift up mine eyes" (Ps 121:1, KJV). For a time, I believed I was physically closer to God in that chapel and in the mountains. (The psalmists had a similar belief, as is evident in many of their writings.) But in important ways, it stimulated my life in faith and then my understanding of life as a time of striving to do the work of faith.

I would never deny that early influences from family or community context had an effect on my life and faith development. But my personal life experiences have also been a towering influence. As a teen, I was convinced that I was not living up to my potential and was called to account by a guidance counselor. As a young person, I came to realize that my early career goals were not consistent with my faith. As an adult, I have learned the most important life lessons from the people I have ministered among, from those in the highest levels of power and prestige to those perceived as the lowest in society, including the unhoused. The lessons have sometimes been jarring and sometimes occasions for rueful laughter. But all have lingered as guides in an attempt to develop my life as a work of faith.

Recently, I have been influenced (again) by Jewish colleagues and friends. They have a word for what I strive to express: *Mikveh*, which loosely translated means *blessing*. You hear the word a lot at memorial services and in moments of gratitude. To be a *Mikveh* is to be a blessing, to enable blessings in others, to live so that others, even God, are blessed.

PUB THEOLOGY

INTRODUCTION

Discussions centered on faith and works raise numerous theological and practical questions: How does one live one's life? How do we gain salvation? There is a division of thought and opinion, as to the belief that salvation is solely received by faith. Others advocate that how you live your life is just as important in one's relationship with Jesus Christ.

ICE BREAKER

Answer quickly: Who has been a major influence in your life and why?

JUMPING-OFF POINTS

- Secular ethical considerations are not always based on the presence or role of a deity. Is "godless faith" possible?
- Is it possible for disputation based on rational thought and logic to reveal biblical truth?
- Does general avoidance of evil action or personal temptation result in a "worthy life"? In other words, is "piety" relevant today?
- Can personal faith ever be fully supported by rational thinking?
- Is there a deadly temptation in assuming that one's life is worthy? Or is there temptation in trying to develop such a life?
- Could you explain how life experiences have challenged you to live a more faithful life?

OUTSIDE READING

Courtney Doctor, "What's the Deal with Faith and Works in James?" May 10, 2020, thegospelcoalition.org/article/faith-works-james/.

Joel Ryan, "What Does James 2:26 Mean by 'Faith without Works Is Dead'?" October 2, 2019, christianity.com/wiki/bible/faith-without-works-is-dead-james-2-26-meaning.html.

Thomas Schreiner, "Faith and Works," thegospelcoalition.org/essay/faith-and-works/.

MEETING 5

A THEOLOGY OF WORSHIP

DEBORAH MOORE CLARK

[Dietrich] Bonhoeffer believed it was the role of the church to *speak for those who could not speak*. To outlaw slavery inside the church was right, but to allow it to exist outside the church would be evil. So it was with this persecution of the Jews by the Nazi state. . . . To serve others outside the church, to love them as one loved oneself, and to do unto them as one would have others do unto oneself, these were the clear commands of Christ. . . . Around [this] time, Bonhoeffer made his famous declaration: "Only he who cries out for the Jews may sing Gregorian chants." As far as he was concerned, to dare to sing to God when his chosen people were being beaten and murdered meant that one must also speak out against their suffering. If one was unwilling to do this, God was not interested in one's worship. (Metaxas, *Bonhoeffer*, 281)

INTRODUCTION

For years, I have been a student of worship. Soon after college graduation, I began to realize my poverty in understanding and leading worship. At the time, I was already employed to lead church music and worship. Despite this fulfilling work and the anchor of having grown up in the church, the daughter of a minister, I realized I was missing something. While backed by years of good experiences and well-intentioned efforts, the epiphany of my insufficiency was swift. In the foreword of my book, *O Come, Let Us Bow Down and Worship*, I confess, "For the first time, I saw that my understanding of worship was shallow, and my contribution to worship, although meaningful, was much less than my best effort."[1] Perhaps you find yourself puzzled with questions about worship and the part you play

---

1. Clark, *O Come, Let Us Bow Down and Worship*, 4.

in it. Perhaps you faithfully participate in worship but find yourself going mindlessly through the motions. Perhaps you've never given worship any serious thought. While entire books are devoted to the theology of worship, this chapter simply isolates and addresses worship's most basic tenets.

WORSHIP IS ACTION

Worship is a verb. When one considers worship as an action word, the myriad ways the gathered church may engage in worship can be imagined and understood as never before. By definition, to worship is to do something. Worship is active and dynamic, not passive or static. In *O Come, Let Us Bow Down and Worship*, I offer a list of words and phrases that describe worship's dynamic nature and actions that might take place within its scope. For consideration, that list is repeated and augmented here. The list follows no apparent order beyond alphabetization.[2] To worship is to

Adore
Act out obediently
Bow
Celebrate God
Clasp hands
Confess
Consciously commune
Converse with God
Dialogue
Encounter
Express awe
Express faith
Feel
Feel awed
Give
Hear (others, self, congregation)
Imagine
Join with others
Kneel

Move
Offer
Participate
Play instruments
Praise
Pray
Read Scripture aloud
Recite creeds
Respond (creature to Creator)
Sacrifice self
Serve
Sing (solo, choral, congregational)
Sing hymns
Smell (incense, burning candles)
Submit
Taste (Communion bread and wine)
Witness

---

2. Ibid., 57–58.

What actions might you add? As a brainstorming activity, please consider additional words and phrases that describe the action of worship and integrate those into this inexhaustive list. To worship is to do *what*?

Archbishop William Temple's (1881–1944) poetic definition of worship became a classic when it was published in 1942. Temple adds more worshipful actions to our expanding list:

> To worship is to quicken the conscience of the holiness of God,
> To feed the mind with the truth of God,
> To purge the imagination by the beauty of God,
> To open the heart to the love of God,
> To devote the will to the purpose of God.
> All this is gathered up in that emotion which most cleanses us from selfishness because it is the most selfless of all emotions—adoration.[3]

Quicken, feed, purge, open, and devote are all action words. Because the conscience, mind, imagination, heart, and will comprise the essence of humanity, these aspects indicate that the whole person is engaged in worship. Holiness, truth, beauty, love, and purpose are attributes of God. To know these is to know God.[4]

A BIBLICAL MODEL FOR WORSHIP

Please read *aloud* Isaiah 6:1-12:

> In the year that King Uzziah died, I saw the Lord sitting on a throne, high and lofty; and the hem of his robe filled the temple. Seraphs were in attendance above him; each had six wings: with two they covered their faces, and with two they covered their feet, and with two they flew. And one called another and said: "Holy, holy, holy is the LORD of hosts; the whole earth is full of his glory." The pivots on the thresholds shook at the voices of those who called, and the house filled with smoke. And I said: "Woe is me! I am lost, for I am a man of unclean lips, and I live among a people of unclean lips; yet my eyes have seen the King, the LORD of hosts!"
>
> Then one of the seraphs flew to me, holding a live coal that had been taken from the altar with a pair of tongs. The seraph touched my mouth with it and said: "Now that this has touched your lips, your guilt has

---

3. Temple, *Hope of a New World*, 30.
4. Clark, *O Come, Let Us Bow Down and Worship*, 58.

departed and your sin is blotted out." Then I heard the voice of the Lord saying, "Whom shall I send, and who will go for us?" And I said, "Here am I; send me!" And he said, "Go and say to this people: 'Keep listening but do not comprehend; keep looking, but do not understand.' Make the mind of this people dull, and stop their ears, and shut their eyes, so that they may not look with their eyes, and listen with their ears, and comprehend with their minds, and turn and be healed."

Then I said, "How long, O Lord?" And he said: "Until cities lie waste without inhabitant, and houses without people, and the land is utterly desolate; until the LORD sends everyone far away, and vast is the emptiness in the midst of the land." (NRSV)

The passage, which illustrates Isaiah's worshipful encounter with God, opens with the historical declaration, "In the year that King Uzziah died . . . ." As John Claypool put it, "A great national crisis had shaken [Isaiah's] security."[5] This crisis was the impetus behind Isaiah's trip to the temple and his ultimate encounter with God.

Isaiah goes to the temple for succor and strength. God is revealed to Isaiah, and the encounter fills the prophet with awe. Acknowledging his sin, Isaiah confesses, "Woe is me!" The great God of Judah meets Isaiah's confession with gracious forgiveness, and then cleanses the prophet for future service, making him whole again. In his encounter with God, Isaiah worships. Isaiah answers his calling, responding to God with words and actions of commitment. Isaiah leaves the temple moved, changed, and motivated, ready to serve.

As I write, a pandemic the likes of which the world has not seen in 100 years rages out of control worldwide. To contain the Covid-19 virus, Americans have isolated at home for ten months, upending normal life. Livelihoods have been ruined and financial insecurity runs rampant. Polarized political differences tear asunder the democratic fabric of our nation, rending our nation's collective soul. Emboldened White supremacy rears its ugly, racist head. Provoked by the irresponsible rhetoric of the president, the US Capitol has been laid siege by an angry mob hellbent on violence and insurrection, its hallowed halls desecrated, Congressional members threatened and terrorized, and citizens killed. The president has been impeached, charged with incitement of insurrection. In America, emotions are raw. We find truth elusive, democracy endangered, and national security shaken. If we need reasons to understand Isaiah's motivation for seeking succor and

---

5. Claypool, "The Secret of Worship," 7.

strength at the temple, we need only look around and within us. Were it not for the pandemic, perhaps we too would be collectively heading to the sanctuary. In our isolation, have we been brought to our knees before God?

Like ours, Isaiah's world was turned upside down. Good king Uzziah was dead. As the story goes, the king had puffed with pride over his many accomplishments, and he was no longer satisfied being merely mortal. Uzziah wanted to be divine. Pride intact, the king entered the temple to burn incense. For Uzziah, it was worship as usual, but when Azariah the high priest and eighty associates confronted him, Uzziah responded in anger and petulance instead of repentance. God judged him, striking him with leprosy.[6] In Uzziah's time, the scourge of leprosy was met with perpetual quarantine and disgrace. Considered unclean, the once good king was ruined and later died in isolation and dishonor. All of these acts had a profound effect on the citizenry of Judah and the prophet Isaiah.

Making things worse, Isaiah knew God was displeased with the empty, worship-business-as-usual actions of the people. The Holy One had come to hate their offerings and festivals. God desired worshipers to wash themselves clean and to "cease to do evil, learn to do good; seek justice, rescue the oppressed, defend the orphan, plead for the widow" (Isa 1:16). Moreover, God wanted the people to resist narcissistic idols of self and to repent of haughtiness, selfishness, and pride.

The Isaiah 6 biblical account provides an exemplary model for Christian worship. Isaiah's encounter is worship at its best because it is God-centered, God-focused, and exalts the Holy One. The following outline of the passage reveals a step-by-step progression through Isaiah's worship experience.[7] This progression suggests a prescriptive framework on which to arrange the actions of our worship. All worship services may be build on this structural form, regardless of style, venue, or theme.

Reference and Action

Isaiah 6:1-4	Commendation (Praise)	*Holy, holy, holy!*
Isaiah 6:5	Confession and Contrition	*Woe is me!*
Isaiah 6:6-7	Cleansing	*Sin blotted out.*
Isaiah 6:8a	Calling	*Who will go?*
Isaiah 6:8b	Commitment	*Here am I: send me.*
Isaiah 6:9-10	Commissioning	*God said, Go!*
Isaiah 6:11-12	Clarification	*How long, Lord?*

---

6. *Nelson's Illustrated Bible Dictionary*, s.v. "Uzziah," 1084.

7. Clark, *O Come, Let Us Bow Down and Worship*, 17.

John R. Claypool, in his sermon "The Secret of Worship," refers to this framework as "interpretive." So what's the secret? The secret lies in how the worshiper understands his or her role in worship.[8]

WHAT ROLE DO I PLAY IN WORSHIP?

Danish philosopher and theologian Søren Kierkegaard (1813–1855) provides a remarkable illustration of the roles played in worship by worshipers, worship leaders, and God. Beyond philosopher and theologian, Kierkegaard was a poet, social critic, and religious author. His writings display a fondness for metaphor, irony, and parables.[9]

Using metaphor, Kierkegaard compares worship to the dramatic medium of plays with the usual participants: actors, prompters, and audience. The actors, enabled and supported by their prompters, engage in dramatic action before the audience, who watches, listens, and reacts. Since the play was an ancient art form, Kierkegaard's comparison was easily understood by the people of his day.[10]

For modern audiences, being part of a group engaged by a play is both a familiar and pleasant form of entertainment. Therefore, if we were asked to compare worship participants to those of a play, we might conclude that worship leaders are actors who perform, prompted by God, before an audience of onlookers, in this case the congregation. Given our needs to critique, judge, criticize, and be entertained, we might further conclude that worship needs to please and entertain the audience of congregants in order to be relevant or worth one's time. These conclusions appear reasonable.

Having now set us up, Kierkegaard turns the comparison on its unsuspecting ear. In worship, Kierkegaard writes, God is the audience. The congregation are the actors. Worship leaders are the prompters. What changes does this new arrangement effect? How might it dovetail with the Isaiah 6 model of worship?

The engagement of players shifts within the metaphor. Comparison turns to contrast. What appeared ordered and obvious becomes disordered. The topsy-turvy arrangement ends any mistaken notion that worship might need to be pleasing or entertaining to a congregation of spectators—because, after all, the congregation is not the audience. This new prototype

---

8. Claypool, "Secret of Worship," 8.

9. "Søren Kierkegaard," en.wikipedia.org/wiki/S%C3%B8ren_Kierkegaard.

10. "The Origins of Theatre—The First Plays," pbs.org/empires/thegreeks/background/24b.html.

highlights God as the sole audience, and it is the Holy One who waits and watches to see how worshipers might respond to the Holy Presence. This new order supports and underscores the fact that to worship is to focus on God. Worship is about God and for God. Remarkably, it leaves open the possibility that God may or may not be pleased with what congregants offer.

To further extend the metaphor, in this new paradigm congregants might assume larger, weightier roles in worship. Responsibility now rests on the shoulders of those gathered, not just on worship leaders. No longer might congregants sit quietly in the balcony or on the back pew, expecting to be partially engaged spectators, waiting to be entertained. Now congregants are exposed to the spotlight of God's expectation that worshipers are to approach God with respect and awe, to fully participate and to act in ways pleasing to God.

No longer are ministers and other worship leaders merely performers before a critical congregation (although leaders are worshipers also). Their primary responsibilities now shift to the work of assisting, edifying, and enabling the saints through leadership, training, and example so that congregants might become full participants in worship who bring acceptable offerings to God.

If critique occurs, God is the one who does it. God is the one to be pleased or displeased. God is the one to be satisfied or not satisfied. God is the one to be praised and honored. It's all about God. God is our reason to gather. God is our reason to worship. Period. When the reviews come in, what might God say of our worship? Pulitzer Prize-winning author Annie Dillard offers this thought-provoking and astonishing thought: "I often think of the set pieces of liturgy as certain words which people have successfully addressed to God without their getting killed."[11]

WORSHIP FOCUSES ON GOD ALONE

Given the focus on God and Isaiah's movement in concert with the Holy One, we can see how the Isaiah scriptural model dovetails smoothly with Kierkegaard's metaphoric illustration. In both the Isaiah model and the Kierkegaard metaphor, God is the singular focus. "God alone is the audience—an audience of One."[12] Claypool asserts that worship "is not

---

11. Dillard, *Holy the Firm*, 59.
12. Swartz, *Dancing with Broken Bones*, 129.

a spectator sport. This is not just a trivial way to pass an hour of the day. The most important thing you ever do is to engage in worship, for that is when God's reality and your reality interact and hopefully, the two 'become one.'"[13]

When worshiping God, the self must be sacrificed. If the selves of worshipers are not subjected, their hedonistic presence skews the focus of worship away from the Holy One. Idols quickly replace God: the needs and desires of people, the chosen theme for the day, the whims of leadership, personalities, and countless other self-interests. Self-interests, both personal and collective, must be minimized and God maximized if authentic worship is to take place. All else is vanity.

What selfish idols get in the way of your worship? What selfish idols get in the way of your congregation's corporate worship?

In Claypool's phrase, "the act of worship becomes trivial and meaningless [when] God is left out, and when this happens, authentic worship ceases to take place, no matter how august the surrounding or the ritual."[14]

CONSEQUENCES OF AUTHENTIC WORSHIP

What might the consequences of authentic worship be?

Twelve Hebrew prophets, whose accounts comprise the final books of the Old Testament—Hosea, Joel, Amos, Obadiah, Jonah, Micah, Nahum, Habakkuk, Zephaniah, Haggai, Zechariah, and Malachi—give us insight into both authentic and inauthentic worship. "The Twelve," along with the prophet Isaiah, cry out against abuses in worship but also prescribe what God desires in worship. In *O Come, Let Us Bow Down and Worship*, I offer this synopsis of their prophetic messages:

> Cries of the Twelve Hebrew prophets frequently link abuses in worship to impoverished and unethical living. Amos, the shepherd from the mountains, condemns empty, vain worship and challenges his audience to do what is right. Micah, the small-town artisan and proletarian, denounces empty, unrelated ceremony and unethical living, petitioning his audience for justice, kindness, and humility. Zephaniah, citizen of Jerusalem and a man of royal descent, cries out against indifference, cites numerous worship abuses, and decries wrong living. His prophecies link worship and right living. The post-exilic prophet Haggai, a virtual unknown, links

---

13. Claypool, "Worship as Involvement," 6.
14. Ibid., 8.

liturgy and life. He preaches that liturgy and life cannot be separated, and because of this, spiritual values, priorities, and cultic worship affect the balance of life.[15]

Isaiah was moved and changed by his encounter with God. Through worship, the prophet sensed God calling him, and his committed response was voiced in words and lived out in actions. Isaiah left the temple moved, changed, and motivated, ready to serve. His past behind him, Isaiah emerged as a new prophet and took his worship experience out of the temple and into the world. I also wrote this about Isaiah:

> The story of Isaiah reveals how the connection between worship and service, liturgy and life, is made in the mind and life of Isaiah. . . . Service is a natural consequence of worship. What is true for individuals is equally true for congregations. Worship breathes life-giving energy into congregations. Worship motivates church communities to serve the world about them. Worship evokes servant action to those in need. Worship musters strength for churches to tackle unusual and challenging ministries. Worship encourages families of faith to keep on when the going gets tough. Worship induces service. Not only is service a consequence of worship, worship is service.[16]

As with Isaiah, we too may be changed in worship, and when what we do *in* and *beyond* worship falls in line with what God desires, our worship is authenticated.

CONCLUSION

In conclusion, I offer a concise theology of worship, which summarizes the meeting's discourse: Beyond all else, worship focuses on God. Worship is composed of a progression of actions that follows a Scripture model: praise, confession and pardon, calling, commitment, and sending out (Isa 6:1-12). All worship services may be built on this structural form, regardless of style, venue, or theme. Authentic worship is reflected in offerings of justice, kindness, and humility, in which God delights (Mic 6:8).

---

15. Clark, *O Come, Let Us Bow Down and Worship*, 227.
16. Ibid., 231.

PUB THEOLOGY

INTRODUCTION

Despite growing up in the church, serving churches in church music ministry, and being a congregant and worshiper myself, I have at times found my worship experience lacking. Perhaps, like me, you find yourself puzzled with questions about worship and the part you play in its action. Perhaps you faithfully participate but find yourself going mindlessly through the motions. Perhaps you've never given worship serious thought and find yourself watching the clock for the worship hour to be over. Whatever your status, it is my prayer that this session, in its attempt to isolate and address worship's most basic tenets, will deepen your understanding of worship, and in turn, center your thinking about your own worship practice. It is also my hope that such study and thought will, in the end, enhance and deepen your worship experience.

ICEBREAKER

Before discussing the questions below—in less than a minute—please begin by stating your name, occupation and favorite hobby or pastime. Please provide a very succinct description of it and share one positive way in which it impacts your life.

JUMPING-OFF POINTS

- To worship is to do what? As you brainstorm, what actions might you add to the list provided?
- As you consider the focus of your church's corporate worship, is the primary focus on God? Does the focus fall elsewhere? On the church family? Personalities? The music? The sermon? What skews the focus away from God?
- Considering the Kierkegaard metaphor, what role do you typically assume in the "drama" of worship?
- If you attend worship services regularly or occasionally but remain unchanged, unmoved, unresponsive, and have nothing compelling to offer the world around you, then perhaps you are not worshiping at all. Could motives that bring you to the worship event be interfering with a true worship experience? To examine motives is an extremely personal activity. What reasons bring you to worship? To socialize? To perform?

To be entertained? To be seen and heard? To edify your standing in the community? To observe? To hear the music? To live out a habit? To please a family member? To assuage guilt? To appease God?
- What consequences do you personally experience when worshiping in your setting? What differences does worship make in your life? Share your discoveries with your discussion group.
- How do you hear God's call to commitment on your life? How does worship figure into this sense of calling and your response?
- Discuss with the group how your congregation is affected by its corporate worship. What are the consequences of worship for your community of faith? What changes does worship effect in your community of faith?

BIBLIOGRAPHY

Clark, Deborah Moore. *O Come, Let Us Bow Down and Worship*. Macon: Smyth & Helwys, 2003.

Claypool, John R. "The Secret of Worship." Transcript of sermon presented at Northminster Baptist Church, Jackson, MS, January 30, 1977.

———. "Worship as Involvement." Transcript of sermon presented at Broadway Baptist Church, Fort Worth, TX, September 23, 1973.

Dillard, Annie. *Holy the Firm*. New York: Harper, 1977.

Metaxas, Eric. *Bonhoeffer: Pastor, Martyr, Prophet, Spy*. Nashville: Thomas Nelson, 2010.

Nelson's Illustrated Bible Dictionary. Nashville: Thomas Nelson, 1986.

"The Origins of Theatre—The First Plays." *PBS*. pbs.org/empires/thegreeks/background/24b.html.

Swartz, David. *Dancing with Broken Bones: Blessed are the Broken in Spirit, for God Can Make Them Whole*. Colorado Springs: NavPress, 1987.

Temple, William. *The Hope of a New World*. New York: Macmillan, 1942.

"Søren Aabye Kierkegaard." *Wikipedia*. en.wikipedia.org/wiki/S%C3%B8ren_Kierkegaard.

MEETING 6

CHURCH AS COMMUNITY
J. ANDREW DAUGHERTY

Why church? The late great Unitarian Universalist theologian James Luther Adams (1902–1994) poignantly and succinctly summarized the reasons people go to church as "ultimacy and intimacy."[1] By intimacy, he signals the deeply human impulse for a connection with others. The horizontal dimension of human union involves profound relationships with other people. By ultimacy, he beckons the longing of the God-shaped hole in the human heart to be creatively bound with a sense of meaning and purpose to something larger than ourselves. This vertical dimension associates us with what we can confidently profess and express about the heavenly realm of transcendence and ultimate meaning.

When the church is being who Christ calls it to be, it's as natural as the rising and falling of our God-given breath: inhale God's life (ultimacy), exhale God's life (intimacy with others). This rhythm of community life is an essential function of the spirituality of discipleship, of *imatatio Christi*: a focus on Jesus of Nazareth and the Christ of faith as a clue to the meaning of the church's mission and the meaning of what it means to be human.

The purpose of the church as a community of the faithful is fueled by and fused by this intimacy and ultimacy that originates in God's heart of transcendent and immanent love. Jesus as the dark-skinned, Jewish rabbi stood in his own Jewish tradition and radically revised it through his teaching of the "kin-dom" of God. He modeled intimacy and ultimacy through his own relationship with the One he called Abba and through the relationships that connected him so deeply to his fully human friends and disciples. The surprising twists and turns of Jesus' teaching and actions ignited his followers to embody God's radical love for the disempowered

---

1. Adams, "James Luther Adams: A Time to Speak," jameslutheradams.org/a-time-to-speak/.

and the dispossessed—for those who were weak and suffering; for those who were poor and poor in spirit.

The centuries-long institutionalization of Jesus' movement can sometimes distract people from this foundational spiritual premise. The classic book by Albert Nolan, *Jesus Before Christianity*, underscores this. Nolan presents a traditioned and innovative view of the difference between the church as an institution and the church as the reincarnation of the spirit of Christ. Put simply, his summary is that Jesus did not come to start a new religion; Jesus came to spark a spiritual movement. The characterization of this movement is further described by German theologian Jürgen Moltmann:

> The church would not witness to the whole Christ if it were not a fellowship of believers with the poor, a fellowship of the hopeful with the sick, and a fellowship of the loving with the oppressed. Its unity would no longer be "predicated of the time of salvation" if it were not to achieve liberation for the downtrodden, justice for those without rights, and peace in social conflicts. It is not "one for itself"; it is one for the peace of divided humankind in the coming of the kingdom of God. In this respect "unity in freedom" and "freedom in unity" become particularly important.[2]

At its best, the church can be a spiritual and social incubator for the kind of unity in freedom and freedom in unity that liberates people personally. It can speak to the solidarity and compassion that propel us to make all things new as a force of social and political justice. The church is always dying and rising again as it follows the ups and downs of Christ's Paschal Mystery.

What is good and beautiful and true for the church at a macro level is what is good and beautiful and true for all people at a micro level. This is the spiritual symbiosis of what gives the church its power by blessing all of God's children regardless of gender identity, age, race, ethnicity, sexual orientation, physical limitation, educational background, or economic situation.

Mom blogger turned philanthropist Glennon Doyle beautifully writes in her iconic womanhood book *Untamed*,

---

2. Jurgen Moltmann, *Church in the Power of the Spirit*, 345–46.

I am a human being. Meant to be in perpetual becoming. . . . If I am living bravely, my life will become a million deaths and rebirths. My goal is not to remain the same but to live in such a way that each day, year, moment, relationship, conversation or crisis is the material I use to become a truer, more beautiful version of myself. I will not hold on to a single existing idea, opinion, identity, story, or relationship that keeps me from emerging new.[3]

What would it be like for the church today to adopt this kind of belief? Doyle names life's seasonal dimensions of death and renewal that inspire change and evolution. Human nature does not accept this as readily. And the nature of church accepts it even less. It's lodged in one of the church's cliches at the highest point of resistance to change: "We have never done it that way before."

Once people decide to join the Jesus movement by joining a community of faith, the Spirit will entice and inspire and startle them into ministries and missions and, yes, radical action that carry the spirit of Christ out into the world where it and the church belong. Such is the Spirit's Pentecostal prerogative, as witnessed in the New Testament narrative of the coming of the Holy Spirit in the book of Acts (2:1-21).

If we listen closely to Luke tell the story, we understand that what happened at Pentecost was not just for an exclusive or elitist few: not just for men; not just for the Jewish people; not just for society's upper crust; not just for those who spoke a certain language. The Spirit came and inspired everybody except for some dubious doubters in the crowd who censured the believers for drinking beer for breakfast at 9 a.m.—even though most locals knew that all the popular pubs around Jerusalem didn't open until 4 p.m. anyway!

As Luke tells it, those gathered were not under the influence of spirits. They were under the influence of the Spirit of God, who gave fresh breath to the stale air of doubt and fear and confusion that had created a mental cloud around despondent and depressed disciples after Jesus' crucifixion. Luke puts this in the boldest terms possible. He uses vivid images of violent wind and tongues of fire to describe the way God blew new life into the fledgling community.

Like a virtuoso vintner, God pressed together the oddest, ripest, and most exotic grapes in the form of people of all kinds. God made this cast of characters into a fine wine that filled the empty earthen jars of hopelessness

---

3. Doyle, *Untamed*, 77.

with hope, physical poverty with spiritual riches, and deepening despair with escalating ecstasy.

"These people are not drunk, as you suppose" (Acts 2:15), says the preacher Peter. He means that it doesn't smell like a party. It only sounds like one. This is about the Spirit, not the spirits, but if we want to exercise some spiritual imagination, it would be something like a sixteen-year-old Lagavulin single malt scotch. There is a smoky, peaty personality to this spirit of Scotland that bespeaks the Spirit of God coming in tongues of flame. That taste of the Holy Spirit's smoky, peaty personality imagined as tongues of fire inspired the new community of Jesus followers to rethink what was possible.

Swiss theologian Emil Brunner's wisdom is apt here: "The Church *exists* by mission, just *as a fire exists* by *burning*."[4] The mission of the church is a mission of a fully divine and a fully human passion. This passion is a fire that warms and comforts just as it ignites hearts to overcome complacency. The work of the church in part is to ensure that religion never becomes an opiate or an anesthetic that values contentment over courage.

Think about this in terms of your own church—or in terms of the church that exists in your spiritual dreams. The famous words of former Archbishop of Canterbury William Temple provide a starting point: "The Church is the only institution that exists primarily for the benefit of those who are not its members."[5] This is a creative challenge in a world where not everyone is a "joiner." And it is a conversant challenge to those who are steeped in the larger tradition of the church (and local church cultures) to such a degree that it becomes an exclusive club rather than an inclusive companionship of Christ's love. To be fair, notions of meaningful church membership and what it means to join a spiritual community are paired with cultural notions of membership—like being a member of Costco or Amazon Prime or AARP. These are parallels for some who ponder the value of joining a spiritual community.

To this matter of church membership and the constitution of a spiritual community, what it means to be a member of a church and what it means to be a member of the Jesus movement could be more equally harmonized. Paul uses a medical or biological metaphor to describe the people of the Jesus movement as "members of one another." It's serious business if one

---

4. Brunner, *Word and the World*, 108.

5. Quoted in Schenck, "Why Does the Church Exist?" frtim.wordpress.com/2013/11/09/why-does-the-church-exist/.

of our body parts goes missing from the rest of our human body. Likewise, in the body of Christ each of us is essential to the whole. The metaphor is emblematic of the evergreen dilemma of the matter of church as a spiritual community and church as a modern organizational institution. Cuban American theologian Justo González articulates a prophetic dimension of what seems to be an ongoing dilemma in this regard: "The function of the Spirit is not so much to create the structures and procedures by which the church must live forever, but rather to break open structures so that the church may be faithful as it faces each new challenge."[6]

No matter the structure of any church as a human institution or as part of a larger denominational network, the governing authority of a congregation is the same governing authority for all congregations around the world. From the first century to the twenty-first century, that authority is God's imaginative Spirit. The Spirit keeps our need for control from becoming idolatrous. The Spirit keeps our need for predictability from becoming stagnation.

These negotiations of tradition typify Kathryn Tanner's assessments that a community's struggle around Christian identity is endemic to questions of how certain applications of tradition are preferred over others. Arguments must be made about how and whether various practices cohere in a particular culture in a certain time and place. The reason is that human agency within the matrices of Christian history can never replace God's free-spirited ways. Whatever continuity a community finds in Christian practices, it must be tested afresh in many times and many places.[7]

Tanner furthermore adds that *a priori* experiences with God are inaccessible. Rooted firmly in postmodern cultural theory, she maintains that any person's spiritual encounters are transmitted through one's own values and experiences. Thus, appeals to tradition become something like one person's word against the other if such appeals are intended only to demand universal conformity to a human authority. "The Holy Spirit moves over the surface of the waters and not in their depths,"[8] Tanner says, meaning that what matters most is the way the tattered strands of Christian practices are stitched together to create a tapestry that a group designates as "traditional."

---

6. Quoted in Segovia and Tolbert, *Reading from this Place*, 146.
7. Tanner, *Theories of Culture*, 135–36.
8. Ibid., 162.

Tanner affirms that the forms of Christian discipleship must be subject to regular revision. Any theological claim that invokes appeals to normative Christian tradition must be respectfully scrutinized. This means, at least in part, that at any given time in the history of a faith community, there are likely both innovators and guardians of particular beliefs, values, or practices. Because Tanner so radically relativizes these elements to the humanly inscrutable free grace of a free God, her proposal favors the innovators of tradition rather than the guardians of it. While she believes both groups are obligated to listen to each other in order to discern what meaning of Christian discipleship to approximate and appropriate in the community, she rightly insists that any person "remains the disciple of God, and not the disciple of God's witnesses."[9]

The church ought to be the nexus of Christ and culture. The church, insofar as it creates the conditions for the vertical (ultimacy) and horizontal (intimacy) dimensions of human experience, provides a conduit for what anthropologist Victor Turner calls *communitas*. *Communitas* is the transformation that happens when people share in the warp and woof of a rite of passage. Episodes of disorientation strip away status and societal roles so that people relate to each other as equals.[10]

Professor Kelton Cobb lists the questions that a local church —as a spiritual movement in the spirit of Jesus and as an institution— courageously seeks to answer at a threshold moment in the life of the American Christian church:

> Where do we go to suspend our normal identities and responsibilities? What occasions do we anticipate will allow us that peculiar kind of anti-structure that rejuvenates us ostensibly for the sake of rejuvenating our society? Where and when do people in our culture experience liminality and *communitas*?[11]

The spontaneity of God's Spirit liberates the church from any illusion to calculate and control all things. The Spirit reminds the church afresh that the best stuff happens when *preparation* meets *inspiration*. In this way, God's Spirit gives a certain "it factor" to the work of the church.

Just as wine has to breathe to reach its ideal flavor potential, if the church is going to add any zest and flavor and imagination to this world,

---

9. Ibid., 138.
10. See Cobb, *Blackwell Guide*, 126, 236.
11. Ibid., 127.

the Spirit needs room to breathe on us and in us and through us. Imagine it this way through these brief poetic lines from Judy Brown:

> What makes a fire burn
> is space between the logs,
> a breathing space . . .
> A fire
> Grows
> simply because the space is there,
> with openings
> in which the flame
> that knows just how it wants to burn
> can find its way.[12]

What the church can do to continue to be community in a time of rapid denominational disaffiliation, as well as continued cultural decline and loss of positional privilege, is to reimagine and reset who the church can still be in the ongoing movement Jesus started. It has never really been about any inauguration of an institution. The original DNA of the church involves the creative spiritual sparks that God through Christ helped fan into full-blown flames from the Acts of the Apostles in the first century to the acts of the church in the twenty-first century. Let the church *be* the church, and start by paying attention to the new directions of how God's holy fire wants to find its way.

PUB THEOLOGY

INTRODUCTION

A church's wisdom as a spiritual community is consciously cultivated by the transformative journey toward an understanding of God as a relationship with ourselves, each other, and the world. It is shaped by the practices, beliefs, and values that constitute the multi-vocality of people and viewpoints (and views from a point) in a collective discernment of how the gospel can be communicated in the times of our lives and the life of our times.

Taking consistent and faithful moral inventory to align the "why" of church with its living witness in a complex and pluralistic culture connects

---

12. Brown, "Breathing Space," judysorumbrown.com/blog/breathing-space.

the inevitable ties of tradition and innovation. It is at such an intersection that guardians, innovators, sinners, and saints manifest a community of belonging and, to use a Pauline phrase, the meaningfulness of being "members of one another."

ICEBREAKER

In a minute or less, describe a person or an event that was significant in your life.

JUMPING-OFF POINTS

- What has most shaped your understanding of what church means?
- When you think of your idea of "the perfect church," what characteristics, beliefs, or practices come to mind?
- What are some constructive critiques you can make about how the contemporary church in America is "getting it wrong"? What needs reasonable or even radical rethinking?
- Consider Kathryn Tanner's observation that there are forms of Christian discipleship that must be subject to regular revision. How and where do you see the distinction and value between "innovators" and "guardians" of beliefs, values, and practices emerging in the church today?
- As noted in the chapter, former archbishop of Canterbury William Temple said, "The Church is the only institution that exists primarily for the benefit of those who are not its members." How might this confirm, challenge, or change the way the church configures itself today for ministry and mission?

BIBLIOGRAPHY

Adams, James Luther. "James Luther Adams: A Time to Speak." *James Luther Adams Foundation*. October 1, 2019. jameslutheradams.org/a-time-to-speak/.

Brown, Judy Sorum. "Breathing Space." *Judy Sorum Brown: Art & Spirit Blog*. November 15, 2013. judysorumbrown.com/blog/breathing-space.

Brunner, Emil. *The Word and the World*. London: Student Christian Movement Press, 1931.

Cobb, Kelton. *The Blackwell Guide to Theology and Popular Culture.* Malden, MA: Blackwell, 2005.

Doyle, Glennon. *Untamed.* New York: Dial Press, 2020.

Moltmann, Jürgen. *The Church in the Power of the Spirit.* Minneapolis: Fortress, 1993.

Schenck, Tim. "Why Does the Church Exist?" *Clergy Family Confidential.* November 9, 2013. frtim.wordpress.com/2013/11/09/why-does-the-church-exist/.

Segovia, Fernando F., and Mary Ann Tolbert, editors. *Reading from this Place: Social Location and Biblical Interpretation in the United States.* Minneapolis: Fortress, 1995.

Tanner, Kathryn. *Theories of Culture.* Minneapolis: Augsburg Fortress, 1997.

MEETING 7

CHURCH AND THE FUTURE

CODY J. SANDERS

Many of us have come to see time as an enemy, developing a type of "chronophobia"—a *fear* of time.[1] Time takes from us those we love, those whom we want to hold on to a little longer. Time diminishes the capacity of our aging bodies and minds. Time takes its toll on the institutions we've worked to strengthen and build as they eventually diminish and erode. We experience time as tyranny when our working lives are governed by clocks and metrics of productivity.[2]

The ways we talk about time often place us in an adversarial relationship to it as a *commodity* of which we can never have enough. "Time is *running out*." "There's *not enough* time." "If I only had *a little more* time." The future becomes a time of dread—to be feared, avoided, and kept at bay. Rabbi Abraham Joshua Heschel observed this fraught relationship we have to time, saying, "*Contempt for time* seems to be characteristic of human thought almost everywhere . . . time, compared with eternity, appears empty, irrelevant and essentially unreal. Things that happen in history are of little significance; only the timeless is truly relevant."[3]

But is this our only option—being essentially in an adversarial relationship with time (or at the least in an *ambivalent* one), taking what comfort we can in the fleeting moments of the present? Or giving up on our relationship to time altogether by seeking comfort in an otherworldly timelessness of the eternal?

---

1. Bjornerud, *Timefulness*, 7.

2. For readers wishing for a history of time's relationship to economics, see Thompson, "Brief Economic History of Time," *Atlantic*, December 21, 2016, theatlantic.com/business/archive/2016/12/a-brief-economic-history-of-time/510566/.

3. Heschel, *God in Search of Man*, 205.

Something that is taken for granted—as is our relationship with "time"—is hard to challenge. If we know anything, we know time. We live it every day. But relationships with time challenge our assumptions, from the perspectives on time being developed in quantum physics to vastly different conceptions of time in other cultures. *Time is more complex than we usually assume.*

I invite you to hold in suspension whatever you currently think you know about time and to entertain other possible relationships with this time/place/concept we call the future as a site of faithful activity for followers of Jesus.

A MORE FAITHFUL RELATIONSHIP WITH TIME

Our relationship to future possibilities is an aspect of Christian discipleship that stretches all the way back to Jesus and his forebearers in the Jewish tradition. Take this example as a starting place: "The time is fulfilled, and the kingdom of God has come near" (Mark 1:15a).[4] Or, as Eugene Boring translates this proclamation from Jesus, "The time is fulfilled, and here comes the kingdom of God." Boring says, "Mark's view [is that] the kingdom is still future but so near that it already affects the present."[5]

That already-but-not-yet, coming-near, just-on-the-horizon nature of the reigning presence of God was the crux of Jesus' preaching throughout the Gospels and has fueled the imaginations of theologians and mystics, philosophers and preachers of the Christian tradition ever since. Take these examples offered by Jennifer M. Gidley, president of the World Futures Studies Federation, on the historical development of futurist thought:

> St. Augustine's *City of God* (426 CE) imagines a future utopic society rooted in the teachings of Christianity and suffuse with love. Abbot and mystic Joachim of Fiore in the 12th century envisioned a future in which the earth is transformed into a place of spiritual activity, inspiring the monks of his order toward faithful action. Spanish theologian Louis de Molina (1535–1600) entered the debate over human free will and God's determination of the future by introducing a notion of contingent and possible futures, not just one predetermined future, influencing concepts

---

4. Except where noted, all Scripture translations are from the New Revised Standard Version.

5. Boring, *Mark*, 49.

of the future for decades after. Dominican monk Tommaso Campanella published *The City of the Sun* in 1602, an esoteric description of a city on a hill with description of a coming age in which more history exists within 100 years than in all the world 4,000 years prior.[6]

Christians have had a long and rich relationship with time and the future. But when have you heard a sermon or read a popular Christian publication on the subject? If you can think of one, what was its central message?

Dominant Christian relationships with the future (in the US, at least) generally fall along two trajectories. In more conserving perspectives, a relationship with time is subverted and the future ignored through a form of Christian escapism into the timeless and eternal (think of the big business the "rapture" has become for segments of Christian publishing). In more progressive expressions of Christianity, time and the future are often subsumed within an American ideology of unbridled optimism and progress: things are always getting better as we grow and develop and invent new technologies.

Both perspectives ignore the importance of attending to the lived experience of our neighbor, whose present and near-future needs are overlooked in favor of eternity. Many such neighbors cannot so naïvely boast of unfettered "progress" making their lives ever better. And both perspectives sever our faithful relationship to possible futures being continually furnished by our faithful activity in the world.

After Jesus says, "The time is fulfilled, and here comes the kingdom of God," at the beginning of Mark's Gospel, the following chapters describe what God's coming near looks like and feels like for people in the present, already being impacted by that future in the presence of Jesus. Any notion of hope that one can derive from those accounts is not a simple escape from time into a timeless eternity where the future doesn't matter, nor is it a vision of hope bound up with the promise of human progress. Hope is always embedded within a concrete eschatological vision of the future of God's reigning presence in the already-but-not-yet, shaping our lives as Christ followers engaging in faithful activity in relation to that future. The church's relationship to the future *matters*. It has from the start. If we want the future to matter for *us* as it did for Jesus and so many others preceding us in the faith, we must enter into more faithful relationships with the future.

---

6. Gidley, *Future*, 26–30.

Afrofuturist thinker Rasheedah Phillips describes the importance of our relationship to time and the future: "The ways in which we are situated in time comes [*sic*] to be reflected in how we think about, talk about, and conceptualize the community, world, and the universe around us."[7] How we think about, live with, inhabit, and are inhabited by time has implications for everything else we do in the world: how we respond to climate change, how we engage in ministries of compassion and justice, how we cultivate more racially just communities, and even how we perceive the Divine in our lives.

Phillips lifts up the notion that many African traditions of time incorporate a notion of *recurrence* and *cycles* rather than a *linear* imaging of time that has come to dominate the Western imagination.[8] In a linear sequencing of time, we are concerned with finality, or what things are leading to. We become beholden to an image of the cessation of time in eternity, or we are mesmerized by the illusion of unfettered human progress always making life better. One or the other of those imaginings becomes our goal, rather than faithfully furnishing a future in which the reigning presence of God becomes more fully palpable in the lives of people and the life of the planet. In linear conceptions of time, past and future are subordinated to the eternal "now" of the present moment, which we imagine is the only "time" that we can inhabit. But the linear past-present-future model of time that seems so natural to us today is a fairly recent invention (emerging about 2,500 years ago in Greece), and it is a relationship with time not embraced by many of the world's cultures.[9] So we have choices to make in the ways we tell time. And those choices have consequences.

TELLING TIME

Part of the church's troubled history with time is a presumption that we are currently living in the far-future of some lengthy linear timeline rather than relating to time through a cosmic perspective in which "a thousand years are like one day" (1 Pet 3:8). That troubled relationship with the future has consequences for how we shape our Christian work and witness in the world.

---

7. Phillips, "Constructing a Theory & Practice of Black Quantum Futurism," 12. Readers may also be interested in Sanders, "What the Church Can Learn from Octavia Butler," *Sojourners*, May 14, 2020, sojo.net/articles/what-church-can-learn-octavia-butler.

8. Phillips, "Constructing a Theory & Practice of Black Quantum Futurism," 20.

9. Gidley, *Future*, 13.

For example, in the 1980s, Ronald Reagan's secretary of the interior, James Watt, was asked a question in a testimony before Congress about the importance of environmental preservation for future generations. Watt responded, "I don't know how many future generations we can count on before the Lord returns."[10] Why be concerned about the future of the earth if we are certain that we'll soon escape earth and time into a timeless eternity? That's how Watt's relationship with the future, shaped by his particular Christian faith, influenced his approach to environmental preservation.

"You know how to interpret the appearance of earth and sky, but why do you not know how to interpret the present time?" (Luke 12:56). These words of Jesus were spoken in anger, and today his words could not be more prescient. The anger he felt at a generation out of touch with a relationship to their own time has troubling resonance for our own generation—a people out of right relationship with the future.

The "doomsday clock" was started in 1947 by the Bulletin of the Atomic Scientists as a way to symbolically represent humanity's proximity to "doomsday," or how close we are to destroying our world, represented by "midnight." The clock has only been reset a total of twenty-four times in seventy-three years. For most of its history, the scientists who set the clock were only concerned with nuclear weapons as the greatest danger to humanity's survival on earth. In 2007, they began taking climate change into their deliberations on how to set the hand of the clock.

At the outset of 2020, the Bulletin moved the hands of the clock to an unprecedented 100 seconds till midnight, "warning leaders and citizens around the world that the international security situation is now more dangerous than it has ever been, even at the height of the Cold War."[11] The press release goes on to name biological and genetic engineering, hypersonic and space weapons, the collection of vast amounts of health-related data by governments and corporations, and a number of other concerns that impinge on the livability of our future. It reads like something from the pages of a science fiction novel, but it represents a real and present threat to our future. The Department of Defense developed a term to describe our

---

10. Quoted in Prochnau and Thomas, "The Watt Controversy," *Washington Post*, June 30, 1981, washingtonpost.com/archive/politics/1981/06/30/the-watt-controversy/d591699b-3bc2-46d2-9059-fb5d2513c3da/.

11. Mecklin, "Closer than Ever," thebulletin.org/doomsday-clock/2020-doomsday-clock-statement/.

relationship to this time of accelerating change and potential threat. It is abbreviated VUCA: volatile, uncertain, complex, and ambiguous.

Every potential future we now face is *complex*, not just *complicated*. The difference between "complexity" and "complicated" is defined by Margaret Heffernan in this way: "Complicated environments are linear, follow rules, and are predictable; like an assembly line, they can be planned, managed, repeated, and controlled." But in our current situation, Heffernan says, "The advent of globalization, coupled with pervasive communications, has made much of life complex: nonlinear and fluid, where very small effects may produce disproportionate impacts."[12] This complexity is experienced in a globalized economy and supply chain, increasingly unpredictable chaotic weather events created by climate change, the ability of social media to shape "realities" in which people believe they live so differently that it seems we inhabit different worlds, even when we're living right next door to one another. The church once imagined our relationship to the future as a complicated one that we could manage with good planning and capable management. *But a future of complexity is the church's new reality.*

"You know how to interpret the appearance of earth and sky, but why do you not know how to interpret the present time?" (Luke 12:56). In the midst of such complexity, such ambiguity, so many large-scale threats to livability, it is understandable that we would want to escape into a relationship with the future that is stabler, simpler, and easier to understand. But this is not our world. We are a people called into faithful relationship with the future with eyes open to interpret the present time and to furnish a future shaped by the reigning presence of God come near.

FAITHFULLY FUTURING

Folks who think and theorize about the future always have pandemics in mind as the exemplar of disruption and times of chaos. Short of world war or an extraterrestrial invasion, there's not much else that holds the potential of a pandemic to thrust the world into international unpredictability. All of our churches have now moved through one of the most complex and chaotic times that futurists warn about. In the experience of the Covid-19 pandemic—with all of its losses and griefs—we've learned a lot about what it means to live in relationship to a complex future. We need to develop our imaginations as faithful futurists to understand how to mine these lessons

---

12. Heffernan, *Uncharted*, xiii.

from our lived experience so that they inform our relationship to emergent futures.

The Apostle Paul framed a faithful relationship with time this way: "Besides this, you know what time it is, how it is now the moment for you to wake from sleep" (Rom 13:11a). But if you only read this text in English, you miss an important nuance that is clear in the Greek. There are two words translated "time" in the New Testament. One is the Greek word, *chronos*, which basically refers to time in general as well as a span or interval of time. But *chronos* is not what Paul is speaking of here in Romans when he says, "Besides this, *you know what time it is.*" Here the word translated "time" is a much rarer word in Classical and Hellenistic Greek: *kairos*.

In *Stand Your Ground: Black Bodies and the Justice of God*, Womanist theologian Kelly Brown Douglas ends her thorough social and theological critique of America's "stand your ground" culture against Black bodies with a prophetic call to recognize the decisive moment of *kairos* time. Douglas says,

> *Kairos* time is the right or opportune time. It is a decisive moment in history that potentially has far-reaching impact. It is often a chaotic period, a time of crisis. However, it is through the chaos and crisis that God is fully present, disrupting things as they are and providing an opening to a new future—to God's future. *Kairos* time is, therefore, a time pregnant with infinite possibilities for new life.... It is a time bursting forth with God's call to a new way of living in the world. It is God calling us to a new relationship with our very history and sense of self, and thus to new relationships with one another, and even with God.[13]

This is the *kairos* time of ferment and reckoning and justice-seeking that we witnessed in the aftermath of George Floyd's killing by police. It is the time we are being awakened to in the voice of teenage Swedish environmentalist Greta Thunberg, who speaks the truth of climate change to the powers of the world, saying that *this* is the decisive moment for action in our own history that will have far-reaching impact on the entire planet's future. It is the *kairos*-chaos time of the Covid-19 pandemic when, amid unprecedented death tolls, so many churches *came alive* to meet the needs of their communities in ways not previously known possible.

Our potential futures are complex, chaotic, nonlinear, and accelerating. We cannot escape that emerging reality. Our *potential futures*, however, are

---

13. Douglas, *Stand Your Ground*, 206.

where the reigning presence of God exists in the already-but-not-yet, just on the horizon, so close that it is already affecting the present, calling us into faithful relationship with the yet-to-be. If we take our relationship to time seriously, our future can become pregnant with possibilities for churches waking from slumber, able to interpret the present time, and eager to enter into new relationships with our history, our future, our planet, one another, and God.

PUB THEOLOGY

INTRODUCTION

The "future." Is it a place we will arrive upon in a matter of time? Is it a concept we imagine in order to create possible worlds? Does it already exist "out there" somewhere, or do we furnish it through our activity in the present, right now? Given how much Jesus referred to these notions, our relationship to time and the future should matter to churches. How we relate to time and the future will determine what possible worlds we will create through our faithful action in the present.

ICEBREAKER

What does time feel like? When you talk about the future with others, what emotional responses emerge for you, for others, for your church?

JUMPING-OFF POINTS

- When you hear the words of Paul, "Besides this, you know what time it is, how it is now the moment for you to wake from sleep" (Rom 13:11a), how do you sense yourself (or your church) being called to "wake up"? What have you been sleeping through that you now need to face with open eyes?
- When you hear Jesus say, "You know how to interpret the appearance of earth and sky, but why do you not know how to interpret the present time?" (Luke 12:56), can you hear the anger in his voice? Anger is an emotional signal that something we deeply value or people we deeply love are being threatened. In relation to our potential futures, what do you sense might anger you? What threats to your values of love and justice, threats to the survival and wellbeing of the people and the planet, do you need to interpret more faithfully?

- If you can develop a bifocal lens for perceiving time—one of *chronos*, another of *kairos*—how do you imagine noticing the signs of our regular day-to-day progression of time being interrupted by the potential of a *kairos* time that is pregnant, possibly for new life and God's call toward a new way of living in the world? When Kelly Brown Douglas says, "It is God calling us to a new relationship with our very history and sense of self, and thus to new relationships with one another, and even with God," where are you sensing that call in your life or in the life of your church? How will you respond with an eye toward the future?

BIBLIOGRAPHY

Bjornerud, Marcia. *Timefulness: How Thinking Like a Geologist Can Help Save the World*. Princeton: Princeton University Press, 2018.

Boring, M. Eugene. *Mark: A Commentary*. Louisville: Westminster John Knox, 2006.

"Closer than ever: It's 100 seconds to midnight," *Bulletin of the Atomic Scientists*. Accessed January 23, 2020. thebulletin.org/doomsday-clock/current-time/.

Doctor, Courtney. "What's the Deal with Faith and Works in James?" May 10, 2020, thegospelcoalition.org/article/faith-works-james/.

Douglas, Kelly Brown. *Stand Your Ground: Black Bodies and the Justice of God*. Maryknoll, NY: Orbis, 2015.

Falk, Dan. "A Debate Over the Physics of Time," *Quantum Magazine*, July 19, 2016. quantamagazineorg/a-debate-over-the-physics-of-time-20160719/.

Gidley, Jennifer M. *The Future: A Very Short Introduction*. New York: Oxford University Press, 2017.

Heffernan, Margaret. *Uncharted: How to Navigate the Future*. New York: Avid Reader Press, 2020.

Heschel, Abraham Joshua. *God in Search of Man: A Philosophy of Judaism*. New York: Farrar, Straus and Giroux, 1955.

Phillips, Rasheedah. "Constructing a Theory & Practice of Black Quantum Futurism: Part One." In *Black Quantum Futurism: Theory*

& *Practice*, vol. 1, edited by Rasheedah Philips. The Afrofuturist Affair/House of Future Sciences Books, 2015.

Prochnau Bill, and Valerie Thomas, "The Watt Controversy," *Washington Post*. June 30, 1981. washingtonpost.com/archive/politics/1981/06/30/the-watt-controversy/d591699b-3bc2-46d2-9059-fb5d2513c3da/.

Sanders, Cody J. "What the Church Can Learn from Octavia Butler," *Sojourners*. May 14, 2020. https://sojo.net/articles/what-church-can-learn-octavia-butler.

Thompson, Derek. "A Brief Economic History of Time." *Atlantic* December 21, 2016. theatlantic.com/business/archive/2016/12/a-brief-economic-history-of-time/510566/.

SPIRITUAL PRACTICES
TED J. PHILLIPS

INTRODUCTION

In answering some of life's difficult questions, those at the Canadian Virtual Hospice website insist, "Every person has spirituality. It is just part of who each one of us is—woven into and expressed through every thought, feeling, and action."[1] What are the core components of spirituality? What is the overall purpose of cultivating a spiritual life? First, according to the website, you work daily to find significant meaning in your life. Second, you assess and evaluate your relationships with yourself, with one another, and with God as you look inward and interact with the Divine.

Therefore, spiritual practice transforms an individual to have a more personal and deeper relationship with God. In this pub theology meeting, the group will discuss spiritual transformation, a foundational process that God desires to have with each one of us. We will consider what an encounter with God can really look like. We will also review the benefits of spiritual practice and identify the four general types of spirituality. Then, we will look at an overview of the history of spirituality. The final section will provide some examples of practices you could consider incorporating into your regular, daily way of life.

SPIRITUAL TRANSFORMATION

Ruth Haley Barton writes, "Spiritual transformation is the process by which Christ is formed in us . . . for the glory of God, for the abundance of our own lives, and for the sake of others (Galatians 4:19; Romans 8:29;

---

1. "Emotions and Spirituality."

Romans 12:1, 2)."[2] For Christians, the overall purpose of cultivating a spiritual life is that each one of us is transformed to the image of Christ, is converted as a follower of Jesus, and is dedicated to assist with the work and growth of the church. In short, we become disciples of Jesus Christ. Romans 12:2 indicates, "Do not be confined to this world, but be transformed by the renewing of your mind, so that you may discern what is the will of God—what is good and acceptable and perfect."[3] Barton adds, "Thus, any approach to transformation that seeks to bring about real change must go beyond merely grasping information at the cognitive level to full knowledge that impacts our deepest inner orientations and trust structures, false-self patterns, and any obstacles that prevent us from fully surrendering to God."[4] The process begins at what the Scriptures call "salvation"—entering into faith—and from there, growth can potentially occur. However, we can do only so much on our own. The rest of this mysterious process must come by way of the Holy Spirit through divine revelation. Next, we need to create the correct conditions for this to occur, and we do this by practicing spiritual practices.

WHAT ARE SPIRITUAL PRACTICES?

Spiritual practice is defined as "any regular and intentional activity that establishes, develops, and nourishes a personal relationship with the Divine in which we allow ourselves to be transformed."[5] "Spiritual Practice: Definition Breakdown" describes four categories of action that are directly related to spiritual practice.[6] First, a spiritual practice is *regular*. This means it is something we do every day. Examples of regular practices include daily habits like taking a shower and putting on our shoes. Second, a spiritual practice is *intentional*. This involves deliberately putting a practice into our daily set of normal activities. Examples include study, centering prayer, and meditation. It takes discipline, commitment, and perseverance to include and then maintain a new spiritual practice. We must build into our daily schedules time to engage in a spiritual practice or practices. It does not happen on its own. Third, it nourishes and feeds "a personal relationship

---

2. Barton, "What We Believe."
3. All Scripture quotations are taken from Attridge, *HarperCollins Study Bible*.
4. Barton, "What We Believe."
5. "Spiritual Practice."
6. Ibid.

with the Divine."⁷ When you think about your other personal relationships, it takes ongoing contact, time, and effort. Fourth, spiritual practice puts each of us in right relationship with God and will transform us to be the people God has *called* us to be.

A PERSONAL SPIRITUAL PATH

One of the main purposes of this book is to aid you in your personal spiritual journey. The theology pub that I lead has been one of the most effective processes in my spiritual growth. At these meetings, each of us can question the unquestionable and take the "road less traveled." We can explore our respective, innermost worlds and seek the truth in our own hearts, minds, and souls.

Have you ever considered why Jesus used parables to share his story of loving one another and transforming people? Think about the woman at the well (John 4:4-26), the Good Samaritan (Luke 10:25-37), the blind man of Bethsaida (Mark 8:22-26), the four thousand whom Jesus fed (Mark 8:1-9), and the Syrophoenician woman of faith (Mark 7:24-29). Jesus used stories to show how each person's need or each group's need was met.

Ask yourself this question posed by Alice Clarke: "What does an encounter with God really look like?"⁸ An encounter with God happens through the Holy Spirit. These encounters can be different for everyone. On December 21, 2020, Jupiter and Saturn came close together in what many believe is the Christmas star. My wife and I drove away from the city to a dark location. Through our binoculars, we were able to see the two stars and four moons of Jupiter all aligned. Many believe this is the same alignment that motivated the wise men to go and find young Jesus. For us, it was truly a unique, spiritual experience. There are times when each of us feels and believes that something spiritual has happened. Sometimes this may happen on a retreat or while walking alone through the forest. My wife and I came away convinced that what we witnessed that evening was clearly the work of God in the universe. For us, it was an encounter with God.

---

7. Ibid.

8. Clarke, "What Does an Encounter with God Really Look Like?" catchthefire.com/blog-full/what-does-an-encounter-with-god-really-look-like.

BENEFITS OF SPIRITUAL PRACTICE

Now, we turn our attention to the benefits of using spiritual practices. We must ask for the courage to make room for spiritual practices. We need to be willing to touch the sacred in ourselves every precious day. In *Naked Spirituality: A Life with God in 12 Simple Words*, Brian McLaren shares, "A spiritual life is a Spirit life, a life in the Spirit, and Jesus' life and work come into proper focus when we realize his goal was not to start a new religion—and certainly not to create a new religion that would compete with or persecute his own religion—his own religion, Judaism!"[9] McLaren adds, "His goal wasn't to start a new religious argument about dogma-mountains; it was to fill hearts with Spirit-fountains. His goal wasn't to replace one group of powerful religious grown-ups (like Nicodemus) with another, but to help everyone become like little children through Spirit-birth."[10]

Maggie Lyon states that each day "draws you deeper into who you really are by connecting you with your divine self."[11] The form of spiritual practice is not as significant as "the profound and connective quality of the time spent within yourself."[12] As the saying goes, practice makes perfect. Thus, we must dedicate time each day to one or more practices. First, practice provides clarity during a potentially crazy day. We can visualize better what is required of us. Second, it fosters the effort to complete our work. Energy and vitality are needed to meet our required goals and objectives. Third, practice energizes our mood. When our mood is heightened, everything becomes easier and more enjoyable to do. Fourth, during change, practice grounds us. Think about playing football, singing in a choir, or playing an instrument—muscle memory and practice play a critical role in our performance. Fifth, it helps us view our lives on both a macro and micro level. On the macro level, we can look outside ourselves and see the bigger picture. On the micro level, we gain a deeper understanding of ourselves and transformational relationship with God. Sixth, practice helps keep us "in the moment." We are focused on what is happening right now, and we are not concerned about the past or worried about the future. Seventh, practice "connects you to and reveals your true spirit. Practice is

---

9. McLaren, *Naked Spirituality*, 18.
10. Ibid.
11. Lyon, "The Top 10 Benefits of Spiritual Practice."
12. Ibid.

where you download profound intuitive messages by opening to your own divine spark."[13]

TYPES OF SPIRITUALITY

According to Philip Sheldrake, spirituality is a system of personal beliefs used to search for the meaning of life.[14] "Getting in touch with oneself" is an important part of spirituality. In general, there are four types of spirituality: the ascetical-monastic, the mystical, the active-practical, and the prophetic-critical. Ascetical-monastic can relate to special places, but its primary avenue for spiritual transformation is through the wilderness or other remote settings. Disciplines of self-denial, disinterest in worldly pleasures, and detachment of material existence characterize this spiritual type. Sheldrake writes, "The mystical type of spirituality is associated with the desire for an immediacy of presence to God, frequently through contemplative practice." Removal from everyday existence is not a requirement, and instead it is suggested that the regular world be transformed into something fantastic! In this view, one is looking for illumination. The active-practical type considers normal life as the primary road for the spiritual journey. Jesus said in Luke 17:21, "For in fact, the kingdom of God is among you." This path seeks to find enlightenment in daily activities and seeks to assist others in the world. The prophetic-critical type of spirituality moves past simply helping people to being involved in social transformation. This fourth type was influenced by corrupt social and political systems, world wars, ethnic and social injustice, and the fight for women's rights.

DISCIPLESHIP

Philip Sheldrake states, "the main New Testament image for the Christian life is discipleship or 'following Christ.'"[15] It is a total way of life. Think about Jesus' disciples not as just learners with a teacher but as those who follow after and alongside the teacher. The first element of discipleship is *converting to Christ*. In Mark 1:15, Jesus says, "The time is fulfilled, and the kingdom of God has come near; repent, and believe in the good news." The second scriptural element is *getting your hands dirty* and helping build the

---

13. Ibid.

14. The information in this paragraph comes from both Sheldrake, "Christian Spirituality and Social Transformation," and Sheldrake, *Spirituality*, 15–16.

15. Sheldrake, "Christian Spirituality and Social Transformation."

kingdom of God.[16] Jesus is recorded as choosing his own disciples (Mark 1:16-20; Matt 4:18-22; Luke 5:1-11; John 1:35-42). Mark 1:17 says, "Jesus said to them, 'Follow me and I will make you fish for people.'" Discipleship has four elements. First, discipleship is a response to a call and a gift of God's grace. Second, the title of disciple was not given as a particularly special title, because Jesus gave it to tax collectors, undesirable people, and women as examples (Mark 9:9; Luke 8: 1-3). Third, conversion involved a person leaving everything (Luke 5:11) for the gospel. Finally, the call to discipleship implies sharing in the work of Jesus to bring about God's kingdom.[17] This is the challenge before us. Can we be worthy and dedicated disciples of Jesus in our daily lives?

HISTORY OF SPIRITUALITY

History of spirituality started before the Old Testament, continued into the Old and New Testaments, appears in the letters of Paul and the Gospels, was part of the Reformation, and continues through history into the twenty-first century. During Jesus' time, Christian spirituality was particularly related to an understanding of God and of God's relationship to the world.[18] The earliest expression of spirituality in the Christian community was centered on Jesus through baptism and the Eucharist.[19] However, spirituality existed in the Old Testament too, within Exodus, the Psalms, and the Song of Solomon. Then Jesus used Hebrew texts when he taught and spoke to the crowds who gathered around him. A spirituality of martyrdom persisted with the early Christian church until Emperor Constantine's edict of toleration (313 CE).[20] Origen of Alexandria (185) emphasized a return to the spiritual path back to God, and Augustine of Hippo (354–430) "was the greatest thinker of Western spirituality in the early period."[21] According to Philip Sheldrake, "The period from the fourth to the twelfth centuries was crucial both for the consolidation of the Christian spirituality in general, and for the development of the specifically monastic paradigm

---

16. Ibid.

17. These four descriptions of discipleship are taken from Sheldrake, "Christian Spirituality and Social Transformation."

18. Ibid.

19. Sheldrake, *Spirituality*, 31.

20. Ibid., 32.

21. Ibid., 35, 37.

in particular."²² In addition, the Western church moved significantly away from Eastern Christianity. During the twelfth century, there were major shifts in the social and cultural environments, especially the Renaissance and the rebirth of cities.²³

Martin Luther (1483–1546) first provoked controversy when he posted ninety-five theses on the doors of the Wittenberg Castle Church. He began to translate the Bible into German and developed a "reformed" theology that challenged many of the laws, beliefs, and practices of Roman Catholicism. Luther's most historic thesis was on the purchase of *indulgences*: a process of paying in order to reduce the years in Purgatory on behalf of one's dead relatives. Luther believed in faith, not in actions in terms of God's forgiveness.²⁴ Luther advocated "real presence," which means that the substance of the bread and wine coexist with the presence of the body and spirit of Jesus Christ. This idea of real presence separated Luther from other Reformers, as evident at the Marburg Colloquy in 1529.²⁵

Keith Mathison indicates that John Calvin (1509–1564) "is widely considered to be one of the greatest theologians of the Reformation era."²⁶ Calvin's *Institutes of the Christian Religion*, first published in 1536, remains one of the classical statements of Protestant thought. His doctrine of predestination was his most famous. "Calvin's spirituality has three elements: mystical, corporate and social."²⁷ He insisted that while believers do not receive Christ's physical presence with the bread and the cup, they do experience his spiritual presence when they come to the Lord's Table. "The Holy Spirit is the bond of the believer's union with Christ," writes Mathison.²⁸ Therefore, what the minister does on the earthly plane the Holy Spirit accomplishes on the spiritual plane. The Catholic Reformation was a process that did not respond directly to the Protestant Reformation because it took a broader view. The Council of Trent (1545–1563) was dominated by doctrinal and disciplinary issues, and spiritual considerations were not really discussed. "Catholic Reformation spirituality had two major elements: the foundation of new religious orders, and the development of

---

22. Ibid., 48.
23. Ibid., 74.
24. Ibid., 115.
25. Wax, "Luther vs. Zwingli 2: Luther on the Lord's Supper."
26. Mathison, "Calvin's Doctrine of the Lord's Supper."
27. Sheldrake, *Spirituality*, 117.
28. Mathison, "Calvin's Doctrine of the Lord's Supper."

new forms of lay Christian life and devotion that were interwoven with daily life."[29]

John Wesley (1703–1791) was instrumental in the development of Methodist spirituality. As a student of Lincoln College at Cambridge University in the early 1730s, he organized a group called the "Holy Club."[30] It was similar to our pub theology group because it was designed to help members create a more personal spirituality. They eventually got the nickname "Methodists."[31]

Philip Sheldrake states, "Western Christian spirituality during the nineteenth century was marked partly by an imperceptible shift of energy from Europe toward the New World."[32] This involved both Protestants and Roman Catholics. Near the end of the nineteenth century, three significant elements began to have an impact on spirituality: evolutionary theory, Marxist social analysis, and the birth of modern psychology.[33] During the twentieth century, Christianity and its subsequent spirituality continued to be present globally, and it presented itself in new forms as it adapted to a multicultural society.[34]

EXAMPLES OF SPIRITUAL PRACTICES

A spiritual practice is an ongoing behavior that is done daily to help a person grow spiritually. In addition, the process is designed to prepare a person to move outward into the world more effectively. You probably cannot cover all of these practices in one evening. You and your group can decide which ones most interest and intrigue you and which ones you have the most questions about. Remember that pub theology is an environment where there are usually more questions than answers.

Below is a sample of spiritual practices, and they are not in any order. This is a "starting point" that you can draw from to increase group awareness, energy, and enlightenment.

- Holy Communion
- Love

---

29. "Counter-Reformation."
30. Mathison, "Calvin's Doctrine of the Lord's Supper."
31. Sheldrake, *Spirituality*, 151.
32. Ibid., 170.
33. Ibid., 171.
34. Ibid., 200.

- Study
- Radical Hospitality
- Baptism
- Worship
- Meditation/Reflection
- Centering Prayer
- Confession/Forgiveness
- Smiling
- Music
- Journaling
- Pilgrimage

HOLY COMMUNION

In Meeting 1 of this book, Holy Communion is described as one of the most sacred spiritual practices for Christians. The sharing of food and drink was an important cultural element during both Old and New Testament times. When people sit down to eat with one another, an environment is created where friendship, sharing, and interpersonal growth can occur. Holy Communion is a spiritual practice because it creates a holy space where we can meet God through Jesus Christ. Celebration and remembrance are central because the bread and wine represent *in some form* Jesus, his life, and his teachings. In this spiritual encounter, we have the potential to be transformed in mind and spirit. In addition, our active participation shows our love, faith, and commitment to God and Jesus Christ. *What element of the Communion experience is most meaningful for you?*

LOVE

Mark 12:29-31 says that, when asked about the greatest commandment, "Jesus answered, 'The first is, Hear O Israel: the Lord our God, the Lord is one; you shall love the Lord your God with all your heart, and with all your soul, and with all your mind, and with all your strength.' The second is this, 'You shall love your neighbor as yourself.' There is no other commandment greater than these."

This passage says it as briefly as possible. One of the most important practices a Christian can do is to love one's neighbor every day. Love is a spiritual practice that we can do continuously and intentionally in our daily lives. The power of love flows like a river through the Holy Spirit. Love surrounds us, flows through us, and sets the tone for our daily interactions with the people around us. What does love mean to you as a spiritual practice?

Love is boundless and powerful. The story of the Good Samaritan showed the Samaritan's compassion and love for the wounded person on the other side of the road. The Bible also says that Mary Magdalene was a devoted and loving follower of Jesus. She showed this by being active in Jesus' daily ministry, at his crucifixion, and at the tomb (Luke 8:1-56; John 19:25; John 20:11-18). Jesus himself reflects God's love for us. As the Apostle Paul says in 1 Corinthians 13:13, "And now faith, hope, and love abide, these three; and the greatest of these is love."

STUDY

Study is a spiritual practice that can be done daily or weekly. In the busyness of our lives, we need to create time for study and reflection. The key is not specifically to look for more answers but to sharpen our awareness of ourselves and our relationship with God. Spiritual study can involve a variety of methods, including reading and studying the Bible (see the examples in Barton, "What We Believe about Spiritual Transformation") and other books, worshiping weekly, attending a retreat, or watching a series on PBS like *God in America*. One of the best ways to learn is to study, reflect, analyze, and then consider what modifications and adjustments you might make in becoming a more effective follower of Jesus. *How do you make study a regular spiritual practice?*

In addition to the works listed in the bibliography, here are some books you might consider studying further:

- *The Wisdom Jesus* by Cynthia Bourgeault (2008)
- *The Protestant Reformation* by Hans J. Hillerbrand (1968)
- *Homebrewed Christianity Guide to Church History* by Bill J. Leonard (2017)
- *Falling Forward* by Richard Rohr (2011)
- *Spirituality: A Brief History* by Philip Sheldrake (2013)
- *Learning to Walk in the Darkness* by Barbara Brown Taylor (2014)

RADICAL HOSPITALITY

Radical hospitality is an intentional act of welcoming and provision. You do more than you normally do, not with the people you know but with individuals you do not know. This can be done both where you worship or out in your community at large. In church, this involves more than smiles and handshakes; it is greeting visitors outside before they enter. Radical hospitality is greeting people warmly and personally and creating an environment in worship where each one is welcomed sincerely. There is a danger of visitors feeling overwhelmed. My wife and I are both introverts, and if we visited a church where we perceived that we were approached too strongly, it might mean we would not return. Most individuals enjoy the practice of "passing the peace," but some church members do not like it at all. Therefore, each objective needs to be considered carefully.

Regarding people in the community, the same can be true of radical hospitality. Sensitivity and perceptiveness are two critical qualities to utilize. As an example, there are varied opinions about what to do about people standing on the side of the road asking for help. To be honest, I usually do not give them anything. However, on Sunday mornings as I am driving to church, I stop at a restaurant called Bojangles. I normally order a bacon and egg biscuit and a tea. One Sunday, I ordered two of each item. I was thinking that if someone was already out looking for help, I would share a biscuit and tea. I approached a guy about halfway to church, and I asked him if he would like a biscuit and tea. He was delighted. Next thing I know, I hear him calling out to a friend at another corner. They were happy to share one bacon and egg biscuit between the two of them and one small cup of tea. Since then, I try to keep bottled water and energy bars in my car to offer the people I sometimes meet at street corners. Some other ideas include volunteering to work in a soup kitchen, helping to build a Habitat for Humanity house, regularly visiting a jail, or assisting at a homeless shelter. *What other ideas do you have to promote and engage in radical hospitality?*

Jesus practiced radical hospitality *daily* in his ministry. He shared stories with strangers, fed the poor, healed individuals he did not know, and ate with a variety of people who were not considered the elite of his day. Jesus' purpose was to make each stranger feel significant and deeply appreciated.

BAPTISM

Baptism is a fundamental cleansing ceremony that is discussed in Meeting 2 (page 39). In Matthew 28:18-20, Jesus says: "Go therefore and make disciples of all nations, baptizing them in the name of the Father and of the Son and of the Holy Spirit, and teaching them to obey everything that I have commanded you." John the Baptist preached that baptism was symbolic of repentance and the forgiveness of sins (Mark 1:4-5). Jesus' approach to baptism was to make disciples of his believers. John did his work in the Jordan River, and Jesus followed suit wherever he was. There are spiritual benefits to baptism. First, baptism uses water to reflect a new covenant and relationship with Jesus Christ and God. Christian baptism is symbolic of a new life in Christ. Second, Paul indicates in Galatians 3:26-27, "for in Christ Jesus you are all children of God through faith. As many of you as were baptized into Christ have clothed yourselves with Christ." Salvation comes by faith, and baptism is symbolic of the death, burial, and resurrection of Jesus. It is a profession of faith where the new Christian is letting go of the old self and starting a new life as a follower of Jesus. It is a ritual used by all Christians, although how and when it occurs varies widely. Third, it involves a commitment to community, and this commitment goes both ways. The community of believers supports the new believer, and the new believer becomes an active and integral part of the community of believers. *Reflect on your baptism experience. What was it like? What did it mean to you? What does it mean to you today?*

WORSHIP

Worship is one of our most important spiritual practices. I have included the Theology of Worship statement from Myers Park Baptist Church, our home congregation in Charlotte, North Carolina (created in 2019), as an example of why and how to worship.

> **Why do we Worship?**
> Worship at Myers Park Baptist is the gathering of a diverse, intergenerational, ecumenical community of faith, celebrating God's active and timeless presence in the world. In worship, God re-forms our hearts, minds, and bodies, and ignites our imaginations with sacred stories—stories that invite us to question, explore mystery, express joy and grief, and deepen our faith. We worship to learn how to develop caring, empowering relationships with each other, and to stay centered in God as the world swirls around us. We worship to be inspired and prepared to exemplify the compassion and justice of Jesus in our church family and in the world. Through worship, God frees and transforms us in heart, mind, and body, so we can make a difference within ourselves, in our relationships, and in our community.

How do we Worship?
Focusing on God, worship at Myers Park Baptist unfolds consistently with the Isaiah 6 scriptural model: praise, confession, pardon, calling to respond, commitment, and sending out. Deborah Moore Clark in *O Come, Let Us Bow Down and Worship* indicates all our worship services are built on this ancient structural form, regardless of worship style, venue, or theme. Communal practices within worship—radical hospitality, confession and assurance of pardon, passing the peace, silence and listening, spirited hymn singing, presentations of gifts, and active participation in Communion—transform worshipers into newness with God and one another. Themes for services, based on lectionary scriptures, annually portray the narrative arc of God's redeeming love for humankind.

James K. A. Smith, in *You Are What You Love*, shares,

> Instead of the bottom-up emphasis on worship as *our* expression of devotion and praise, historic Christian worship is rooted in the conviction that God is the primary actor or agent in the worship encounter. Worship works from the top down, you might say. Worship is the arena in which God recalibrates our hearts, reforms our desires, and rehabituates our loves.[35]

In *O Come, Let Us Bow Down and Worship*, Deborah Moore Clark states, "Worship reminds us who we are, who we are not, and who we can become. Worship woos us back to right relationship with the Holy One. If we forsake this opportunity, we fail to live responsibly in relationship with God."[36] Clark later adds, "Worship breathes life-giving energy into congregations."[37] Worship can involve many elements, including celebration, confession, singing, the message, and going out into the world to make a difference. (You can find an examination of these concepts in Meeting 14, "Theology of Worship.")

MEDITATION/REFLECTION

Meditation and reflection are spiritual practices. The usual purpose of meditation and reflection is the restoration and rejuvenation of the mind, spirit, and body. This is done by calming the mind and relaxing the body. There

---

35. Smith, *You Are What You Love*, 77.
36. Clark, *O Come, Let Us Bow Down and Worship*, 9.
37. Ibid., 231.

are many types of meditation: breathing and chanting as well as Buddhist, Hindu, Chinese, and transcendental meditation. When you meditate and reflect, you normally sit on the floor or in a chair (but be sure the chair is not too comfortable). You close your eyes and breath normally unless you are doing a breathing meditation. In chanting, you silently hum, sing, or chant a mantra. A mantra can be short or long. In transcendental meditation, you silently repeat a mantra that has been especially determined for you by your TM teacher.

Meditation and reflection are practiced once or twice daily to help you remove your focus from your daily activities, thoughts, and feelings. The benefits of meditation and reflection can be grouped into two categories: spiritual and personal. Spiritual benefits include improved clarity, more defined focus on God, enhanced awareness of the Holy Spirit, an even-keeled spirit, and the opportunity for a quieter and deeper relationship with the internal you. Personal benefits of meditation and reflection are better self-awareness, improved concentration, more energy, less stress, heightened mood, and an overall healthier lifestyle. Guided meditation, where a facilitator leads a meditation, can be quite effective in a group environment like a retreat setting. *Have you ever tried meditation? What was it like? Do you do it daily?*

CENTERING PRAYER

The purpose of centering prayer is to deepen our relationship with the living Christ. It prepares us to receive the gift of contemplative prayer. Richard Rohr, in *Everything Belongs*, writes, "My starting point is that we're already there. We cannot attain the presence of God because we're totally in the presence of God. What's absent is *awareness*."[38] Centering prayer is normally silent prayer. The point is for you to be silent and listen for the voice of God who is within us and around us. Generally, you kneel or sit, and this is not passive prayer but focused silence. "The focus of centering prayer is the deepening of our relationship with the living Christ."[39] *If you have not tried centering prayer, try it daily for one week and see what impact it makes on you. Will you commit to doing this for an entire week?*

---

38. Rohr, *Everything Belongs*, 29.
39. "Centering Prayer."

CONFESSION/FORGIVENESS

Protestants have faith in which they can go directly to God through prayer with their confessions and requests for forgiveness; Roman Catholics use a confidential process where an individual speaks privately to a priest in a confession booth. According to *Greater Good Magazine*, "Psychologists define forgiveness as a conscious, deliberate decision to release feelings of resentment or vengeance toward a person or group who has harmed you, regardless of whether they actually deserve your forgiveness."[40] Forgiveness does not mean that a person has to forget, and it does not condone or excuse the other person's action. Confession is the moment where we seek God's presence, revealing our shortcomings and our unhealthy habits, and we ask for forgiveness. The Old Testament writers said that the people who left Egypt and wandered in the wilderness for forty years needed forgiveness numerous times. In Psalm 32:5, the psalmist says, "Then I acknowledge my sin to you, and I did not hide my iniquity; I said, 'I will confess my transgressions to the LORD,' and you forgave the guilt of my sin." Christians believe that there is no limit to forgiveness, assuming that there is real repentance. In Matthew 18, Peter asks Jesus how many times they should forgive another member of the church who has wronged them. Jesus said to him, "Not seven times, but, I tell you, seventy-seven times" (v. 22). *How do you feel when you sincerely ask for forgiveness?*

SMILING

Are you surprised to see smiling as a spiritual practice? Smiling is one of the best things you can do for yourself and for everyone else you encounter each day, and it needs to be a warm, sincere, and welcoming smile. Smiles reflect joy, warmth, and love, and if you are smiling, it increases the probability that the person you are smiling at will smile back at you. When you consider the importance of nonverbal communication, smiling is one of the most important ways to show you care. *How do you regularly smile? What happens to you when you smile at someone?*

MUSIC

Tom Morris writes, "Music is an art that brings both beauty and miracles."[41] Music is a spiritual practice that everyone can take advantage of.

---

40. "What Is Forgiveness?"
41. Morris, "Music and Joy."

Musical melodies can be simple in composition or extremely complex. Music can range from religious to pop, jazz, classical, and country, to name a few. Consider the brilliance of Mozart, Dolly Parton, Neil Young, and the Beatles. Each one of us can listen to music and benefit from the rhythms and the lyrics. Music can create an atmosphere that is conducive for listening inward to oneself. Music can transform us and help give clarity of purpose both inwardly and outwardly.

The singing of hymns can be an important spiritual practice for those who are singing and for those who are not singing. Singing uses the three senses of sight, hearing, and touch. The singing of anthems sometimes involves a degree of musical talent, while the singing of hymns is for everyone. Colossians 3:16 says, "Let the word of Christ dwell in you richly; teach and admonish one another in all wisdom; and with gratitude in your hearts sing songs, hymns, and spiritual songs to God." Everyone can fully take part in the singing of songs, hymns, and spiritual songs. Someone may not be able to carry a tune, but they can participate. Everyone can listen to the music and read the words in a hymn, and this fosters a closer connection to God. Music can facilitate us feeling both joy and sadness in life, compassion for those around us, love for one another, and a desire to be an active participant in this world. *How does music as a spiritual practice affect you?*

JOURNALING

Journaling can be a spiritual practice. Let your mind be free and start writing. Do not worry about appearance or grammar because no one will see this but you. In the beginning, freely write (whatever comes into your mind) for five minutes. Just like walking, jogging, or running, start small and build up over time. You can also use a "prompt" like "Today, I learned . . . ." As a suggestion, you might start by writing by hand instead of typing on a computer. When you write something in a journal, the process has a kinetic energy that is different from the touch and feel of a keyboard. In addition, journal writing is like meditation and mindfulness since it reminds us to stay in the moment. If you try this spiritual practice, commit to it for at least two weeks and then evaluate its impact. *Did it make a difference? If so, how?*

PILGRIMAGE

Pilgrimage can be an amazing spiritual practice. *Merriam-Webster* defines pilgrimage "as being a pilgrim, especially one who travels to a shrine or a sacred place." Jesus' ministry was all about traveling in the countryside and having meals and discussions with the people he met. Pilgrimage cultivates us spiritually, culturally, mentally, and physically.

Here are three examples of places where individuals can participate in a pilgrimage. First is the Appalachian Trail. It extends through fourteen states, and the average walk-through time is five to seven months.[42] Participants have communicated that there are some days when they do not see a single human being. Though "thru-hiking" the trail is a grueling and demanding experience, there are benefits of self-examination: walking *alone* along the trail for hours or even a day or two, eating with other travelers one meets along the way, and accepting the danger of wildlife along the trail. This pilgrimage is not for the faint of heart.

Second is the El Camino de Santiago in Spain (also called the Way of St. James). This walk is 500 miles long. It starts at Jean Pied de Port and ends at the Cathedral of Santiago de Compostela. People who originally started the trek did so to seek the forgiveness of their sins.[43] A professor who worked with my wife did the entire walk after he retired from teaching and indicated that it was unforgettable.

Third is the pilgrimage to Jerusalem and the Holy Land of Israel and Palestine. There, travelers can visit the places where Jesus lived and conducted his ministry. They also can visit the wonderful city of Jerusalem.

Whether you travel across the United State or in other countries, travel gives all of us the opportunity to see the beauty of God's creation. You can visit the mountains, the Grand Canyon, state and national parks, or even special places where you live. Whether you travel to some distant place or go to a location near your home, you can sense God's presence if you are open to it.

In 2020, 2021, and even now as I write in 2022, Covid-19 has changed how people travel, even hindering travel as variants surge in different areas. It will be interesting to see how travel and pilgrimage rebound in the years to come. *What has been your experience with pilgrimage and travel? What benefits have you received? How can you "travel" even if you aren't able to explore a place that is far from your familiar surroundings?*

---

42. "Thru-Hiking."
43. Martin, "Walking the Camino de Santiago: A Beginner's Guide."

CONCLUSION

Spiritual practices include any intentional activity designed to develop and nourish our personal relationship with Jesus Christ. "Do not conform to the pattern of this world, but be transformed by the renewing of your mind" as we approach the Divine (Rom 12:2, NIV). Through these practices, we seek to go to the innermost part of our being and develop a powerful and gentle relationship with God. We encounter God by way of the Holy Spirit. Sometimes we can sense the presence of God as we listen silently and patiently. However, there are other times when we might be at a rock concert or looking up at the majestic sky and still sense God. As previously mentioned, four types of spiritual practices help support a system of personal beliefs: ascetical-monastic, mystical, active-practical, and prophetic-critical.

Jesus calls all of us to be his disciples. It is a total way of life that includes both conversion and the building of God's kingdom on earth. A disciple does not just sit and learn from a teacher. Jesus' disciples were not just learners with a teacher but people who followed after and alongside their teacher. Thus, the overall purpose of discipleship is to learn, be converted, and then assist in the building of the ministry of Jesus.

Spiritual practices are a critical part of living and growing in our spiritual lives. Each of us determines what types of spiritual practices we want to incorporate on an ongoing and intentional basis. Practices like baptism, Communion, and pilgrimage do not occur each day. Practices like meditation, love, journaling, and centering prayer can be done daily. Finally, there are many other practices that are not included here. What spiritual practices do you include in your personal and spiritual growth? How do they influence your life?

PUB THEOLOGY

INTRODUCTION

This chapter has presented an overall history of spiritual practices to give some context for how and when these practices developed. In addition, we covered numerous benefits of spiritual practices. First, practice helps us become like little children. As an example, think about the many times you have walked through the forest and reminded yourself of the subtle beauty of God. Two, spiritual practice focuses the quiet time that you spend with yourself. Whether you are meditating or taking a stroll along a park path, this time is reserved for the restoration of your mind, body, and spirit. Practice can help heighten your mood. When the potential "cobwebs" start disappearing from your mind, you will feel better and your mood will be brighter and lighter. With spiritual practice, you have a clear understanding of both the macro and micro levels of the practice. In the macro level, you can move outside of yourself and have a wide perspective, while the micro level focuses on your innermost self. All of this can be utilized when you remain in the present moment. You do not dwell in the past or worry about the future.

ICEBREAKER

In a minute or less, describe a favorite childhood memory.

JUMPING-OFF POINTS

- What is a spiritual practice?
- What are the benefits of spiritual practices?
- What spiritual practices do you use and why?
- Are there any spiritual practices that you choose not to use? If yes, why?
- What practices spark your imagination and wonder?
- Share a pilgrimage experience.
- What spiritual practices give you a visceral or gut reaction? Why might this be important?
- What is the significance of doing spiritual practices as a body of believers?
- After discussion with your group, what spiritual practices might you try for yourself, and why?

BIBLIOGRAPHY

Arndt, William F., and F. Wilbur Gingrich. *Greek English Lexicon of the New Testament*. Chicago: University of Chicago Press, 1957.

Attridge, Harold W. *The HarperCollins Study Bible*. New York: HarperOne, 2016.

Barton, Ruth Haley. "What We Believe About Spiritual Transformation." *Transforming Center*. 2011. transformingcenter.org/2011/01/what-we-believe-about-spiritual-transformation/.

"Centering Prayer." *Contemplative Outreach.* centeringprayer.com/.

Clark, Deborah Moore. *O Come, Let Us Bow Down and Worship.* Macon: Smyth & Helwys, 2003.

Editors of *Encyclopaedia Britannica.* "Counter-Reformation." *Britannica.* britannica.com/event/Counter-Reformation.

"Emotions and Spirituality." *Canadian Virtual Hospice.* virtualhospice.ca/en_US/Main+Site+Navigation/Home/Support/Support/Asked+and+Answered.aspx.

Lyon, Maggie. "The Top 10 Benefits of Spiritual Practice." huffpost.com/entry/spiritual-practice_b_1231569.

Martin, Craig. "Walking the Camino de Santiago: A Beginner's Guide." *Outside.* August 12, 2013. outsideonline.com/1917861/walking-camino-de-santiago-beginners-guide#close.

Mathison, Keith. "Calvin's Doctrine of the Lord's Supper." *Ligonier.* November 1, 2006. ligonier.org/learn/articles/calvins-doctrine-lords-supper/.

McLaren, Brian. *Naked Spirituality A Life with God in 12 Simple Words.* New York: HarperOne, 2012.

Morris, Tom. "Music and Joy." *Huffpost: The Blog.* November 26, 2010. huffpost.com/entry/music-and-joy_b_788663.

Rohr, Richard. *Everything Belongs.* New York: Crossroad, 2003.

Sheldrake, Philip. "Christian Spirituality and Social Transformation." *Oxford Research Encyclopedias: Religion.* August 31, 2016. doi.org/10.1093/acrefore/9780199340378.013.231.

———. *Spirituality: A Brief History.* Chichester, West Sussex: Wiley-Blackwell, 2013.

Smith, James K. A. *You Are What You Love.* Grand Rapids: Brazos, 2016.

"Spiritual Practice: Definition Breakdown." *Spiritual Practices.* spiritual-practice.ca/what/what-2/.

"Thru-Hiking." *Appalachian Trail Conservancy.* appalachiantrail.org/explore/hike-the-a-t/thru-hiking/.

Wax, Trevin. "Luther vs. Zwingli 2: Luther on the Lord's Supper." *The Gospel Coalition*. February 11, 2008. thegospelcoalition.org/blogs/trevin-wax/luther-vs-zwingli-2-luther-on-the-lords-supper/.

"What Is Forgiveness?" *Greater Good Magazine*. greatergood.berkeley.edu/topic/forgiveness/definition.

MEETING 9

THE LORD'S PRAYER . . . THE PERFECT PRAYER?

CHAZ SEALE AND PEGGY SEALE

We all know that there are many ways to pray. Some say prayer is just talking with God. We can do that by reading the Bible, sitting in stillness, meditating, praying with specific requests—basically, whatever fits our personal style and the specific purpose of the prayer.

To varying degrees, we all struggle to find what suits us the best. The Lord's Prayer, also known as the Our Father and occasionally as the Perfect Prayer, holds a place in most of our minds. As presented to Jesus' disciples, it is repeated frequently. Repeating the Lord's Prayer may be likened to saying the rosary, which to many is also enough for a life in prayer.

To answer questions surrounding the Lord's Prayer, or any Scripture, pub theology undertakes a concise yet thorough study. This chapter examines what lies beyond the general usage, the form, and the words. Our method analyzes how the Scripture relates to our individual connections with God. This is our way to uncover Scripture's depth and true meaning to each of us.

Let's begin with childhood. Most of our childhood years included nursery rhymes and jingles that we memorized through repetition. Naturally, many of these may remain with us throughout our lives. In Christian households, and even in many that were only slightly "churched," the Lord's Prayer is the primary prayer this is rooted in our minds. As with many things we memorize, this prayer is learned by rote repetition, often with little thought given to its individual elements or history. This "Perfect Prayer" has quite a history, and as with many important biblical passages, its origin and correct translation are complicated. The Lord's Prayer was so important to many early Christian communities that Christians were instructed to say the prayer three times a day. (Not a bad idea!) It remains a treasure trove for intellectual biblical scholars—and even amateurs like us.

To begin, there are two versions of the Lord's Prayer. The shorter version is found in Luke 11:2-4 (NRSV) and is presumed to have been written by St. Luke, who also wrote Acts. The passage reveals that Jesus said to his disciples,

> When you pray, say:
> Father, hallowed be your name,
> Your kingdom come.
> Give us each day our daily bread.
> And forgive us our sins,
> for we ourselves forgive everyone indebted to us.
> And do not bring us to the time of trial.

The longer version is found in Matthew 6:9-13. For the sake of simplicity, we will use it as the version for our study. It's interesting to note that Matthew's author is unknown, but it was probably a Jewish male writing somewhere around 80 CE. Jesus says in Matthew,

> Pray then in this way:
> Our Father in heaven,
> hallowed be your name.
> Your kingdom come.
> Your will be done,
> on earth as it is in heaven.
> Give us this day our daily bread.
> And forgive us our debts,
> as we also have forgiven our debtors.
> And do not bring us to the time of trial,
> but rescue us from the evil one.

Often the prayer is completed by the following doxology, which is included in only some translations: "For thine is the kingdom, and the power, and the glory, Amen."

Beyond these two versions, a more in-depth search reveals that different forms of early Christianity used various translations but normally retained significant similarities. A primary example relating to Americans is *The Geneva Bible* 1599, which appears to have been a basic text in early America.[1]

German theologian Jeremias attempted to retranslate the Lord's Prayer back into its original Aramaic form by comparing the two New Testament versions of the prayer (Matthew 6 and Luke 11) and drawing upon his extensive knowledge of the Aramaic language.

Here is an English translation of Jeremias's Aramaic reconstruction:

Dear Father,
Hallowed be thy name,
Thy kingdom come,
Our bread for tomorrow / give us today,
And forgive us our debts / as we also herewith forgive our debtors,
And let us not succumb to the trial.[2]

The Rev. Dr. H. Stephen Shoemaker's studies show that "We do not have the original form of the prayer in Jesus' Aramaic tongue. Ancient Greek manuscripts show some variances in the prayer before it reached its final two versions in Matthew and Luke. Luke's version is most likely the closer to Jesus' original prayer."[3]

The study of the various versions and the significant differences from the prayer's original text is no doubt an interesting intellectual endeavor. It clearly drives questions like these: What is the real text? How many times was this prayer changed? Is the study of our modern translation faulty? However, again for simplicity, we need to separate this analysis for another study and to accept the differences as normal for biblical texts.

Let's turn our attention to the story around the Lord's Prayer and why most followers of Christ consider it to be so important. In the Sermon on the Mount on the Sea of Galilee, Jesus spoke to a large crowd consisting of the throngs who were following him. It was truly a pivotal time in Jesus' work, worthy of many pub theology sessions.[4] It's no surprise that this crowd included Jesus' highly diverse group of disciples, all of whom were selected after John the Baptist baptized Jesus. During this time, Jesus speaks about how people should relate to each other and to God through the

---

1. Matthew 6:9-13 [GNV], *Bible Gateway*, biblegateway.com/passage/?search=Matthew+6%3A9-13&version=GNV.

2. Jeremias, The Lord's Prayer, 17.

3. The Rev. Dr. H. Stephen Shoemaker, personal email to authors, February 23, 2021.

4. For more, see Chan, "Complete Summary of Jesus' Sermon on the Mount."

Beatitudes, parables, and the Lord's Prayer. Some believe Luke's version of the Lord's Prayer was addressed to the larger crowd, but in Matthew greater emphasis is given to the request from Jesus' disciples for extra help with prayer. It appears they separated themselves with Jesus, apart from the crowd. "His disciples came to him" (Matt 5:1), and he "began to speak, and taught them" (5:2). Any debate over others also attending this teaching doesn't diminish the importance of the event, which addresses a question nearly all of us have pondered: "How should I pray?"

Both in Luke and Matthew, it appears that Jesus is asking for the Lord's Prayer to be prayed exactly as he states it—and there's a reason for that. Obviously, this is not the only place where Jesus prayed. For example, in Luke we read that Jesus prayed before his baptism (3:21), after healing the sick (5:16), before selecting the twelve apostles (6:12), and before the confession of Peter (9:18). In the four Gospels, there are nine recorded prayers from Jesus' lips. Although we're not focused on these passages, they may have also been instructional, just as they are today to Jesus' followers.

Here is where the meaning of the Lord's Prayer comes to the forefront of our study. We notice that the Lord's Prayer is largely in the first-person plural and relates to our thoughts and concern for all others, not just ourselves. This understanding appears to support the concepts behind Jesus' overall teachings to the larger crowd: "*Our* Father . . . Give *us* this day *our* daily bread . . . forgive *us our* debts, as *we* also have forgiven *our* debtors . . . do not bring *us* to the time of trial." Rick Hamlin writes, "It's as though Jesus was reminding the disciples and us that you can't pray for yourself by yourself without somehow praying for others. Put it another way: . . . We're all in this together."[5]

Elsewhere in Matthew (Mt 6:5-9), Jesus warns the disciples not to pray "like the hypocrites [who] . . . love to stand and pray in the synagogues and at the street corners, so that they may be seen by others. . . . [And] do not heap up empty phrases as the Gentiles do; for they think that they will be heard because of their many words." Phrases like "Do not be like them," "for your Father knows what you need before you ask him," and "Pray then in this way," which precede the Lord's Prayer in Matthew, support this understanding.

---

5. Hamlin, "The Truth about the Lord's Prayer."

BLESSED ARE THE POOR IN SPIRIT, FOR THEIRS IS THE KINGDOM OF HEAVEN

To further emphasize that Jesus is teaching us to think broadly when we pray—that is, beyond ourselves—he starts his teaching with a statement about the poor in spirit, those who are spiritually poor. One analysis states, "He is declaring that, before we can enter God's kingdom, we must recognize the utter worthlessness of our own spiritual currency and the inability of our own works to save us."[6] Let's look at each element of the Lord's Prayer in Matthew.

OUR FATHER IN HEAVEN

Rev. Shoemaker wrote, "Jesus' use of Father, or Abba in the Aramaic, was highly unusual for his time. It spoke to the remarkable intimacy and trust Jesus had with His God, a perfect parent."[7] The use of "father" has become more controversial during these times. Many churches have replaced this word with "God" to avoid depicting God as belonging to one sex. It's easy to relegate this change to a feminist movement seeking genderless Scripture, but that doesn't seem fair. When discussing God, the use of a gendered term would have been natural during the patriarchal times of Jesus, and the intention was simply to state that we are all the children of God. The statement does not necessarily assign God a distinctive sex. However, fathers (males) have indeed lorded over and often abused their families throughout most of human history. Many stories in the Bible are examples of this. Accepting an alternative term for the word "father" can be helpful. For the purposes of this discussion, however, we will continue to use "father," recognizing that the term "God" may, in time, become more universal.[8]

The consistent usage of the terms "our" and "us" is even more relevant and is crucial to this prayer. The Rev. Dr. W. Benjamin Boswell's sermon on this point states, "'Our' in this prayer implies we cannot pray this prayer in isolation. How could we pray about forgiveness if we are not in relationship with other people?" He continues, "when we pray this prayer, we are not just praying for ourselves but for each other," which also implies that this

---

6. "What does it mean to be poor in spirit?"
7. Shoemaker email, February 23, 2021.
8. "The Lord's Prayer: line-by-line commentary."

prayer should most often be prayed in communion with others.⁹ Beyond these two words, the phrase continues with "in heaven," wherein Jesus reaffirms that God is our celestial Father, "both with us in spirit and above us in the perfect realm of Heaven."[10]

HALLOWED BE YOUR NAME

Hallowed means *holy* or *sanctified* and therefore set apart from sin. God's name is holy, as stated here: "There is no Holy One like the LORD" (1 Sam 2:2). In this instance, we are revering God, treating the "heavenly Father" with respect, and positioning ourselves as God's humble followers. In this posture, the prayer states conclusively that we should recognize one true God. Many religions might agree with this, even though they arrive at it from different directions.[11]

YOUR KINGDOM COME

This petition, asking God to do something for everyone, contains two twists. First, it talks about wanting our lives and the life of the world, in a current sense, to have heavenly characteristics of faith, hope, and love (1 Cor 13:13). Another way of looking at the phrase comes from Richard Rohr. Speaking at our church, Rohr stated, "'Thy kingdom come' really means 'My kingdom go!'"[12] Second, "Your kingdom come," an evangelical petition, asks that believers might live with God for eternity where a state of nirvana exists (Rev 21:1-4).

YOUR WILL BE DONE, ON EARTH AS IT IS IN HEAVEN

If heaven is the perfect desire for humans to live for eternity, then this phrase is a desire to bring compassion and justice as well (Isa 30:18). This is a trusting statement in which we ask for God's will to take charge and guide us. God's ultimate guidance is simply to love one another as stated in God's commandments and emphasized by Jesus: "love the Lord your God with

---

9. The Rev. Dr. W. Benjamin Boswell, quotation from sermon preached at Myers Park Baptist Church, July 24, 2021.

10. "The Lord's Prayer: line-by-line commentary."

11. "What does 'hallowed be thy name' in the Lord's Prayer mean?"

12. Richard Rohr, notes from presentation at Myers Park Baptist Church, April 29, 2012.

all your heart, and with all your soul, and with all your mind. . . . You shall love your neighbor as yourself" (Matt 22:37, 39). Trusting God's strength for ourselves and others is one way we surrender to God.

GIVE US THIS DAY OUR DAILY BREAD

We need to eat to live, but it isn't only food that sustains us; "one does not live by bread alone, but by every word that comes from the mouth of the LORD" (Deut 8:3). This petition asks God for *all* that nourishes us. The term *bread* may be used as a symbol for that which sustains us, meaning all the aspects of how we are dependent on God: physical, spiritual, and mental. One thought is that this is an evangelical call to spread God's message: "whoever feeds on this bread will live forever" (John 6:58).

AND FORGIVE US OUR DEBTS, AS WE ALSO HAVE FORGIVEN OUR DEBTORS

This section of the Lord's Prayer may be the toughest to pray and follow. Because it talks about forgiveness, it talks about God's foremost request of us. It's a little easier to receive forgiveness than to forgive. To forgive, however, has the transformative power to break our pride and keep us humble.

When reading this part of the prayer, some of us may wonder whether we must forgive others or God will not forgive us. Shoemaker comments, "God is forever and always forgiving us, but here are the dynamics of forgiveness and forgivingness in the human heart. The heart has a swinging door through which forgiveness flows in and out. If we who are forgiven shut the door and refuse to forgive others, the door is now shut to God's flowing forgiveness."[13] From this, some infer that we must forgive others to be forgiven, which might be true but might also miss the mark of the passage. The alternative is to be judgmental or resentful and withhold forgiveness, which is strongly refuted elsewhere in Scripture. But if God loves all people, this is a strong admonition for us to follow suit and, by definition, be closer to God.[14]

We can't leave this phrase without addressing the fact that "trespasses" is often replaced by "debts" (as in NRSV) or by "sins." These words don't appear to be synonyms, so, as John M. Miller asked in a sermon, "Which of

---

13. Shoemaker email, February 23, 2021.
14. See "And Forgive us Our Trespasses, as we Forgive those who Trespass against Us."

these three words did Jesus mean? It could make a big difference, couldn't it?" We won't debate this here, but it seems to these humble authors, at least, that Jesus is admonishing us to forgive anything and anyone that has harmed us.[15]

AND DO NOT BRING US TO THE TIME OF TRIAL

Some wonder whether these words imply that God sometimes leads us into trials and temptations. The book of James clears up any misunderstanding: "No one, when tempted, should say, 'I am being tempted by God'; for God cannot be tempted by evil and he himself tempts no one" (Jas 1:13). After all, temptation is a basic element of our world. We all need help in this area. Even Jesus did. When we're tempted, we're more likely to sin, which is not God's intent for us. This passage has a strange implication, since God doesn't lead us into sin or bring us to trying times. We do that on our own with our free will or as a part of living in a broken world. God provides us an alternative when we focus on God: "God is faithful, and he will not let you be tested beyond your strength, but with the testing he will also provide the way out so that you may be able to endure it" (1 Cor 10:13). Taking the higher ground here, we may recognize that we are not tempted by God but are being directed to overcome our weaknesses and accept God's capacity to maneuver us away from temptation and sin, no matter what circumstances we may face.[16]

BUT RESCUE US FROM THE EVIL ONE

In this context, evil could again mean "temptation" or perhaps the idea of delivering us from the "devil" or "evil one," who is depicted throughout the Bible as the one always attempting to lead us away from God. Whichever meaning you accept, we seem to be always at risk of succumbing to evil. Common vernacular would point to simply asking God to protect us from doing or being around bad things, whatever they may be. Regardless, this petition acknowledges that God is always available to help deliver us from all our fears (Ps 34:4). The phrase is an acceptance that God is available at any time to separate and protect us from evil.[17]

---

15. Miller, "Lord's Prayer: Sins, Debts, or Trespasses?"
16. See "Matthew 6:13."
17. Ibid.

FOR THINE IS THE KINGDOM, AND THE POWER, AND THE GLORY

While studying various versions of the Lord's Prayer, we consulted multiple sources, including the Didache Bible, a second-century Book of Teachings that may date back to the apostles. This resource exposes the fact that neither Luther nor the Roman Catholic versions of the prayer include these concluding words. Several sources state that the final phrase comes from both the Didache and other Greek texts that ended prayers with a blessing. "Most recent editors have accordingly omitted it, as probably an addition made at first (after the pattern of most Jewish prayers) for the liturgical use of the Prayer."[18] In many cases, "the practice stuck."[19]

AMEN

Even the term *Amen* seems to stir up controversy, despite it being a standard Hebrew ending of a prayer that would seem consistent with Jesus' heritage. Several sources and authors speak of the word as meaning *truly* or *verily* or *so be it* and believe that it, too, was added later.

WHAT DOES THIS MEAN?

The Lord's Prayer has three basic elements. It positions God as all powerful and pervasive in all things. It is a series of petitions. And it's definitively a guide on what to pray when considering everyone and when not aiming our prayer at a specific purpose. It's a prayer of community. Rev. Boswell, in a sermon on this topic, stated, "Praying the Lord's Prayer is not about achieving a goal or receiving answers. It is about being formed into people who want what God wants, who desire what God desires, who give like God gives, and who forgive like God forgives."[20]

The phrases "perfect prayer" or "greatest prayer," per John Dominic Crossan, who also calls it the "strangest prayer," don't mean that the prayer is all-encompassing. It is a prayer that is meant to bring us together under God's presence, protection, and power. It allows us to focus as one on the good that can exist in the world when we "let go and let God" guide us to forgive and stand against the evils that exist in our own thoughts and

---

18. Ibid.
19. "For Thine Is the Kingdom—Conclusion to the Lord's Prayer."
20. Boswell, sermon, July 24, 2021.

actions. Crossan goes a step further for Americans, stating that the Lord's Prayer is a "radical vision for justice," similar to our country's Pledge of Allegiance that aspires "liberty and justice for all."[21]

PUB THEOLOGY

INTRODUCTION

The Lord's Prayer is one of many ways to pray. In fact, many of us memorized the prayer in childhood, along with countless other blessings, prayers, rhymes, and jingles. This chapter examines what lies beyond the prayer's general usage, the form, and the words. Although two biblical versions exist, we use the longer version found in Matthew 6:9-13 in this study of the prayer and the story surrounding it.

ICEBREAKER

In a minute or less, describe a favorite individual hobby or a favorite group activity.

JUMPING-OFF POINTS

- What do the various versions of the Lord's Prayer mean to you?
- How important is the story that surrounds the Lord's Prayer?
- Was this prayer always so important, or did historical usage expand it?
- What slight or major variances in translation do you deem most important?
- What does the Lord's Prayer mean to you personally?
- Do you feel the same praying the Lord's Prayer alone as you do when praying it with others? Why do you think this is so?

BIBLIOGRAPHY

"And Forgive us Our Trespasses, as we Forgive those who Trespass against Us: The Large Catechism—Martin Luther." *Bible Hub*. biblehub.com/library/luther/the_large_catechism/and_forgive_us_our_trespasses.htm.

---

21. Quoted in Csillag, "Understanding the Lord's Prayer with John Dominic Crossan."

Beaumont, Douglas. "The Lord's Prayer: 'Adding To' or 'Subtracting From' Scripture?" May 26, 2015. douglasbeaumont.com/2015/05/26/the-lords-prayer-adding-to-or-subtracting-from-scripture/.

Boswell, Rev. Dr. W. Benjamin. Sermon preached at Myers Park Baptist Church. July 24, 2021.

Chan, Phil. "Complete Summary of Jesus' Sermon on the Mount." January 13, 2013. phillipchan.org/summary-of-jesus-sermon-on-the-mount/.

Csillag, Ron. "Understanding the Lord's Prayer with John Dominic Crossan." *HuffPost*. May 25, 2011, huffpost.com/entry/10-minutes-with-john-domi_n_770261.

"For Thine Is the Kingdom—Conclusion to the Lord's Prayer," *University Lutheran*, August 11, 2017, universitylutheranchurch.org/2017/08/11/for-thine-is-the-kingdom/Hamlin, Rick. "The Truth about the Lord's Prayer." *HuffPost*. Updated May 18, 2013. huffpost.com/entry/the-truth-about-the-lords-prayer_b_2902631.

Jeremias, Joachim. The Lord's Prayer, trans. John Reumann, Facet Books Biblical Series (Philadelphia: Fortress, 1964).

"The Lord's Prayer: line-by-line commentary." *lords-prayer-words.com: traditional & contemporary prayers*. lords-prayer-words.com/commentary/our_father_who_art_in_heaven.html.

"Matthew 6 [GNV]: 1 Alms. 5 Prayer. 14 Forgiving our brother." *Bible Gateway*. biblegateway.com/passage/?search=Matthew%20 6&version=GNV.

Miller, John M. "The Lord's Prayer: Sins, Debts, or Trespasses?" Sermon at The Chapel Without Walls, Hilton Head Island, SC. October 20, 2019. chapelwithoutwalls.org/sermons/2019/10/20/the-lords-prayer-sins-debts-or-trespasses.html.

Mitchell, David C. "The Lord's Prayer in Aramaic." June 10, 2020. brightmorningstar.org/lords-prayer-in-aramaic/.

Mulholland, James. *Praying Like Jesus*. San Francisco: Harper Collins, 2001.

Rohr, Richard. Notes from presentation at Myers Park Baptist Church. April 29, 2012.

———. Email to authors. February 23, 2021.

"What does 'hallowed be thy name' in the Lord's Prayer mean?" *Bible Portal.* March 18, 2019. bibleportal.com/articles/what-does-hallowed-be-thy-name-in-the-lords-prayer-mean.html.

"What does it mean to be poor in spirit?" God Questions: Your Questions. Biblical Answers, gotquestions.org/poor-in-spirit.html.

MEETING 10

A HISTORICAL AND THEOLOGICAL RESPONSE TO SYSTEMIC RACISM: A PROCESS OF LIBERATION

OLIVER M. THOMAS

Systemic racism, also known as institutional racism, is a form of racism that is embedded as normal practice within society or an organization. It can lead to such issues as discrimination in criminal justice, employment, housing, health care, political power, and education, among other issues.[1]

INTRODUCTION

We Christians and citizens of the United States live in the tension between oppression and freedom. The tension is present in our history and our daily lives. The US, often said to be founded as "a Christian nation," was established on texts of freedom. However, while these texts were being written, communities of Black and brown people were being oppressed. To critically discuss systemic racism in the US, people of faith must commit themselves to understanding the entanglement of historical, theological, and sociopolitical realities. A pub theology group is an avenue for inviting individuals and communities to navigate this tension by imagining and constructing different possibilities; by deconstructing theological and sociopolitical realities in order to imagine new/different undertakings; and by constructing new experiences as a process of liberation.

As I have written in *Toward a Pedagogy of Critical Liberative Theological Consciousness*, liberation is a process of continually freeing ourselves from

---

1. Carmichael and Hamilton, *Black Power*, 4.

individual and communal bondage as we act in/on our environment.² In a pub theology group, liberation may manifest within various activities. Among them are rereading history, asking thoughtful questions, reflecting on lived experiences, and delving into scriptural (re)interpretation. As your pub theology group engages with this topic, I invite you to peel back the layers of your historical, theological, and social existence in order to embark on a process of liberation that might lead to holistic transformation. The intentions of this chapter are for you to become aware of, reflect on, and develop a response to systemic racism.³

A PROCESS OF LIBERATION

The culture of the US is shaped by historical, theological, and sociopolitical systems of oppression that gave birth to institutional racism. As a Black man and a being in the world, I remain arrested by the idea that one group of people would claim their freedom while simultaneously oppressing another group of people. On the one hand, the Declaration of Independence was not written with Indigenous, African, and Mexican communities in mind. On the other hand, abolitionists, former slaves, and free African Americans reinterpreted the Declaration of Independence. They read it as a text articulating democracy and freedom *for all*. In the twenty-first century, with a government entity like the US Immigration and Customs Enforcement (ICE) and a social movement like Black Lives Matter (BLM), it is clear that the US lives in the tension between the lived experience of oppression and the promise of freedom. In education and ministry, I navigate this tension by studying the teachings of James H. Cone,⁴ Black liberation theology, and the Gospels (Matthew, Mark, Luke, John). Individuals in a pub theology group can (and should) do likewise as they begin the process of liberation,

---

2. Thomas, "Toward a Pedagogy of Critical Liberative Theological Consciousness," 82.

3. As you study the historical, theological, and sociopolitical realities of racism in the United States, I recommend *The Oxford Handbook of African American Theology*, edited by Katie G. Cannon and Anthony B. Pinn; *Black Theology: A Documentary History* (2 vols.), edited by James H. Cone and Gayraud S. Wilmore; *Major Problems in the History of the American South* (2 vols.), edited by Sally G. McMillen, Elizabeth Hayes Turner, et al.; *Racism without Racists*, by Eduardo Bonilla-Silva; *Southern Politics in State and Nation*, by V.O. Key and Alexander Heard; and *White Rage: The Unspoken Truth of Our Racial Divide*, by Carol Anderson.

4. As you study James H. Cone, I recommend beginning with these texts: *God of the Oppressed*; *Risks of Faith: The Emergence of a Black Theology of Liberation*; *Speaking the Truth: Ecumenism, Liberation, and Black Theology*; and *The Cross and the Lynching Tree*.

deconstructing their lived experiences alongside the *unfinished* story of the church and the US.

THE IMPACT OF STORYTELLING ON THEOLOGICAL REFLECTION AND LIBERATION

Storytelling is the heartbeat of pub theology because it calls on members to engage the process of liberation through listening, self-reflection, and dialogue, which are essential to theological reflection as an evolving praxis. It allows members of the group to share their lived experiences, their history, and their faith formation. As a gateway to structured dialogue, storytelling opens the door to developing a political, theological, and social awareness of the world in which we live by naming the dynamics of injustice, oppression, and power[5] and cultivating agency for social change. Equally, it invites listeners to connect the proverbial dots between historic and present realities. As a member of your pub theology group, I want to share the impact of storytelling on theological reflection as a way of peeling back the layers of systemic racism.

STORYTELLING WITHIN AFRICAN AMERICAN CULTURE, HISTORY, AND RELIGION

Within the African American cultural, historical, and religious tradition, storytelling is a way of inviting listeners—and readers—to imagine the possibilities for human liberation and divine interaction.[6] The Exodus narrative of Moses leading the "children of Israel" out of Egyptian bondage (i.e., slavery) is one example. The story is so ingrained in the African American tradition that Harriet Tubman, a conductor on the Underground Railroad, was nicknamed "Moses" because she led enslaved people out of American bondage. She believed the struggle to liberate her people was a divine calling and a communal responsibility. Black people have told and continue telling the story of Harriet Tubman to conjure yearnings for justice and freedom in an oppressive society. The Exodus narrative and the

---

5. Thomas, "Toward a Pedagogy of Critical Liberative Theological Consciousness," 64.
6. Cone, *God of the Oppressed*, 74–75.

story of Harriet Tubman are stories that shaped Black liberation theology in the US.[7]

For Christians, parables are stories filled with complexity, nuance, and comparisons that encourage listeners and readers to imagine multiple possibilities for understanding individual, communal, and social worlds. The telling of parables, as a teaching method, has been practiced for hundreds of years in the Christian tradition. The central texts for reading parables are the Gospels (i.e., Matthew, Mark, Luke, John). Jesus of Nazareth, a rabbi (translated *teacher*) and the central figure of the Gospels, taught in parables. Yet the use of parables is not limited to the Gospels and Christianity. Parables are used by religious and nonreligious traditions alike because they encompass the common, familiar, everyday experiences of individuals and communities to teach multiple lessons.[8] I emphasize the Gospels and the liberatory mission of Jesus because my theology and the theology of James H. Cone are grounded in the story of Jesus.

Jesus' liberatory mission is articulated in Luke 4:18-19. The text reads, "The Spirit of the Lord is upon me, because [God] has anointed me to bring good news to the poor. [God] has sent me to proclaim release to the captives and recovery of sight to the blind, to let the oppressed go free, to proclaim the year of the Lord's favor." Jesus identified with the marginalized and the oppressed in his community. Furthermore, he professed that God gave him the authority to empower the subjugated, speak truth to power, and pursue justice in his sociopolitical context. In other words, Jesus committed his life, in solidarity with the oppressed, to confront the powerful, whether the powerful were the Jewish religious authorities or the Roman government authorities.

WOULD YOU ALLOW ME TO SHARE MY STORY?

My story and the story of my ancestors are examples of the connectedness of individual, communal, and societal matters. My ancestors were enslaved Africans, free Africans and African Americans, Native Americans (i.e., Tuscarora), and slaveholding Europeans in Bertie County, Windsor, North Carolina. Plainly stated, my story is shaped by the history of European colonization in North America. As a child, I heard stories of my African,

---

7. Ibid., 147–49.

8. Sensoy and DiAngelo, *Is Everyone Really Equal?*, xxv–xxvii.

African American, and Native American ancestors' resistance to, subversion of, and survival from oppression. I also heard stories of these same ancestors being abused, beaten, and dehumanized by my European ancestors.

My knowledge, emotions, and images regarding these stories are driving forces for my beliefs and actions. Whether I am ministering in the church or teaching in the classroom, liberation is at the core of my pedagogy and theology. I am a person of faith believing that the practice of theological education for liberation is an act of hopeful resistance that centers the lives of the oppressed. As a Black man and minister, I know that biblical stories and some religious teachings are habitually used to oppress, dehumanize, and discipline bodies in ways that are contrary to mental, physical, emotional, and spiritual freedom. Storytelling, for good or bad, has the power to change lives. Stories of leaders in the civil rights movement, for example, reveal the intersections of history, lived experience, and Scripture.

As a Master of Divinity student, I studied African American educators and ministers who were prominent leaders during the civil rights movement of the 1950s and 1960s. One of those leaders, Rev. Dr. Benjamin E. Mays, was the focus of my thesis. Rev. Dr. Mays was a Baptist minister and educator, affectionately known as the "Schoolmaster of the Movement." In studying him, I discovered that he mentored Rev. Dr. Martin Luther King Jr. and Rev. James H. Cone. The more I studied Mays, the more I learned of his influence on Cone and the powerful influence of Cone on Christian theology in the US and the world. As a result, my story and theological commitment to liberation has been forever changed by the stories of James H. Cone, Martin Luther King Jr., and Benjamin E. Mays.

CONTEXTUALIZING JAMES H. CONE

James H. Cone, a Protestant (i.e., African Methodist Episcopal) shaped by the civil rights and Black Power movements, recognized the power of storytelling within the church and other liberatory spaces. As a theologian and a teacher, he was committed to telling the story of oppressed people and connecting their lived experiences to the story of Jesus. In a theological way, Cone wrote counter narratives that critiqued the watered-down story of Jesus and whitewashed story of American racism. For him, the actions and teachings of Christianity *should* be congruent with the liberatory teachings and actions of Jesus, which wrestle with and respond to the silenced stories of the oppressed, particularly Black Americans.

The story of Black Americans is a story of treacherous and tumultuous marginalization. The current realities of the first quarter of the twenty-first century are not unlike the realities of the mid-twentieth century or the latter part of the nineteenth century. Openly practiced racism, police brutality, state-sanctioned violence against nonviolent protesters, and resistance movements are recognizable similarities between the present and the past. In the 1960s, Black people lived under the constant assault of Jim Crow "law and order," which enforced racial segregation and White supremacy. In many states, Black people did not have the right to vote. In other states, if they had the right to vote, they lived with the threat of being killed for choosing to exercise their right. Restaurants were segregated. Water fountains were segregated. In the southern US, many poor Black people were sharecroppers, one step removed from slavery, trying to make a living working for paternalistic landowners. The civil rights movement was one response to the assault on Black lives. The movement was intended to dismantle racial segregation and White supremacy, change all systems of oppression, and retard the history of inequality in the US. It began with the cries of Black people. It became a campaign for all.

Amid the struggles for liberation in America, James H. Cone emerged as a *contested* leader of cultural, theological, and social change. Cone's contributions to the historical project of liberation were contextualized in his work with Black communities in the US.

WHAT WAS CONE'S STORY?

As a minister with the African Methodist Episcopal Church and a Black man wrestling with his rage, Cone found himself betwixt the nonviolent approach of Martin Luther King Jr. of the civil rights movement and the "by any means necessary" approach of Malcolm X of the Black Power movement. Beginning with his lived experience in Bearden, Arkansas, he "sought to deepen [his] conviction that the God of biblical faith and Black religion is best known as the Liberator of the oppressed from bondage."[9] Cone articulated the ways his interpretation of Scripture was rooted in his experiences with a marginalized people. He also expressed the ways the scriptural interpretation of many White theologians was rooted in their experiences with a dominant people. "The God of biblical faith and Black

---

9. Cone, *God of the Oppressed*, ix.

religion is partial toward the weak," he wrote.[10] With the Bible and lived experience dialectically sourcing his theological reflections, Cone argued that God, in Jesus Christ (past, present, future), liberates the oppressed.

Cone began defining Black liberation theology with his publication *Black Theology and Black Power*. His central argument was that there is no contradiction between the social justice orientation of the gospel of Jesus Christ, the Black Power movement, and the civil rights movement. Cone argued that Black Power is for liberation; Jesus Christ is for liberation; therefore, Black Power is a contemporary expression of the gospel of Jesus Christ in America.[11] In so doing, he ruptured and positively altered the theological world by combining Black *with* theology—the freedom struggle of the oppressed *with* the gospel of Jesus Christ. He continued his work with *A Black Theology of Liberation* and reached a crescendo with *God of the Oppressed*. The central concern of *God of the Oppressed* is the liberation of the Black community from White supremacy and racism in the US. Guided by his Christian faith from his childhood to his death on April 28, 2018, the Rev. Dr. James H. Cone taught and wrote within the context of the Black Freedom movement, opposing White racist churches, racist theologies, and systemic racism.

HOW DOES MY STORY INTERSECT WITH CONE'S?

History and the gospel of Jesus Christ are lenses through which I connect with the life and liberative work of James H. Cone. I did not live the historic moments he experienced, but we share a history of systemic oppression. As two Black men born in the US, reared in the South, we share a history of slavery, Jim Crow, the civil rights movement, Christianity, and the struggle of being Black in a world of White supremacy. I believe the teachings, theological interpretations, and activism of Cone are guideposts for theo-social transformation in the twenty-first century.

RESPONDING TO SYSTEMIC RACISM AND INTERSECTING OPPRESSIONS

As a social institution, Christianity has shaped and continues to shape the worldviews of individuals and communities in helpful and harmful ways.

---

10. Ibid., x–xi.
11. Gross and Cone, "Black Liberation Theology, in Its Founder's Words."

Within the academy, Black liberation theologians and critical scholars of education are striving to (de)construct educative practices that are detrimental to individuals as well as communities and (re)construct educative practices that are liberative. Unfortunately, religious teachings such as "Slaves, obey your earthly masters with fear and trembling . . ." (Eph 6:5) have been and are used to oppress as opposed to liberate. During the era of slavery, European teachers, preachers, politicians, and economists employed this teaching to oppress Black bodies. But critical pedagogues, though they would not have defined themselves as such, used (re)constructive texts. For example, "Thus says the LORD: Let my people go . . ." (Exod 8:20) was a central teaching used by abolitionists such as Sojourner Truth and revolutionaries such as Nat Turner to liberate enslaved bodies.

Censuring LGBTQ bodies is a present-day example of oppression. "You shall not lie with a man as with a woman; it is an abomination" (Lev 18:22) is a central teaching used to condemn LGBTQ persons. They are discriminated against in various aspects and institutions of our society because they are not affirmed as equal members. They are denied civil rights as a result of being their true selves. But critical theologians such as Bishop Yvette A. Flunder of the City of Refuge United Church of Christ, Oakland, California, and Bishop William J. Barber II[12] of the Greenleaf Christian Church, Goldsboro, North Carolina, use (re)constructive texts to affirm LGBTQ persons. "For it was [God] who formed my inward parts; [God] knit me together in my mother's womb" (Ps 139:13) and "For there are eunuchs who have been so from birth . . ." (Matt 19:12) are central teachings used by Bishops Flunder and Barber to liberate censured bodies. Matthew, the author of the Gospel, is quoting Jesus. And the term *eunuch* was a first-century term for homosexual.[13]

As slaves, former slaves, activists, and leaders, in different times and spaces in the Black community, read and listened to the story of Jesus by way of the Gospels, they connected with his vision of liberation and his moral principles. Leaders like Malcolm X and Martin Luther King Jr. did not perceive Jesus as a White man, but they perceived that his teachings, life, and legacy were co-opted by a White supremacist ideology. Black liberation theology (re)claims the Jesus born to an oppressed community and

---

12. Bishop William J. Barber II is co-chair of the Poor People's Campaign: A National Call for Moral Revival with Rev. Dr. Liz Theoharis.

13. Ellison and Douglas, eds., *Sexuality and the Sacred*, 110.

extends his mission to liberate the oppressed from systemic racism and oppression.

Black liberation theology centers the marginalization of Black people, but its work is not limited to the Black community. It is for the Black community in that it is concerned with the poor, the marginalized, and the voiceless. However, it *is not* primarily concerned with the Black community in that it is concerned with *all* poor, marginalized, and voiceless. Today, for many within and without the Black community, Jesus and the Gospels remain a moral compass for equality, equity, and justice in society.

Unlike White American theology, which is and has been shaped by the cultural, political, and theological ideology of the dominant group (i.e., the ruling class), Black liberation theology is and has been shaped by Black people's collective identity as theological, political, and cultural victims in North America. Black people have responded to the sociohistorical problem of American slavery, Jim Crow, and enduring oppressive ideologies through the medium of stories (storytelling) as a way of conjuring images of God's liberating power and freedom for the oppressed not fulfilled in the historic present. Thus, the existence of God is not a theoretical idea divorced from the realities of oppression. Jesus, the "Son of God," came to set the oppressed free in his age (i.e., People of the Way), the present age (e.g., civil rights movement, Repairers of the Breach), and the age to come (i.e., the perpetual process of liberation). Intricately woven into the Black freedom struggle are claims about who God is, what God has done, what God is doing, how God has done it, and how God can bring about liberation through the actions of people.

CONCLUSION

For members of a pub theology group, the process of liberation calls for a critical reading of history, Scripture, lived experience, and sociopolitical realities to uncover oppressive teachings. The communal efforts of Black liberation theologians are firmly rooted in the lives of individuals, communities, and the (re)imagining of the socially constructed world. Knowing Christianity is the largest religious tradition in the US and conservative Christians (i.e., evangelicals) are driving public policies, which are reversing the advances of civil rights legislation for people of color, women, youth, and other marginalized groups, a pub theology group is fertile ground for holistic theological and social transformation. As we participate in the group, we must commit to demonstrating a critical theological consciousness that is transformative for the lives of *everyday* people (and all of creation).

Our knowledge of history, both communal and personal, helps us combat stories that subjugate some while disproportionately empowering others. The history of domination and marginalization in the US, both present and past, is intricately connected to the history of individual members of dominant and marginalized groups. Knowing one's personal and communal history is an integral part of the educative process, of naming the "historic present"[14] to oppose the "dominant material relations of the ruling theological ideas in a given society."[15] For a liberative theological consciousness, Cone offers wisdom for critically engaging the relationship between personal and collective histories toward the fulfillment of all humanity.

In the vein of Black liberation theology, I do not assume there is a "one size fits all" approach to critical liberative theological consciousness. Liberation is a process that takes seriously the sociopolitical experiences of individuals and communities. To this end, I want to offer guiding questions as a path for peeling back the layers of individual and collective histories, conditioned by domination, so as to take "the [road] less traveled"[16] as we submit ourselves to a process of converting from an old way to a new way of being in the world. So, too, the guiding questions I suggest are derived from my lived experiences, a critical reading of history, Black liberation theology, and liberative themes gleaned from *God of the Oppressed* fully researched in my dissertation "Toward a Pedagogy of Critical Liberative Theological Consciousness: Cultivating Students as Agents of Social Change."

The guiding questions invite a transformation of relational power by challenging members of the group to name theo-social inequality, analyze theo-social inequality, and struggle toward new theo-social constructions in community. The adoption of this theological approach is linked to the wisdom of communion as a way of transforming structures of domination. In the Gospel of Luke and the Acts of the Apostles, communion led to the sharing of life and property. It also altered communal living in ways that led to forms of Christian socialism in the first century and the twentieth century. By way of communion, we experience conversion by learning from one another, reflecting with one another, trusting one another, and

---

14. Freire, *Pedagogy of the Oppressed*, 19–21.
15. Cone, *God of the Oppressed*, 38–39.
16. Frost, "The Road Not Taken," 163.

acting with one another. Communion calls us to discover the ways we are shaped by intersecting oppressions as we deconstruct systems of dehumanization so that *all* experience the fullness of humanity. (See the questions in "Jumping-off Points" below.)

PUB THEOLOGY

INTRODUCTION

In *God of the Oppressed*, James H. Cone wrote, "Human beings are made for each other and no people can realize their full humanity except as they participate in its realization for others." Transforming the oppressive certainties of systemic racism is about changing the policies that create and cause intersecting oppressions in our society. We Christians and citizens of the United States can transform the oppressive certainties of systemic racism in our church, community, and country if we have the will to participate in a process of liberation.

ICEBREAKER

In a minute or less, share why one person is (or was) a good or a best friend. (You can select a friend from any time in your life.)

JUMPING-OFF POINTS

In my dissertation "Toward a Pedagogy of Critical Liberative Theological Consciousness," I ask this question: How does my lived experience(s) influence the way(s) I interpret Scripture and act consciously to transform systemic oppression (i.e., racism)? The guiding questions I suggest here are derived from my lived experiences, research, and a critical reading of history, Black liberation theology, and liberative themes.

- What are the implications of storytelling on Christian experience?
- How does one's knowledge of history and their lived experiences inform their understanding of the relationship between *everyday* life and theology?
- How does one's knowledge of history and their reading of Scripture shape their theological reflections?
- How does one trouble, or even resist, the traditional teachings of the church in the context of systemic racism?

- How are individual lives in community and society conditioned by intersecting oppressions?
- How do one's actions communicate the liberatory mission of Jesus that we read in Luke 4:18-19?
- How does one define the relationship between faith and political action?

BIBLIOGRAPHY

Brock, Rochelle. *Sista Talk: The Personal and the Pedagogical.* New York: Lang, 2010.

Cone, James H. *Black Theology and Black Power.* 50th anniversary ed. Maryknoll: Orbis, 2018.

———. *A Black Theology of Liberation.* 20th anniversary ed. Maryknoll: Orbis, 1986.

———. *God of the Oppressed.* Revised ed. Maryknoll: Orbis, 1997.

Ehrman, Bart D. *The New Testament: A Historical Introduction to the Early Christian Writings.* 4th ed. Oxford: Oxford University Press, 2008.

Ellison, Marvin M., and Kelly Brown Douglas, eds. *Sexuality and the Sacred: Sources for Theological Reflection.* 2nd ed. Louisville: Westminster John Knox Press, 2010.

Freire, Paulo. *Pedagogy of the Oppressed.* 30th anniversary ed. New York: Continuum, 2003.

Frost, Robert. "The Road Not Taken." In *Selected Poems,* 163. New York: Gramercy Books, 1992.

Gross, Terry, and James H. Cone. "Black Liberation Theology, in its Founder's Words." Interview on *Fresh Air.* March 31, 2008. Produced by Terri Gross and Danny Miller. Podcast, 13:05. npr.org/player/embed/89236116/89236797.

Harmon, Amy, Apoorva Mandavilli, Sapna Maheshwari, and Jodi Kantor. "From Cosmetics to NASCAR, Calls for Racial Justice Are Spreading." *The New York Times.* June 13, 2020.

Long, Thomas G. *The Witness of Preaching.* 2nd ed. Louisville: Westminster John Knox Press, 2005.

Macedo, Donaldo. "Reinserting Criticity into Critical Pedagogy." In *Critical Pedagogy: Where are We Now?*, edited by Peter McLaren and Joe Kincheloe, 391–95. New York: Lang, 2007.

McKim, Donald K. *Westminster Dictionary of Theological Terms*. Louisville: John Knox Press, 1996.

Rohr, Richard. *Immortal Diamond: The Search for Our True Self*. San Francisco: Wiley, 2013.

Sensoy, Özlem, and Robin DiAngelo. *Is Everyone Really Equal? An Introduction to Key Concepts in Social Justice Education*. New York: Teachers College Press, 2012.

Thomas, Oliver Melton-Christian. "Toward a Pedagogy of Critical Liberative Theological Consciousness: Cultivating Students as Agents of Social Change." PhD diss. University of North Carolina at Greensboro, 2020. ProQuest (27744843).

SALVATION AND LIBERATION: A RADICAL FAITH

BILL J. LEONARD

"Whether they hear or refuse to hear (for they are a rebellious house) they shall know that there has been a prophet among them." (Ezra 2:5 [NRSV])

They were exiles, those first Baptists in the new world, the scourge of "Christian America." Roger Williams personified their plight, at least for a moment. In 1636, the Puritan representatives of a "Christian Commonwealth" threw Williams, the quintessential dissenter, out of civilized Massachusetts because he rejected the establishmentarian idea of the "civil magistrate's right to govern in ecclesiastical affairs."[1] To avoid deportation back to England, Williams ventured into the "howling wilderness" in the forests of New England, where he "was sorely tossed for fourteen weeks, in a bitter winter season, not knowing what bread or bed did mean."[2] In exile, he said, he was "denied the common air to breathe in, and a civil cohabitation upon the same common earth; yea and also without mercy and human compassion, exposed to winter miseries in a howling wilderness." The Narragansett Indians saved him, and he bought land from them to found Providence and, by 1638, the First Baptist Church in America in the colony of Rhode Island.

Of that endeavor and its religious radicalism, Williams wrote,

> I having made a covenant of peaceable neighborhood with all the sachems and natives round about us, and having, in a sense of God's

---

1. Backus, *History of New England from 1620 to 1804*, 53.
2. Ibid., 39.

merciful providence unto me in my distress, called the place Providence, I desired it might be for a shelter for persons distressed for conscience. I then considering the condition of divers of my distressed countrymen, communicated my said purchase unto loving friends . . . who then desired to take shelter here with me.[3]

It was a colony, a church, born in exile. Rhode Island became a sanctuary for seventeenth-century religious fanatics, holy rollers, and assorted theological perverts. And the Massachusetts moral majority was glad to see them go. As one Puritan preacher declared, "all . . . Anabaptists and other Enthusiasts, shall have free liberty to keep away from us . . . the sooner the better."[4]

Roger Williams was a prophetic pain in the Puritan religious establishment from the beginning. No sooner had he gotten off the boat than he was disseminating certain "erroneous and dangerous" opinions. For one thing, he said that the Native Americans, not the English king, were the sole owners of the American land and should be justly compensated for it. For another, he declared that the authority of civil magistrates extended only to "bodies and goods," not to "souls and religion."[5] Anticipating American religious pluralism, Williams declared that "Jews, Turks, [Muslims], or anti-christians" could indeed "be peaceable and quiet subjects, loving and helpful neighbors, fair and just dealers, true and loyal to the civil government."[6]

The New England Puritans justified the exile of Baptists and the execution of Quakers as proper protection for the only true gospel. Williams suggested that if New England churches were truly Christ's, they would neither need nor desire political protection. God would take care of God's own by the power of the Spirit and the Word of the Lord. Again, we confront Williams's and early Baptists' offensive, prophetic faith: true religion can take care of itself. It need not be defended save by the spiritual life of its people. Finally, the Puritans had enough of it; Williams was exiled.

Roger Williams led colonial religious dissenters to that radical, exilic faith. Then he established another Baptist tradition. He quit! He is a proto-Baptist at best, but he set a course, radically inventing religious America in all its pluralism and religious diversity. He was not alone. Dr. John Clarke, Baptist physician and preacher, joined Williams in Rhode

---

3. Backus, *History of New England, with Particular Reference to the Baptists*, 1:75.
4. Mead, *Lively Experiment*, 13.
5. Williams, *Bloudy Tenent of Persecution for Cause of Conscience Discussed*, 218.
6. Ibid., 112–13.

Island, founding the town of Newport and the First Baptist Church there by 1640. Clarke, who never left the Baptist fold, wrote the charter of Rhode Island, the first colony to extend complete religious liberty to all its citizens. The charter states that "No person within said colony at any time hereafter shall be in any wise molested, punished, disquieted or called into question for any differences of opinion in matters of religion . . . ."[7]

Where did Clarke, Williams, and early Baptists get such views? From secular humanists born of the Enlightenment? Hardly. Theirs was not so much a faith *for* radicals as it was a radical, prophetic faith: a faith so daring that even they did not fully comprehend where it would take them; a vision that we have not yet fulfilled in all its implications; a faith that is out there in front of us, challenging our continuing love affair with establishments, prestige, and power; and a faith at its best in exile.

First, they said that faith cannot be compelled. The word of God must be preached, not enforced by state or an official, culture-privileged religion. For those early Baptists, the idea of uncoerced faith was inseparable from the freedom of conscience. Faith is personal, not political, and each individual is responsible to God alone for the faith he or she does or does not have. Such radical faith had implications even for those who did not believe. God alone was sovereign judge for the conscience of believer and nonbeliever alike. Baptism—the outward sign of inward faith—was to be administered only to those who could testify to a work of grace in their hearts. John Clarke wrote, "I testify that . . . a visible believer or Disciple of Christ Jesus, is the only person that is to be baptized OR DIPPED."[8] Baptists' views on religious liberty were indivisible from their concern for uncoerced faith.

Second, these Baptists declared that faith cannot be nationalized. There are no Christian nations, they insisted—only Christian people, bound to Christ not by citizenship but by faith. Again, Clarke wrote that no "believer or servant of Jesus Christ hath any liberty, much less authority from his Lord to smite his fellow servant, nor with outward force or arm of flesh, to constrain, or restrain his conscience."[9]

Baptists, like other colonial dissenters (Quakers, Mennonites), were an obstinate lot, sometimes acting with prophetic insight, sometimes blind to the gospel bursting out all around them. The church has always had its

---

7. Quoted in Leonard, *Baptist Ways*, 76–77.
8. Ibid., 77.
9. Ibid.

share of prophetic individuals as well as people who misunderstand and "take offense" when the gospel appears right in front of them.

Prophets abounded among colonial Baptists. Obadiah Holmes, a New England Baptist pastor arrested and flogged for preaching Baptist views, looked his assailants in the eyes and audaciously declared, "You have struck me with roses."[10] John Leland, eighteenth-century Virginia Baptist preacher, declared, "Experience . . . has informed us that the fondness of magistrates to foster Christianity, has done it more harm than all the persecutions ever did. Persecution, like a lion, tears the saints to death, but leaves Christianity pure; state establishment of religion, like a bear, hugs the saints, but corrupts Christianity . . . ."[11]

The early Baptists were unashamed spokespersons for Christ; they did not hesitate to tell people—high and low, rich and poor—to be saved. They hoped the United States would become a nation of Christians, but only by the free preaching of the gospel, not by implicit or explicit government support. Historian Penrose St. Amant wrote insightfully, "Both the problem and the glory of our Baptist heritage are rooted in the authority of the Word of God and in the freedom of . . . (the human) mind and conscience to understand it."[12]

The Revolution came and went. The Constitution with its Bill of Rights was secured, and suddenly, the Baptists awakened mid-nineteenth century to discover that things had changed—that they had become the second largest Protestant denomination in America. The remnant became a majority and the exiles became an establishment. The dark side of the Baptist heritage loomed large. The issue was human slavery. Suddenly, a people who defended the liberty of human conscience were torn apart over the liberty of human beings.

In the South, many Baptists who claimed and worked toward religious liberty also accepted, even promoted, what came to be called "biblical defenses" of slavery. Reverend Richard Furman is a case in point. In 1822, a freed slave named Denmark Vesey was arrested and hanged for allegedly plotting to overthrow slavery in Charleston, South Carolina. (There is scholarly debate as to whether there was a "plot.") Vesey was one of the founders of the Emanuel African Methodist Episcopal Church, and most of the thirty-four other defendants came from that church. (They were hanged

---

10. Quoted in Gaustad, *Baptist Piety*, 29.
11. Quoted in Leonard, *Baptist Ways*, 131.
12. St. Amant, "Southern Baptists," 15.

too.) The church was closed until after the Civil War, when it was rebuilt and became a leading congregation in the AME. In June 2015, the church was the scene of the brutal murder of eight African American congregants by a young White supremacist, reminding Charleston and the nation that religious liberty continues to have dangerous racism-based overtones.

A few months after the execution of Vesey and the other defendants, Dr. Richard Furman, pastor of First Baptist Church, Charleston, wrote to the South Carolina governor and proposed a state day of "prayer and humility" to thank God for delivery from a slave rebellion and a recent hurricane that struck the South Carolina coast. In that same document, Furman set forth the first "biblical" defense of slavery, insisting,

> Had the holding of slaves been a moral evil, it cannot be supposed, that the inspired Apostles, who feared not the faces of men, and were ready to lay down their lives in the cause of their God, would have tolerated it, for a moment, in the Christian Church. If they had done so on a principle of accommodation, in cases where the masters remained heathen, to avoid offences and civil commotion; yet, surely, where both master and servant were Christian, as in the case before us, they would have enforced the law of Christ, and required, that the master should liberate his slave in the first instance. But, instead of this, they let the relationship remain untouched, as being lawful and right, and insist on the relative duties. In proving this subject justifiable by Scriptural authority, its morality is also proved; for the Divine Law never sanctions immoral actions.[13]

Misusing the Bible, those pro-slavery Baptists overlooked one important thing: they continued to preach the gospel of salvation to Black and White alike. True enough, they qualified it by insisting that salvation changed only the slaves' eternal status, not their earthly condition, but try as they might, they could not keep the liberating power of the *full* gospel from finding its way into the hearts and hopes of the slaves. So, in 1804, a Black woman named Winney, a Kentucky slave belonging to Miss Esther Boulware, was disciplined by her mistress and the Forks of Elkhorn Baptist Church for saying publicly that "she once thought it her duty to serve her master and mistress but since the Lord had converted her, she had never believed that any Christian (could keep) Negroes or slaves." She got in more trouble for saying she believed "there was thousands of white people wallowing in Hell for their treatment to Negroes—and she did not care if there was many

---

13. Furman, "Exposition of the Views of the Baptists," 382–83.

more . . . ."[14] That slave woman talked free, didn't she? Even in slavery, she claimed the hope and promise of liberation, born of the waters of baptism.

Likewise, in the terrible days of Jim Crow laws and "separate but equal" facilities, Baptist churches represented one of the few institutions that African Americans could call their own. In the autonomy of those communities of faith, preachers spoke out against the oppression of a people, even in the face of bombings, church burnings, threats, and death. The Baptist heritage of freedom flourished even when it divided Baptists, Black and White. The prophetic freedom of the gospel that stands at the center of Baptist ideals cannot long be inhibited, even by Baptists themselves. What does all this mean for us? Three things, at least.

First, beware of the majority. Since the crucifixion of Jesus, sometimes the religious majority has come out on the back side of grace. An orthodox majority exiled Roger Williams, and an orthodox majority boarded up Baptist churches in New England and Virginia. An orthodox majority hanged Quaker Mary Dyer on Boston Common in 1660, and an orthodox majority defended slavery by the authority of Holy Scripture. Majority religion often undermines or overlooks the heart of faith.

Second, let us take seriously and nurture the dissenting tradition of the Baptists and other faith traditions. Dissent means (1) "to differ in sentiment or opinion, especially from the majority"; (2) "to disagree with the methods, goals, etc., of a political party or government; take an opposing view"; and (3) "to disagree with or reject the doctrines or authority of an established [or state-privileged] church [or religion]."[15]

In *Dissent in American Religion*, historian Edwin S. Gaustad laid out the imperative of dissent, writing, "Should a society [whether church or state] actually succeed . . . in suffocating all contrary opinion, then its own vital juices no longer flow and the shadow of death begins to fall across it. No society—ecclesiastical or political, military or literary—can afford to be snared by its own slogans."[16] Gaustad acknowledged that dissent can be "irritating, unnerving, pigheaded, noisy, and brash. It can also be wrong." Yet, citing Reinhold Niebuhr, he concluded that "consent makes democracy possible; dissent makes democracy meaningful."[17]

---

14. Quoted in Sweet, *Religion on the American Frontier*, 329.
15. "Dissent," *Dictionary.com*, dictionary.com/browse/dissent.
16. Gaustad, *Dissent in American Religion*, 2.
17. Ibid., 2.

For me, two Baptist saints/mentors illustrate the dissenting point, the courage of faith and freedom. In 1946, Wake Forest University alumni Henlee Barnette, with a new doctorate in Christian ethics, was invited to teach at Birmingham's Howard College, now Samford University. Untenured, he organized the first association of Black and White ministers in Birmingham, Alabama. For his trouble, his contract at Howard was not renewed. Dissent had its price in that Baptist College. Barnette later became an ethics professor at the Southern Baptist Theological Seminary, Louisville, Kentucky, from which he marched with Martin Luther King Jr. and worked for integration and equal voting rights for African Americans and other minority groups. A generation later, Barnette lived to see his son James Barnette appointed chaplain of Samford University. He loved the irony of it all.

In 1971, Dr. John Thomas Porter, civil rights leader and pastor of the Sixth Avenue Baptist Church, sued the city of Birmingham, challenging the segregationist policies at Edgewood Cemetery, which forbade a Black Catholic soldier killed in Vietnam from being buried in that hallowed ground. Porter won, and a Baptist preacher's dissent against public policy opened a final resting place for a Catholic soldier. Today, Porter's remains lie in that same cemetery. Small acts. Great consequences. Solid dissent.

Third, Barnette, Porter, and a whole collection of radical Baptists have taught us this: Turn loose the gospel. Let it do whatever God intends it to do. Governments do not protect the gospel; the gospel protects us. Governments do not save the gospel; the gospel saves us! Let's take a chance. Let's turn it loose again, that good news of Christ. Who knows where it will take us? For it is more radical than any of us will ever understand.

This brings me to the Bible and the heart of that good news, a confession born of St. Paul's audacious words to the Romans: "There is therefore now no condemnation to those who are in Christ Jesus. For the law of the spirit of Christ has set you FREE from the law of sin and death" (Rom 8:1, KJV). Good news, don't you think? For exiles.[18]

---

18. Portions of this essay were first published in Leonard, *Word of God Across the Ages*, 103–12.

PUB THEOLOGY

INTRODUCTION

From the beginning, religious liberty has united and divided Americans. Historically, Americans tend to grant religious liberty grudgingly, that is, new movements often have a difficult time making their case and claiming their First Amendment rights. Colonial religious establishments whether Puritan in New England, and Anglicanism in the South, often dealt harshly with dissenters. By the twenty-first century, debates over the boundaries of religious liberty seemed constant, from tax breaks for religious groups to clergy to refusing to provide wedding cakes for LGBTQ marriages to violence against mosques, synagogues, churches, and temples. Hence the following questions for discussion.

ICEBREAKER

In a minute or less, describe what type of church were you raised in. If you were not raised attending a church, describe an activity your family did together.

JUMPING-OFF POINTS

- How does Roger Williams's view of religious liberty apply to certain twenty-first-century ideas and debates?
- Why has religious pluralism, advocated by Roger Williams and other colonial religious libertarians, remained such a controversial freedom in the United States?
- Is Williams's assertion that there are no "Christian nations" a valid understanding of church and state relationships?
- In what ways do contemporary Christians sometimes develop "biblical" support for certain culture-based practices?
- How would you define "conscience" and its place in your own life?

BIBLIOGRAPHY

Gaustad, Edwin Scott. *Baptist Piety: The Last will and Testament of Obadiah Holmes*. Tuscaloosa: University of Alabama Press, 2005.

———. *Dissent in American Religion*. Chicago: The University of Chicago Press, 1973.

Leonard, Bill J. *Baptist Ways: A History*. Valley Forge: Judson Press, 2002.

———. *The Homebrewed Guide to Church History: Flaming Heretics and Heavy Drinkers*. Minneapolis: Fortress, 2017.

Manis, Andrew M. *Southern Civil Religions in Conflict: Civil Rights and the Culture Wars*. Macon, GA: Mercer University Press, 2002.

Sobel, Mechal. *Trabelin' On: The Slave Journey to an Afro-Baptist Faith*. Princeton, NJ: Princeton University Press, 1979.

MEETING 12

QUEER THEOLOGY

NANCY E. CULP

INTRODUCTION

I grew up Southern Baptist in a small town in South Georgia. I learned Bible stories by heart and was so steeped in preaching and teaching, at church and at home, that it became part of my identity. In high school, I dedicated my life to full-time Christian ministry. I believed my life to be one of Christian service. After much discernment, I found myself at a Baptist seminary, and within three months of beginning this seminary journey, I discovered two life-changing things about myself: that I no longer believed the teachings of the Southern Baptist denomination and that I was gay. Either of these soul-shifting discoveries would have been enough to disrupt my life course, but the combination caused my path to disappear before me.

How could I not be Southern Baptist? It was all I had ever known of church. How could I be gay? Strangely, that question was the easier to answer because I could find no fault in the love and freedom I felt in my soul. For the first time in my life, questions about God and church and the Bible were held in safe trust with a growing circle of seminary friends. These friends helped me ask hard questions about God, the church, and being gay.

When I found a pub theology group at a Baptist church years later, I was sure I had landed in a faith community of welcoming people of God. If these people were authentic, loved God, and were part of a Baptist church, perhaps I had found home. After years of feeling outside the fold, I now believe the openness and acceptance I found through pub theology brought me back to God—and that Baptist church brought me back to church.

Why share this story of my decades of trying to bring church, God, and queer together? As we enter a conversation about queer theology, perhaps my story will strike a spark in you that will help you explore your own beliefs about sexuality, gender identity, the church, and God—as well as how you formed your beliefs and how you live into them now.

If we belong to a faith community, it is within that community that we learn much of what we believe about ourselves and others. This can become quite confusing when one is grappling with a changing identity, especially if the message from the church as you have known it stands in contradiction with the message of God's love. Sometimes we need to unlearn what we have been taught. We need to see again how our spiritual sources have informed us, learn how to ask hard questions, and discover how we can successfully live into the evolving story of being queer and loving God.

This pub theology session will offer a framework to explore queer theology. We will learn about LGBTQ+ labels and language and why any of that matters. We will open the Bible, the sacred Scripture for Christian churches, to read what it says. And we will pose numerous questions to allow for further pondering of queer theology.

WHY QUEER?

Merriam Webster's first definition of *queer* is "differing in some way from what is usual or normal." Decades ago, my grandmother would say, "I just feel queer today," which simply meant she didn't feel well. *Merriam-Webster* goes on to list five descriptors of queer as "relating to, or being a person whose gender identity . . ." comes under the definition of "sometimes disparaging and offensive." Is it any wonder that the word *queer* holds different meanings for people and gets different responses?

For many years, the word *queer* was used as a slur against same-sex attracted people, particularly men. Considering the definitions describing queer as differing, disparaging, and even offensive, the word carries heavy weight. Perhaps this is why Cody Sanders tells us that "queer is a word with life. You cannot hear it without an emotional—and visceral—response. The word does something to you. It acts upon you."[1] Several years ago, when I was leading a conference on LGBT Elders and Alzheimer's, another presenter claimed that in ten years we would be using only the word *queer*. This one word would become an umbrella term, encompassing all forms of sexual and gender identity. And so it has come to be.

Queer includes it all. As Sanders says,

---

1. Sanders, *Queer Lessons for Churches on the Straight and Narrow*, Kindle ed., preface, par. 1.

Queer calls our attention to the limitation on our linguistic capacity to define others. It challenges the binary terms we use to categorize human beings and experience with words like straight/gay and male/female. Queer should disturb us, shake us up a bit, skew our perception. Just when you think you've "got it," queer calls us to question what we felt sure we knew, to form, de-form, and reform our knowledge of sexual and gender difference.[2]

Perhaps a discussion of our need to define others can be taken into a pub theology conversation.

WHY ALL THE LETTERS?

Let's level the language playing field by sorting through the letters of the LGBTQ+ lexicon. Lesbian, gay, bisexual, trans, and queer are just words—letters arranged to describe something. But words carry weight, history, and influence. Over time and the course of people's lives, politics and culture may cause words to change. We form opinions and judgments of words and the meanings we have been taught. Words matter. Language matters.

So what do the letters in LGBTQ+ represent? Let's start with some descriptions from the Human Rights Campaign.[3]

- Lesbian: a person who identifies as female who experiences a romantic or sexual attraction to persons who identify as female.
- Gay: a person who is sexually or romantically attracted to members of the same gender. Persons who identify as men, women, or nonbinary may use this term to describe themselves.
- Bisexual: a person who is sexually or romantically attracted to more than one sex, gender, or gender identity. Though not interchangeable, the terms "bisexual" and "pansexual" are sometimes conflated.
- Transgender: an umbrella term for a person whose gender identity and/or expression differs from the gender that is noted on their birth certificate.
- Q (queer or questioning): Queer refers to persons who identify under a broad spectrum of sexual/gender identities and/or orientations. Questioning refers to those who question, or are exploring, their sexual orientation or gender identity.

---

2. Ibid., preface, par. 12.
3. "Glossary of Terms," hrc.org/resources/glossary-of-terms.

- +: The + sign is used to extend inclusion to all sexual attractions, asexual, intersex, and/or gender identities. Sometimes, the acronym LGBTQIA+ is used to account for intersex or asexual identities.

Other terms connected to the queer community include
- Ally: describes someone who actively supports LGBTQ+ people.
- Cisgender: a term for a person whose gender identity and/or expression is the same as the gender noted on the birth certificate.
- Homophobic: a term describing the fear and hatred or discomfort with people who are attracted to members of the same sex.

This list does not explore the other letters in the ever-evolving acronym that inevitably ends with the "+." That +, however, in its attempt to include all who identify differently with sex and gender, immediately excludes those same people.

We hear about gender identity and sex. We've all been asked to check a box indicating our sex: male or female. The world no longer identifies with such simplistic binary words. It no longer applies that identity is either/or. So what's the distinction between sex/sexual orientation and gender?

Sexual orientation refers to one's primary attractions and desires for physical, sexual, spiritual, or emotional intimacy. Gender identity is used in reference to one's social, psychological, spiritual, and behavioral experience. Further, it is also an expression of gender as male or female, both, neither, or those for whom gender is experienced in a more fluid state, not captured by the male/female binary. These terms have become part of our lexicon as authentic voices arise to identify the many ways God has created humanity.

PRONOUNS: WHY DO THEY MATTER?

We hear many people introducing themselves by the pronouns they prefer. Why is it important to identify in such a way? What does it say about us to respect others' identification of pronouns? What are commonly used pronouns?

Pronouns refer to either the person talking (I or you) or someone being talked about (she, him, it, them). In current culture, one's pronouns cannot always be visually identified and should not be assumed.[4] We now can express the pronouns we prefer and respect others when she/he/they

---

4. See "Why We Ask Each Other Our Pronouns."

identify her/his/their preferred pronouns. The most commonly used pronouns present a binary construct: she/her/hers, he/him/his while they/them/theirs can refer to more than one person or to an individual who doesn't identify with binary pronouns. Some people prefer to eliminate pronouns completely and use just the name, e.g., Nancy wrote about Nancy's experience of Nancy's childhood.

Connecting pronouns to theology informs how we identify with God. If we believe we are created in the image of God, what is that image? Does God align with a sexual/gender binary? When we anthropomorphize God, do we create a human standard to identify God? Do we create God in our image? In our sense-making humanity, a visual image seems to ground our understanding of God. What is your image of God? If you can see yourself in the reflection of God, how does that create a relationship of love and acceptance?

WHAT DOES THE BIBLE SAY AND WHY DOES THAT MATTER?

How we approach Scripture reflects what we have been taught about our relationship with the Bible. For queer theology, revisiting the Bible with love opens new understandings of God's message. Nadia Bolz Weber tells us that "if meditated on, wrestled with, and questioned properly, the Bible hands over the goods."[5]

As Christians, we are called to grow in love and understanding, using the Bible as our primary text. Author Pamela Lightsey asserts,

> we understand the God of the Bible because of human reason, by our ability to think and do critical reflection. The ability to know God via reason is so important it is listed in the catechism of the Catholic Church. So important was reason as a source for doing theology among Methodists that it is listed among what is often referred to as the Wesleyan quadrilateral: reason, experience, scriptures and tradition.[6]

As we engage with the Bible and queer theology, holding reason and emotion in a grace-filled balance allows us an authentic experience with the Scriptures. Lightsey goes on to say,

---

5. Weber, *Shameless*, 5.
6. Lightsey, *Our Lives Matter*, 46.

Our interpretation is never perfect, but a work in progress. We need to ask probing questions of the text and context. There is simply no one simple and exact reading of the text and its events. Most Christian arguments that attempt to respond to the elements of queer lives use some combination of scripture, reason, experience, and tradition."[7]

Jesus rejected attempts to exclude others with the verses quoted to him from the scribes. With fresh spirit and an overarching intent to love, Jesus taught them new concepts. His message then and now teaches "love God, love your neighbor" (Matt 22:36-40 and Mark 12:30-31). Jesus sought to bring people into the circle—not to exclude them. Episcopal Bishop Michael Curry says, "when love is the way, we actually treat each other, well . . . like we are actually family."[8] Love holds the key for interpretation of Scripture.

Of more than 30,000 verses in the Bible, primarily seven are used to cast judgment on the queer community and are infamously referred to as the clobber passages. Verses such as these do not convey God's divine design for the creation of humanity or Jesus' instruction to love your neighbor. It may be noted here that Jesus does not directly address any queer topic.

Mel White, author and founder of Soul Force, an organization that seeks to end political and religious oppression of LGBTQIA people, tells us these particular verses are "misused to convince 'queers' that our longings are sinful, to keep us in our closets, and to condemn us to hell if we ever dared to accept our sexual orientation or gender identity as another of God's mysterious gifts."[9]

The "founding clobber fathers," as Mel White names them, forgot much about how these verses, or the entire canon, came to be. "They forgot that originally the clobber passages describe rape or attempted rape (Gn 9:20-27, 19:1-11), female prostitution (Lv 18:22, 20:13), male prostitution and pedophilia (1 Cor 6:9-10, 1 Tm 1:10), and the sexual practices of the Isis cult in Rome (Rom 1:26-27)."[10]

Open a Bible, any version, any translation, and read the verses just noted. Read the verses before and after them. Explore the context of these stories. Be an informed child of God as you feel the weight of how these

---

7. Ibid., 49.

8. Quoted in Peters, "Bishop Michael Curry's Royal Wedding Sermon."

9. White, "What happened in the room where it happened," in *Clobber the Passages*, par. 18.

10. White, "My Story," in *Clobber the Passages*, par. 5.

stories have been used throughout society to condemn queer folks. Mel White presents how these verses have influenced legal decisions, mental health determinations, and, all too often, a church's rejection of beloved queers in his book *Clobber the Passages*. As you read these verses, consider what you were taught and what you believe now.

CONCLUSION

We have explored queer theology from Scriptures that have been misused and taken out of context to clobber queer folk. If we hold the sacred Scripture in grace to teach us and show us how God designed us to be, and if we take into account the many verses that teach us how to love God, one another, and ourselves, our responsibility to accept and include all God's creation becomes clear. The sacred space of pub theology can inspire a conversation about queer theology that helps us explore our own beliefs about sexuality, gender identity, the church, and God—as well as how we formed our beliefs and how we live into them now.

When we consider how much of what we believe about ourselves and others comes from experiences with faith communities—e.g., churches, synagogues, and mosques—the questions begin to arise about how God loves us and how we love each other. This can become confusing if the message from the church stands in contradiction with the message about God's love. Sometimes we need to unlearn what we have been taught. We need to see again how our spiritual sources have informed us, learn how to ask hard questions, and discover how we can successfully live into the evolving story of being queer and loving God.

PUB THEOLOGY

INTRODUCTION

This chapter has given us a framework to explore queer theology in pub theology. We have learned about LGBTQ+ labels and language and why they matter. We have opened the Bible, the sacred Scripture for Christian churches, to read what it says.

Writer and activist Sonya Renee Taylor introduces us to an "Unapologetic Agreement" that invites us to ask questions when we encounter something that seems contrary to our learned beliefs. Let's use this agreement as we ask questions about queer theology: "Part of sorting through ideas and beliefs is to ask questions about those ideas. That includes asking ourselves hard questions: 'Why do I believe this? What am I afraid of? What am I gaining or losing by trying on a new perspective?'"[11] These are good questions that get us to good answers in our conversations about queer theology.

ICEBREAKER

After reading the material in Meeting 12 about queer theology, what is your most pressing question?

JUMPING-OFF POINTS

- Pamela R. Lightsey writes, "Queer theology offers an opportunity to include rather than exclude more voices within our various communities."[12] How do you make your language, behaviors, and beliefs inclusive rather than exclusive?
- When were you first aware of queer theology? What is your history with gender identity? What is your identity as a sexual being?
- According to Pamela Lightsey, "We cannot rely solely on what has been written in the Biblical text. We understand that not everything about God has been recorded by humanity and that therefore God stands within and outside the text."[13] What do you believe about the Bible? Do you believe only what others have taught you or what you have discerned through many sources?
- Nadia Bolz Weber writes, "God created humanity in mind-blowing diversity, so how could any theology assume that God is pleased only with a certain type of human. This view of God has led so many of us to deny our natures, identities, and desire to not anger an easily disappointed God. The result is suffering and it is not of God's making."[14] What do you believe about how God created humanity? What did God create in you as a reflection of God's nature? What beliefs do you hold about queer people that reflect God?

---

11. Taylor, *The Body Is Not an Apology*, 90.
12. Lightsey, *Our Lives Matter*, 27.
13. Ibid., 45.
14. Weber, *Shameless*, 57.

- We all live at multiple intersections of identity.[15] What are your intersections of identity? How do your multiple identities affect each other? Some intersections of identity could be race, nationality, gender, sex, economics, or spirituality. Name yourself according to these identifiers, and feel how that settles in your body. Allow yourself to embrace how others would receive you in these intersections of your identity. For example, I would identify as racialized White, American, lesbian, cis-female, middle-class, non-attached spiritual seeker.

BIBLIOGRAPHY

Human Rights Campaign. hrc.org.

Lightsey, Pamela R. *Our Lives Matter: A Womanist Queer Theology.* Eugene, OR: Pickwick Publications, 2015.

Sanders, Cody J. *Queer Lessons for Churches on the Straight and Narrow.* Macon, GA: Faithlab, 2013.

Taylor, Sonya Renee. *The Body Is Not an Apology: The Power of Radical Self-love.* Oakland: Berrett-Koehler, Inc., 2018.

Vines, Matthew. *God and the Gay Christian.* New York: Convergent Books, 2014.

Weber, Nadia Bolz. *Shameless: A Sexual Reformation.* New York: Convergent Books, 2019.

White, Mel. *Clobber the Passages: Seven Deadly Verses.* Palm Desert: Wideness Press, 2020.

ADDITIONAL RESOURCES

On reading the Bible holistically

Bell, Rob. *Velvet Elvis: Repainting the Christian Faith.* Grand Rapids: Zondervan, 2015.

———. *What Is the Bible?* New York: HarperOne, 2017.

Enns, Peter. *The Bible Tells Me So.* New York: HarperCollins, 2014

———. *The Sin of Certainty.* New York: HarperOne, 2016.

---

15. See Taylor, *The Body Is Not an Apology*, 87.

Evans, Rachel Held. *Inspired.* Nashville: Nelson, 2018.

Kegler, Emmy. *One Coin Found: How God's Love Stretches to the Margins.* Minneapolis: Fortress, 2019.

On LGBTQ+ acceptance in the church

Baldock, Kathy. *Walking the Bridgeless Canyon.* Reno: Canyonwalker Press, 2014.

Brownson, James V. *Bible, Gender, Sexuality.* Grand Rapids: Eerdmans, 2013.

Gushee, David. *Changing Our Mind.* Canton, MI: Read the Spirit Books, 2014.

On queer theology

Althaus-Reid, Marcella. *Indecent Theology.* Abingdon: Routledge, 2002.

———. *The Queer God.* London: Routledge, 2004.

Cheng, Patrick. *Radical Love: An Introduction to Queer Theology.* New York: Seabury Books, 2011

———. *Rainbow Theology: Bridging Race, Sexuality, and Spirit.* New York: Seabury Books, 2013.

Edman, Elizabeth. *Queer Virtue.* Boston: Beacon Press, 2016.

Hartke, Austen. *Transforming: The Bible and the Lives of Transgender Christians.* Louisville: Westminster John Knox Press, 2018.

Kim-Kort, Mihee. *Outside the Lines: How Embracing Queerness Will Transform your Faith.* Minneapolis: Fortress, 2018.

… MEETING 13

WHITENESS

W. BENJAMIN BOSWELL

I no longer use the term "White privilege." Leaders and activists in the Black community have impressed upon me that White people should not describe the experience of being the beneficiaries of four hundred years of systemic oppression toward Black people as a "privilege." It would be more fitting to use the term "White advantage" or "White power," but I no longer use those terms either. In addition, I no longer use the terms "White supremacy," "White fragility," "White rage," "White resentment," or "White backlash," because they are repetitive and redundant. All of the ideas that we often combine with the term "White" to make compound phrases are already contained within the word "Whiteness."

What is Whiteness? Contrary to popular belief, Whiteness is not a skin color or pigmentation. Whiteness has no basis in biology or science. Whiteness is not an ethnicity and was not given to us by God like the color of our eyes or hair. Whiteness is something we made up. It is a social construct; worse, it is a lie—a mythology. There are no White people, as James Baldwin once said; there are only people who think they are White.[1] Whiteness is a human invention, and we continue to perpetuate this ideology today. However, simply because it is a lie and a social construct does not mean that Whiteness has no real-life power or consequences—quite the opposite.

WHITENESS IS THE DOMINANT CULTURE

Black people talk about what it means to be Black all the time, but White people almost never talk about what it means to be White. Why? We don't talk about being White because we don't have to—because Whiteness is the dominant culture of our society. It is the water in which we swim. Many White people have come to believe that we are living in a "post-racial

---

1. Baldwin, "On Being White . . . and Other Lies," 164–67.

society" and claim that they are "colorblind" or "not racist." However, colorblind ideology simply reinforces the violent and oppressive power of Whiteness by making White people feel good about advancements that Black people have made while hiding and ignoring the ongoing harmful legacy of systemic racism. Power is more powerful when it's hidden, unmarked, unspoken, ignored, denied, avoided, or lurking in the shadows.

When White people talk about racism, our conversations are often shallow discussions that barely plunge below the surface. The reason for this shallowness is that we have been conditioned to believe race is something other people have that we do not—something that is a problem for "people of color." White politicians and religious leaders used to refer to the problem of systemic racism and Whiteness as the "Negro problem" or "Black problem." These deflections afforded White people the ability to discuss the subject of race as if we are detached from it, when what we are detached from is reality—the reality of racial oppression.

Detachment from reality stems from the fact that White people are a part of the dominant culture and imagine we are "normal" and do not have a race. Therefore, we often live in a constant state of denial about our own history, our own racial identity, and the ongoing legacy of Whiteness and systemic racism in American society. A paralyzing pathology of denial leads White people to frequently discuss race as if it as an abstract external issue that others are struggling through—something other people possess that we do not have. As a result, we tend to participate in conversations about race without ever discussing or addressing our own racial identity, let alone the harm that Whiteness has caused so many.

WHERE DID WHITENESS COME FROM?

Not only do White people only have a racial identity, we invented the concept of race intentionally to exert power over other people. Rarely do we ask, "Why was race created?" "What was Whiteness created for?" Whiteness is a lie that European settler-colonists created to enforce the idea that they were superior because of the color of their skin, and they created this lie in order to steal things and harm people. We need to be honest about that reality and tell that story. Many White people mistakenly believe that racism is the result of hatred, but hatred is the result of racism. European settler-colonists invented the concept of Whiteness (or the racial hierarchy) to steal land, labor, people, and political and economic power.

At its most basic, Whiteness is an anti-Black ideology of domination and oppression. Therefore, it is no wonder White people do not want to look at Whiteness. To do so is to disrupt and disturb our sense of self in ways that cause an existential identity crisis. This experience of existential crisis is often unbearable for us, so we, wittingly or unwittingly, blind ourselves to it, ignore it, hide it, avoid it, and crawl back under the warm blanket of denial. Denial is the primary emotional state of White people in America. It is an advantage to be able to live in denial. It only possible for us to avoid reality because we are the dominant culture that has benefited from the long legacy of the terrorism and oppression of Black people.

In White-dominant settings like churches, schools, businesses, and organizations, we often find White people in a paralyzing pathology of denial, living and working in close proximity with Black people who are experiencing constant trauma. Denial and trauma do not communicate well. Denial does not know what to do with trauma. Trauma is a threat to denial. People in denial are in danger of further traumatizing people who are in trauma. Therefore, those who are in denial (White folks) must take the first step. You don't ask a person who has been abused by their spouse to sit down and have a nice chat with their abuser. We enter into therapy for trauma and we enter into anger management for violence. As White people, we must relearn our history so that we know and understand that we have almost always been the abusers—and benefited directly from the abuse of others.

Whiteness can be defined as anti-Blackness, but this ontology of anti-Blackness not only harms people of color but also harms White people in many ways. Whiteness was created to oppress Black people most directly, but it was also created to subjugate poor White people. White, rich, landowning men in Virginia (and elsewhere) needed a way to protect their wealth and property. There was real and present danger that poor White people might align themselves with the enslaved and form a revolution to overthrow the rich White landowners, redistribute their wealth, and create a more just society for all.

In those days, there were no governments, police forces, barbed-wire fences, security systems, or automatic weapons wealthy landowners could use to protect themselves and their property. But they had an even greater weapon: the weapon of ideology. Whiteness was the perfect wedge issue—the ultimate wedge issue of all wedge issues—that rich White landowners used to divide poor Whites and poor Blacks from one another. By convincing poor White people that even though they were poor, they were more like the landowners and therefore better than Black people because of their White skin, rich White men could prevent revolution and protect their property by oppressing the Black population and controlling the White population at the same time. As President Lyndon B. Johnson once said, "If you can convince the lowest white man he's better than the best colored man, he won't notice you're picking his pocket. Hell, give him somebody to look down on, and he'll empty his pockets for you."[2]

HOW DOES WHITENESS WORK?

Whiteness operates by setting up a racial hierarchy of power and value with White, rich, landowning males at the top, then White women, and then every other color, ethnicity, gender, and economic status all the way down the ladder to the bottom, where we find Black, Brown, and Indigenous transgender women. However, neither Black and Brown people nor their families and communities are the ones with the problem. We are. White people created this mess, and White faith communities should be at the forefront of supporting and participating in efforts to address systemic racism and injustice—not just for the sake of our Black and Brown neighbors but also for the sake of our own humanity.

Toni Morrison once said, "White people have a very, very serious problem, and they should start thinking about what they can do about it. Take me out of it."[3] Every time White people enter into the conversation about racism and social injustice without dealing with our own White racial identity or attending to Whiteness, we end up being harmful because we cannot help but operate from a paternalistic and patronizing worldview. We think we are doing a favor for people of color when we talk about race, but we are the ones with the problem!

Southern author Lillian Smith claims that European settler-colonists and immigrants made a "Grand Bargain"[4] when they settled in this country or arrived in America. Today, one might more aptly describe this bargain as a "Faustian deal with the Devil." Our European ancestors, who came from England, Ireland, Italy, Scotland, Sweden, France, Norway, Germany, etc., made a great and horrible trade. They realized the path as outsiders in America would be very difficult, but they were offered an opportunity to

---

2. L. B. Johnson, quoted by Bill Moyers, "What a Real President Was Like."
3. Morrison, interview.
4. Smith, *Killers of the Dream*, 154–68.

trade their ethnic identities in order to become American. What they often did not realize, however, was that by trading for the ethnicity of Whiteness, they were surrendering their humanity to participate in a system of domination and oppression. We dehumanize ourselves when we participate in the dehumanization of others.

In a letter to the great freedom fighter Angela Davis, James Baldwin wrote, "White people will never, so long as their whiteness puts so sinister a distance between themselves and their own experience and the experience of others, feel themselves sufficiently human, sufficiently worthwhile, to become responsible for themselves, their leaders, their country, their children, or their fate."[5] White people have lost our humanity by participating in the dehumanization of our Black and Brown neighbors, and therefore White religious communities must become places of rehumanization where White people can take responsibility for Whiteness and recover our humanity. Our work is to take responsibility for our history, rediscover our humanity, and learn to live justly in solidarity with all other human beings.

James Baldwin famously said, "White people are trapped in a history they don't understand and until they understand it, they cannot be released from it."[6] Europeans, who imagined themselves to be Christians, are the people who invented Whiteness, which is why the Whiteness we see in America is often indistinguishable from what it means to be American or Christian. America, Christianity, and Whiteness are entangled together because Christianity is the mother of Whiteness and America is its adopted father.

REJECTING WHITE CHRISTIANITY

Whiteness was born through the monstrous marriage and unholy union of church and empire. It has older siblings (imperialism and colonialism) and children of its own (Jim Crow and mass incarceration), but Whiteness remains the well-nurtured love child of Christianity and America's 400-year-long adulterous affair. Therefore, it is the responsibility of White people to disentangle the evil of Whiteness from Christianity and America. However, this will not be an easy task, and many of our most precious

---

5. Baldwin, "An Open Letter to My Sister, Miss Angela Davis."
6. Baldwin, *The Fire Next Time*, 8.

theological beliefs, as well as our social and political ideas, will need to be discarded and/or reimagined along the way.

Whiteness is not natural or neutral. I've searched thoroughly for something positive in Whiteness that could be redeemed, but there is nothing positive in Whiteness. It is simply evil—pure evil. It cannot be redeemed. It can only be resisted. In *Enchiridion*, Augustine said that "evil is the privation of the good," which means it has no goodness in it. Whiteness showed its violent face in Nazi Germany, which we have no problem describing as evil. However, we forget that Hitler borrowed many of his ideas from White supremacists in America. There is no hope in Whiteness, but there is hope for White people. Whiteness cannot be redeemed, but White people can. In order to do that, we must jettison Whiteness and become human again. We must be rehumanized.

James Baldwin wrote,

> When the dream was slaughtered and all that love and labor seemed to have come to nothing, we scattered . . . . We knew where we had been, what we had tried to do, who had cracked, gone mad, died, or been murdered around us. Not everything is lost. Responsibility cannot be lost; it can only be abdicated. If one refuses abdication, one begins again.[7]

There is hope for White people because White people always have the opportunity to stop abdicating responsibility, to stop living in denial, and to begin to take responsibility for Whiteness and for building a beloved community of justice and equality.

This will require White people listening to Black and Brown voices, histories, and experiences, beginning to understand Whiteness and confront our Whiteness, and then imagining how we can help to dismantle Whiteness in our spheres of power and influence. James Weldon Johnson wrote, "The Black people of this country know and understand white people better than they know and understand themselves."[8] I found that to be absolutely true and deeply embarrassing. Black people were forced to learn to understand White people for the sake of their own survival in a White supremacist society.

What I learned from reading Black authors and intellectuals and studying the work of Black creatives is that when we examine Whiteness through their eyes, a mirror of truth is put up before us that allows us to see

---

7. Baldwin, *Just Above My Head*, 429.
8. Johnson, *Autobiography of An Ex-Colored Man*, 25.

ourselves more clearly than we ever have before. The conjoining of racism and White supremacy is not a problem for the Black community. Instead, it is our problem—a White problem. It is a problem our ancestors created—a problem we benefit from. It is a problem that is our responsibility to work to eliminate for the sake of love and justice and for the sake of our own freedom and salvation from the ideology of Whiteness.

As a pastor, I have discovered that predominantly White faith communities, like the church, have never reckoned with terror and the ongoing legacy of the 400-year history of anti-Black violence and oppression. Instead of seeking to understand or reckon with this history, White faith communities, like most White Americans, continue to live in a constant denial about history and their own participation in Whiteness. We have a tremendous amount of work to do. White faith communities can begin by seeking to understand the history of how the ideology of White supremacy was created and sustained by White religious people and by working together to discover how to take responsibility for our Whiteness.

BECOMING "RACE TRAITORS"

White faith communities must come to understand that addressing racial and social injustice is not an optional activity, or even one among many good programs. It is our first and foremost work. This is the most pressing work we are called to do. I recommend that White religious communities in America immediately cease all other ministries, programs, or activities so we can devote our time, energy, and attention to this work of understanding and reckoning with our Whiteness. Then, and only then, will we be able to know what we can do to address racial and social injustice and be good neighbors in the work of building the beloved community.

Noel Ignatiev said, "Treason to whiteness is loyalty to humanity."[9] We do not need more White people who believe they are called to be "allies" to the Black freedom movement. We need a generation of White people who are co-conspirators in the movement who identify Whiteness and learn to become "race traitors" who act treasonously against the evil of Whiteness in all its forms. We need White faith communities who will engage in the work of rehumanizing White people by enlisting them in the cause of treason against Whiteness and inviting them to divest from and dismantle the very thing that they have benefited from most—killing Black and

---

9. Ignatiev and Garvey, eds., *Race Traitor*, 10.

Brown people. We need a generation of people who are racialized as White but have committed themselves to abolishing Whiteness.

It all starts with making a conscious decision to stop living in denial and to start looking at Whiteness, and our participation in it, so that we can shift the burden of responsibility for systemic racial oppression off of Black and Brown people and back to us. We are the people with the problem, and, as Baldwin said, "White people . . . have quite enough to do in learning how to accept and love themselves and each other, and when they have achieved this—which will not be tomorrow and may very well be never—the Negro problem will no longer exist, for it will no longer be needed."[10] May it be so.

PUB THEOLOGY

INTRODUCTION

Talking about race always brings out our emotions because White people have been trapped in a lie for so long that we've lost touch with reality. Give yourself and your conversation partners a lot of grace. You can acknowledge that race is a social construct, and that Whiteness is a lie Europeans created to steal land, resources, people, and power while at the same time giving people the space to think through their own racial identity formation. The most profound revelations and transformations come through the power of stories. Facilitators of pub theology groups should do their own anti-racist work and come prepared to share stories from their own racial autobiographies to get the conversation started and be patient with the group as the open up and share these intimate parts of themselves.

ICEBREAKER

When did you first come to realize and understand your racial identity?

JUMPING-OFF POINTS

- What do you think James Baldwin meant when he described White people as "those who think they are white"?
- Baldwin also says "whiteness is a moral choice." Is Whiteness a choice?
- What is the responsibility of people who are racialized as White?

---

10. Baldwin, *The Fire Next Time*, 22.

- How can we work to disentangle Whiteness from Christianity and America?
- What does it mean to be a "race traitor" or to participate in treason to Whiteness out of loyalty to humanity?
- What are some ways we can disavow or defect from Whiteness?
- How can you work to dismantle systemic racism and Whiteness in your sphere of power and influence (i.e., family, neighborhood, church, school, business, city)?

OUTSIDE READING

The Fire Next Time by James Baldwin

OUTSIDE EXERCISE

Write a personal racial autobiography, attending to all the ways you have been formed racially, encountered race, or engaged with race and racism throughout your life.

BIBLIOGRAPHY

Baldwin, James. *The Fire Next Time.* New York: Vintage Books, 1993.

———. *Just Above My Head.* New York: Dial Press, 1979.

———. "On Being White . . . and Other Lies." *The Cross of Redemption: Uncollected Writings*, edited by Randall Kenan, 135–38. New York: Pantheon, 2010.

———. "An Open Letter to My Sister, Miss Angela Davis." *The New York Review.* January 7, 1971. nybooks.com/articles/1971/01/07/an-open-letter-to-my-sister-miss-angela-davis/.

Birdsong, Mia. *How We Show Up: Reclaiming Family, Friendship, and Community.* New York: Hachette, 2020.

Glaude, Eddie, Jr. *Begin Again: James Baldwin's America and Its Urgent Lessons for Our Own.* New York: Crown, 2020.

Ignatiev, Noel, and John Garvey, eds. *Race Traitor.* New York: Routledge, 1996.

Johnson, James Weldon. *The Autobiography of An Ex-Colored Man.* New York: Penguin Classics, 1990.

Johnson, Lyndon. Quoted in Bill Moyers, "What a Real President Was Like." *Washington Post*. November 13, 1988.

Morrison, Toni. Interview. *The Power of Questions*. PBS. May 7, 1993. charlierose.com/videos/18778.

Roediger, David, ed. *Black on White: Black Writers on What It Means to Be White*. New York: Schocken, 1998.

Smith, Lillian. *Killers of the Dream*. New York: Anchor Books, 1949.

STOLEN COOKIES: A TAKE ON BLACK LIVES MATTERING

MIA M. MCCLAIN

In my writings, it is important to name my audience. For this pub theology session, I am talking to people of White-dominant Christian spaces who purport to be progressive and would, in earnest, profess to want to know about Black lives mattering: how to talk about it and how to do the intellectual exercises around understanding it. I find it important to name the audience, and who isn't the audience, in these times. In general, I do not need to talk to Black people about Black lives mattering. I may need to remind certain Black folk that the mattering of Black lives should include *all* Black lives; i.e., those who identify as Black and queer, trans, lesbian, gay, bisexual, pansexual, and a host of other identities that transcend the aforementioned.

In the context of pub theology—a group at Myers Park Baptist Church that has been, to my knowledge, predominately White and the group that has conjured the spirit of this publication—I am using the premise of speaking to well-meaning White folk as my portal. I will use scriptural references and storytelling to illuminate the struggle of Black people in this country. I will also call upon the work of poets, theologians, biblical scholars, and mystics to make my claim that the mattering of Black lives is an undeniable Christian issue that need not be pushed underground any longer. Movements are flawed, including the civil rights and Black Lives Matter movements. Movements can't root you. You have to be grounded in a different kind of understanding. Through this exploration, I hope I'm able to give you a (not the) foundation for understanding.

WHO STOLE MY COOKIES?

In a classic hit song that has swept this nation for decades, an important and urgent question is posed. It is a song that can be sung into infinitude, never finding an answer or resolution to the question at hand. This question requires a sophisticated mind to unravel one of life's most philosophical quandaries. It is a question that calls us to confrontation as we interrogate every single person around us, friend and foe alike. "Who stole the cookie from the cookie jar?"

You, too, may have been asking this question for decades, never finding an answer. Perhaps you participated in this singalong activity as a kid. The song typically begins with a lead investigator asking a group of deviant suspects about some illegal activity involving a missing cookie.

"Who stole the cookie from cookie jar?" the accuser asks, followed by the name of one of the suspects. One by one, each suspect confirms the question and then denies the "accusation":

"Who me?" the suspect asks, inviting confusion.

"Yes, you!" the group and the accuser respond.

"Couldn't be!" the suspect pronounces.

"Then who?"

The call-and-response singalong can be infinitely repetitive, with the tendency to go on and on because no one wants to admit that they are the one who stole the cookie from the cookie jar. It's a silly little exercise on the surface that is often more about musicality and rhythm than honesty. By the end of the ditty, we're still left wondering who stole the cookie from the jar. There is no acknowledgment of the sin. There is no reparation for the transgression. There is simply the myth of a mystery, looming over the heads of everyone in the circle, feeding and encouraging skepticism and provoking disgust among them.

Perhaps you have not played this game, but you've had your lunch stolen from the fridge at work, or someone in your home ate your favorite piece of cake that you had been saving for dessert. When things like this happen, you may go around asking your office mates, "Did someone eat that slice of pizza that was sitting on the top shelf in the fridge?" or you may ask one of your house mates, "Which one of you ate that slice of almond cake I brought home from the wedding?" Often, the frustration is not with the missing food alone but with the betrayal—with the lack of care. You're upset because somebody is lying. You're upset because somebody is not owning up to their transgression.

The cookie jar is an elementary version of the age-old "blame game"—the game we are trained to play to make sense of our misfortunes. When we're late for work, or we slip and fall in a building, or the car runs out of gas on the highway, our first thought is to immediately figure out who is at fault other than us. Have you ever tripped over a tree root while walking on a sidewalk and looked back at the root with spite like it's the tree's fault you tripped? The tree doesn't 'fess up, just like the cookie stealer is never revealed. There is no resolution, just anger and frustration.

Many of us live our lives on the margins. Many live lives as the ones missing the cookie, never getting an answer to who stole our stuff. If we ever figure it out, there is never an acknowledgment of the transgression on behalf of the transgressor. There is never an apology, never an admittance of the deed that devoured our public worth and disenfranchised our communities.

Anybody who's ever been evicted because the rents are rising in their gentrifying neighborhood knows what it's like to ask, "Who stole my cookie?" and never get an answer or apology. If you've ever had your leftovers eaten by a family member who didn't ask permission, you know what it's like to ask, "Who stole my cookie?" If you've ever had money go missing from your wallet or unknown charges show up on your credit card, you've probably asked, "Who stole my cookie?" and never gotten an answer or apology.

Esau, son of Isaac, has his cookie stolen from his jar in Genesis 25. Born first to his mother Rebekah, he came out of the womb red; in Hebrew the word used is *admoni*, a play on the word "Edom." (This is relevant because his descendants would go on to become the Edomites, enemies of the Israelites.) Jacob, Esau's younger twin brother, came out of the birth canal grabbing Esau's heel. It's a bizarre scene, and it's really not written to be about Esau's misfortune. In the end, this is a setup for Jacob's story and for the story of his people, the Israelites—the people who are at the center of what Christians call their sacred text.

Jacob's story pops up in writings around the seventh century BCE when the Judeans are in exile, but we know the narrative was part of the oral tradition long before it was written down. It is interesting that much of Jacob's story shares similarities with other texts, Scripture, and folklore—such as the battle between brothers. As in the Cain and Abel story, there is tension between the brother who is a hunter (Esau) and the brother who is a shepherd (Jacob). As firstborn, Esau is promised to inherit leadership of the family and a double share of inheritance. This is his birthright. One day,

Jacob corners Esau in a moment of hunger and vulnerability and coaxes him into selling his birthright—his inheritance. Esau, presented as dull and impetuous, is outsmarted by his brother on an empty stomach.

It has been noted that children in school don't learn well on empty stomachs. The ability to retain pertinent information is nearly impossible if one is experiencing dire hunger or thirst. A lot of impetuous decisions happen when one doesn't have access to necessities. Jacob knows something about this, and in an effort to get ahead in life, he manipulates his older brother.

Like Esau, poor, marginalized, Black, Brown, and Indigenous folks in this country have been painted as lazy and dull, unable to keep up economically and socially, and easily duped and manipulated. The blossoming of neoliberalism in the 1980s signaled manipulators into convincing marginalized folks to believe their misfortune has been because of their own doing, their own shallow mindedness, their own inability to pull themselves up by the bootstraps. "But we ain't even got no boots," I heard somebody say. Generations after the first "Jacob" looted the cookie jars of Indigenous folks in this country through theft of land, and generations after the first "Jacob" looted Africans and their descendants through exploitation of labor, Black, Latine, and Indigenous folks find ourselves crying out, "Who stole our cookies, and how do we get them back?" "Who ran off with my birthright, and how do I get it back?"

GENERATIONAL DECEIT AND GENERATIONAL TRAUMA

The myth of White superiority, stemming from the roots of Anglo-Saxon exceptionalism, is carved out by a first-century Roman historian named Tacitus. We journey back to the year 98 CE when, in his publication *Germainia*, Tacitus makes the case that a certain subpopulation of Germany is more ethnically pure and thus morally and physiologically superior, laying the foolish foundations of ethnic supremacy that would spread like a virus across the globe. This myth is further explored in the 2015 publication *Stand Your Ground: Black Bodies and the Justice of God*, in which Dr. Kelly Brown Douglas explicates Tacitus's ferocious and foolish declaration of superiority, linking it to the events of the Holocaust many centuries later and carrying this idea of Anglo-exceptionalism across the Atlantic.

Now, many may be bored with this history lesson—an unfortunate reality of how much our educational system has failed us as we sit around foolishly baffled at how history we hardly know keeps repeating itself. I write not to bring peace but a sword—a weapon of knowledge that will prick us out of the ignorance that keeps us bound and circling the block on the issue of Black and Brown lives mattering in this country and globally.

Douglas reminds us that the early interlopers in this land "carried their Anglo-Saxon heritage across the Atlantic Ocean with a self-righteous pride. Believing they were the true and chosen heirs to a divine Anglo-Saxon mission, they were determined not to betray their Anglo-Saxon roots, as they thought the English had done."[1] Thus, Anglo-Saxon exceptionalism became Anglo-Saxon chauvinism became the Manifest Destiny became the Trail of Tears became indentured servitude and chattel slavery became Jim Crow laws, redlining, voter suppression, militarized police forces, a corrupt prison system, a lack of gun control, a recreating and repackaging of unjust systems. And now we find ourselves here today, once again, performing shock, ritualizing our tears, lighting our candles, patting ourselves on the back for surface-level solidarity, wondering why we keep having to call out injustice, wondering why we keep having to sit through sermons and lectures and conversations about Black lives mattering, wondering why Black and Brown and Indigenous folks keep yelling, "Who stole our cookies, and how do we get them back?" "Who ran off with my birthright, and how do I get it back?"

I imagine Esau asking the same thing when he finds his brother Jacob has not only deceived him but has deceived their father, Isaac, as well. Stealing the birthright wasn't enough to secure power. Jacob needed Isaac's blessing. The birthright meant nothing without the blessing. Deathbed blessings and curses were important in the lives of ancient peoples. The father's blessing was believed to release a power that could not be recanted—a tangible power that defined the destiny of the recipient. Not only does Jacob take advantage of Esau; Jacob takes advantage of his visually impaired and aging father by pretending to be Esau so that his father will give him the blessing meant for his brother.

This is the breach. This is the betrayal. It lingers, spilling into the future, from Genesis 25 to Obadiah 1. It lingers, spilling into the subsequent generations, creating ongoing tension and strife between Jacob's people and Esau's people, between the Israelites and Edomites. It lingers, acting as a haunting allegory for the ongoing generational deceit and trauma experienced between Black and White people in this country.

---

1. Douglas, *Stand Your Ground: Black Bodies and the Justice of God*, Kindle ed., ch. 1.

THE CYCLICAL UN-MATTERING OF BLACK LIVES IN AMERICA

Have you ever been betrayed? Maybe your sibling didn't steal your portion of the wealth your parents left behind or manipulate you in a moment of vulnerability. But have you ever experienced a breach in trust? Have you ever been the victim of deception? in a friendship? in a marriage? at your workplace? Have you ever been stolen from—pillaged and looted—and left to fend for yourself? Have your children suffered as a result? Have your grandchildren been bursting with anger because of it?

To understand the Black-led movements for rights and mattering, one must understand the existence of the anger bursting from the guts of the oppressed and ransacked peoples of this world. It is an intergenerational anger—one that is passed through the bloodline. It transcends the present moment. The oppressed are not merely angry for themselves; they are angry for their ancestors and for their children. The present intersects with the past and the future as we are brought to urgent moments of reckoning.

The nineteenth-century African American poet James Monroe Whitefield writes in his poem "America":

> America, it is to thee,
> Thou boasted land of liberty, —
> It is to thee I raise my song,
> Thou land of blood, and crime, and wrong.
> It is to thee, my native land,
> From whence has issued many a band
> To tear the black man from his soil,
> And force him here to delve and toil;
> Chained on your blood-bemoistened sod,
> Cringing beneath a tyrant's rod,
> Stripped of those rights which Nature's God
>   Bequeathed to all the human race,
> Bound to a petty tyrant's nod,
>   Because he wears a paler face.[2]

How is it that this same rage—albeit poetically woven into something palatable to many an ear—is still present today? How is it that this rage and deception and failure to repair what has been broken is still present

---

2. Whitfield, "America," 36–40.

today? We might ask the same thing of the deadly friction between Esau's and Jacob's people.

FROM GENESIS TO OBADIAH

As the rest of the Genesis story unravels, Jacob's twelve sons will follow in his footsteps, deceiving their brother, Joseph, and selling him into slavery. The cycle of deception continues in various forms throughout the sacred text. Deception lingers, and before you know it, centuries have passed and the Judeans and the Edomites remain at war with each other when we meet the prophet Obadiah in his wrestling.

The date of Obadiah's composition is often presumed to be sometime after the Babylonian Empire attacked Jerusalem. Hebrew Bible scholar Lauress Wilkins Lawrence reminds us that

> Obadiah's community had been traumatized by those events . . . . In response to that trauma Obadiah wrote a prophecy against a foreign (non-Israelite) nation, a kind of writing several biblical prophets used as a way to reassure the people of Judah that God would save them by destroying their enemies. Prophecies against foreign nations were preached to Israelite audiences more to comfort them than to condemn their neighbors.[3]

In twenty-one verses—the shortest book in the Hebrew Bible—the prophet Obadiah captures this ongoing battle between Jacob's people and Esau's people—between the Judeans/Israelites and the Edomites. Here we find generations battling one another, generations of Edomites trying to get revenge or, perhaps, justice, and generations of Israelites and Judeans trying to defend a blessing that was not originally for their ancestor. Is it the Judeans' fault that what they've built was built on a lie? Is it Jacob's descendants' fault that the blessing they cling to was passed down through fraudulent methods? Likewise, is it the European descendant in America's fault that the privileges granted were achieved and made legacy through dishonesty, fraud, theft of land and bodies, and refusal to acknowledge the transgression?

Black folks are saying, "*You* stole the cookie from the cookie jar!"

Many White people in this country who are fragile about their identity may respond, "Who me?"

---

3. Lawrence, "Where Have All the Women Gone?," 143–49.

"Yes, you!"
"Couldn't be!"
"Then who?"

The reality is that the Judeans might not have stolen the cookie, but the lack of acknowledgment by Obadiah and others that the cookie was stolen is a gross denial of the deception that occurred at the hands of Jacob in Genesis 25. So the war between the two nations lingers. The Edomites are painted as vengeful, ruthless enemies who have no reason to be as enraged as they are. Similarly, Black and Brown folks in this country are often painted as vengeful and ruthless as they protest for basic rights and respect of land and body, wondering if the breach will ever be repaired, wondering if the empty cookie jar will ever return to fullness in our lifetimes, or if we'll keep accepting the cookie crumbs from a government that refuses to acknowledge that we matter.

The un-mattering of Black lives lurks as we walk on soil soaked with unacknowledged transgressions. As the dampness of the earth coats the sullen soles of our feet, the soil turns to quicksand, and we find ourselves fighting to keep our heads above waters that were designed to swallow us. We are reminded that our existence is the product of a curse lasting generations every time we drive past monuments of duplicity.

Centuries of suffering could have been avoided had Jacob apologized! Generational curses would have been prevented had Jacob apologized! Intergenerational trauma might have ceased to exist had reparations been offered for what was stolen!

This is what happens when transgressions aren't attended to. This is what becomes of us when we ignore the breach far too long. This is what becomes of our children who inherit our transgressional behaviors and our grandchildren who grow up woven in the web of lies and deceit.

The people are saying, "You stole my cookies," and they are getting crumbs in return.

THE BLACK MESSIAH AND BLACK LIVES MATTER

At the time of my drafting of this piece, there has been a sudden (or more pronounced) push in White-dominant progressive churches to understand and profess that Black lives matter. In the quest to act in solidarity, well-meaning folks racialized as White rush to read all the latest anti-racist books and have (what they believe to be) productive discussions on the problems of Whiteness and race in America. This impulse isn't bad; it is a necessary beginning point. However, the point of interrogation is often rooted in colonial epistemologies that allow folks the comfortable space to theorize and intellectualize what is an embodied experience. Blackness is an embodied identity, and to understand the various movements around Black rights and mattering, one must embrace an embodied method of learning. What usually happens is that the book club or the small group ends and there's a rush to pronounce a statement or action of unity that is to function as the bow atop a gift box. "Look, Ma! We finished! We are anti-racists! Black Lives Matter!" This rush—or what I like to call White anxiety—stems from a deep-seated need to prove that one is the "good White" or the "good Christian" (or in the case of Myers Park Baptist, the "good Baptist"). This anxiety overexerts. It overcompensates because, often, the embodied work has not been done. The day-to-day relational work has not been engaged. Furthermore, much of the anti-racist scholarship that White Christians tend to engage ignores the reality of Jesus' identity, a crucial piece in comprehending the mattering of Blackness in the context of the faith.

In his 1968 publication *The Black Messiah*, African American minister and political activist Albert Cleage[4] sets the scene at his church after the unveiling of a mural of the Black Madonna in the chancel on Easter Sunday. Cleage explicates that

> it wasn't so long ago that such a conception would have been impossible for us. Our self-image was so distorted that we didn't believe that even the Almighty God could use us for his purpose because we were so low and despised. Now we have come to the place where we not only can conceive of the possibility, but we are convinced, upon the basis of our knowledge and historic study of all the facts that Jesus was born to a black Mary, that Jesus, the Messiah, was a black man who came to save a Black Nation.[5]

---

4. Albert B. Cleage Jr. (1911–2000) was a Black Christian minister, political candidate, newspaper publisher, political organizer, and author. He founded the Shrine of the Black Madonna Church, a Pan-African Orthodox Church in Detroit, Michigan, as well as the Shrine Cultural Centers and Bookstores in Detroit, Atlanta, and Houston. Cleage changed his name to Jaramogi Abebe Agyeman in the early 1970s and became increasingly involved with Black nationalism and Black separatism, rejecting many of the core principles of racial integration. He also founded a church-owned farm, Beulah Land, in Calhoun Falls, South Carolina, and spent most of his last years there.

5. Cleage Jr., *Black Messiah*, 85.

If you are to understand Jesus as the Brown, poor, and marginalized carpenter that he was, and you purport to be a Christian—or, more pointedly, a follower of the teachings of Jesus—then Black lives have to matter. If your salvation—or your liberation—is connected to a Brown, poor person from Nazareth, then Black and Brown lives have to matter for you. Therefore, the issue isn't about understanding a movement; the issue is about understanding a Black Christ. By "Black," I do not mean in the sense of race. There was no "race" during the life and times of Jesus. There was no race until it was constructed on American soil, a tool of White supremacy to oppress and disenfranchise others for the sake of maintaining power. Jesus' "Blackness" is connected to his "Jewishness"—to his status as an oppressed member of an imperial society that actively sought to relegate certain citizens to the margins. He is of a people beaten and bruised, whose widows were left to starve, whose ancestors were held captive by several empires—the Egyptians, the Babylonians, the Persians, the Romans. He is of a people who had to watch their temple be destroyed—who, perhaps, would wonder in different words, who stole their cookies and how do they get them back? Jesus' past Jewishness is connected to his present Blackness is connected to his future identities as poor, oppressed, and marginalized peoples.

Black liberation theologian James Cone further explicates Jesus' identity in his 1975 publication *God of the Oppressed*:

> It is only within the context of Jesus' past, present, and future as these aspects of his person are related to Scripture, tradition, and contemporary social existence that we are required to affirm the Blackness of Jesus Christ. . . . But unless Black theologians can demonstrate that Jesus' Blackness is not simply the psychological disposition of Black people but arises from a faithful examination of Christology's sources . . . we lay ourselves open to the White charge that the Black Christ is an ideological distortion of the New Testament for political purposes.[6]

We can affirm Jesus' Blackness through the way his status as a Jew under the abusive domination of Rome over 2,000 years ago interacts with the Black person's status under the abusive domination of America and the unjust systems that hold her up today. Thus, Black lives must matter for those who call themselves disciples of the carpenter.

---

6. Cone, *God of the Oppressed*, 122.

If you are asking yourself, "What does race have to do with this?" then perhaps you do not understand oppression. Perhaps you do not fully comprehend the history of America, a land that flourished having been nourished by Black bodies and watered with Black tears. When poet James Weldon Johnson writes, "we have come over a way that with tears has been watered" in the bridge of the second stanza of "Lift Every Voice," he isn't talking about natural condensation; he is talking about Black tears.[7] When Johnson says, "We have come, treading our path through the blood of the slaughtered," this blood is the plant food that we must reckon with when we say, "Black Lives Matter." This is the embodied experience. The watering and feeding of this nation that has made it thrive all these centuries comes from the Black and Brown body, collective and individual. It comes from the pain, from the blood, from the tears, and even from the joy that somehow carved its way in the purple mountains.

SO WHAT ABOUT BLACK LIVES MATTER?

I suppose one may have expected to encounter an unpacking of the movement #BlackLivesMatter. I suppose my original task was to give a light overview of a movement that is one of many and cannot be captured authentically on paper. When it was started by Patrisse Khan-Cullors, Alicia Garza, and Opal Tometi—Black women, "two of whom self-describe as queer-identifying, and one of the women comes from a Nigerian-immigrant family"[8]—it was in response to the acquittal of Trayvon Martin's murderer, George Zimmerman, in 2013. It was and is designed to be "an ideological and political intervention in a world where Black lives are systematically and intentionally targeted for demise . . . an affirmation of Black folks' humanity, our contributions to this society, and our resilience in the face of deadly oppression."[9] It has grown beyond these origins and, as with many movements, has displayed the complications that come along with diversity of thought and praxis in the African diaspora. Lisa L. Thompson notes, "the very compilation of [the leaders'] trifecta exemplifies the labyrinth of Black identity in the US."[10] This presses the reality that being "Black" in America

---

7. Johnson, "Lift Every Voice and Sing."
8. Thompson, *Ingenuity*, 1.
9. "Herstory," *Black Lives Matter*, blacklivesmatter.com/herstory/.
10. Thompson, *Ingenuity*, 1.

is not a monolithic experience and that no one movement is going to lead all of our people to freedom.

There have been many spin-off movements, one of which notably focused on Black trans lives. There has been friction. There have been splits as well as the unfortunate reality of holding certain leaders accountable in ways that may damage the overall progress of the movement. Additionally, the movement has become commodified. Capitalist companies are making millions of dollars off the #BlackLivesMatter brand, throwing it up on their websites during Black History Month or after another unarmed Black person has been killed by the cops, to pacify the masses and to prosper financially. We've also seen how many levels of government have co-opted the phrase-turned-movement for similar purposes. In 2020, we witnessed several mayors commissioning public street murals of the words "Black Lives Matter." The art was approved with swiftness, which echoes the rapidity with which many institutions that want your dollars have hopped on the BLM bandwagon. The hoopla around the "Black Lives Matter" street art provided a perfect distraction from the lack of policy changes and conversations around defunding the police. The performative esprit de corps of the mayors and their minions solidified the governmental takeover of a once-radical call for intervention and affirmation. Furthermore, the founders of Black Lives Matter are often left out of these symbolic gestures, and the movement continues to be watered down.

I give a capsulized view of #BlackLivesMatter from my perspective as a Black person talking to White people, wanting them to ponder why I don't believe their quest for solidarity with Black and Brown folks should start here. Black lives mattered long before 2013—long before 1965 or 1865— and I have a feeling the founders would agree. As mentioned at the top of this piece, it isn't the movement alone that grounds one's understanding of the mattering of Black lives. When the movement fades, when the leader is assassinated, when the savior is hung from a cross, what will ground your understanding of liberation?

FEAR AND HOPE

It has been said that Jacob lived in fear of his brother. When their paths were to cross many years after the act of deception, Jacob hired an army of folks to back him up and support him. I have to believe it was because deep down inside, Jacob knew that what he did to his brother was not just. Esau lived with a taste for revenge that burdened his soul and lingered for generations.

Their relationship was never healed because there was no admittance of a breach. But is there a hope? There is a hope for healing, perhaps not fully captured in this story but contained in the stories we can write for our lives. Jacob does eventually wrestle with God, his identity, and his fragility in later chapters. Some may say it's too little to late—that reparation requires more than joining a book club; that the seeds of injustices are far too deep in the ground by this point. But is there a hope? There is a hope that lies within the possibility that the story doesn't end with the betrayal or the transgression or the deception. There is a hope that a different ending can be conceived through persistent acknowledgment of the harm done against marginalized communities in this country. We cannot heal until we explore the breach. We cannot move forward as a community, as a church, as a city, or as a country until we explore the breach. We cannot profess to love our neighbors until we explore the breach. That is first step of restorative justice practice: identifying and taking steps to repair harm.[11]

We must acknowledge the generational harm if we are to explore the breach. We mustn't merely acknowledge with our voices. We must acknowledge with our resources. We must understand the significance of verbal admittance and resourceful reparation. We must repair what has been broken. It starts within us. Justice starts with us.

In summer 2020, the city council of Asheville, North Carolina, unanimously voted to give financial reparations to Black residents by way of investments in areas where Black Americans still face discrimination and disparity in opportunity. In Charlotte, North Carolina, the Ministry of Outreach at Myers Park Baptist Church granted a founding gift of $20,000 to Restorative Justice CLT, an emerging organization that seeks to firmly set Charlotte on a path to addressing the persistent opportunity and wealth gaps that stem from a long history of discrimination and injustice in the city. There is a hope. Justice is not just a big philosophical concept. Black lives mattering is not some intellectual exercise that you can read about in one session and move on to something else. Apologies and acknowledgment are difficult, especially when we're used to playing "the blame game,"

---

11. Restorative Justice is a theory of justice that emphasizes repairing the harm caused by criminal behavior. It is best accomplished through cooperative processes that allow all willing stakeholders to meet, although other approaches are available when that is impossible. This can lead to transformation of people, relationships, and communities. The key principles of Restorative Justice as listed on restorativejustice.org: A. Crime causes harm and justice should focus on repairing that harm; B. The people most affected by the crime should be able to participate in its resolution; C. The responsibility of the government is to maintain order and of the community to build peace.

but they are possible. Amends are possible. Healing is possible. The breach doesn't have to remain forever. It can shrink, one reparative act at a time.

I don't want my children to be asking "who stole our cookies" twenty years from now. I don't want my grandchildren to be pounding the painted pavements of cities, begging for their birthright in the middle of a pandemic. I want them to have it. I want them to have it fully; I want them to have it wholly; and I want them to have it in peace. No crumbs but whole cookies. This generation of activists and scholars, pastors, and artists are demanding whole cookies. This is the mattering of Black lives. This is the plight of the systemically disenfranchised. Will you hear their plea and answer?

PUB THEOLOGY

INTRODUCTION

Welcome to more than a discussion around race and faith. You may have been pondering or are continuing to ponder why the topic of Black lives mattering—or any marginalized lives mattering—is important for a pub theology conversation. When I think of pub theology, I don't just imagine a basic Bible study at a bar or restaurant; pub theology can also be public Theology—an exploration of the divine in conversation with public life and the lived experiences of everyone, especially the least of these. Indeed, the task of public theology should be at the forefront of what we do as followers of a carpenter from Nazareth who's lived experiences and the lived experiences of those around him shaped everything he taught during his time on earth.

ICEBREAKER

How often do you think about your racial and ethnic identity as it related to a) where you live, b) your economic status, and c) your health care?

JUMPING-OFF POINTS

- Has there been a time in your life when you felt unseen or unheard? How did your body feel? What was your plan of action?
- How does your body react when you hear the pleas of others? Do you jump into action? Do you sit with your own privilege?
- What can we learn from Jacob and Esau?

- What can we learn from Jesus' identity and how his story transcends time and place?
- Do you have an understanding of rage? If so, how might that understanding help shape your perception of movements for Black lives?

OPTIONAL READING

Genesis 25 and 27

Obadiah 1

Cone, James. *God of the Oppressed*. Maryknoll, NY: Orbis Books, 1975.

Morrison, Toni. *Beloved*. New York: Alfred A. Knopf, Inc., 1987.

Thurman, Howard. *Jesus and the Disinherited*. Boston: Beacon Press, 1949.

BIBLIOGRAPHY

Angelou, Maya. *Letter to My Daughter*. New York: Random House, 2008.

Cleage, Albert, Jr. *The Black Messiah: On Black Consciousness and Black Power . . . a strong and uncompromising presentation by one of American's most influential Black religious leaders*. Trenton, NJ: Africa World Press, 1989.

Collins, Patricia. *Black Feminist Thought*. New York: Rutledge Classics, 2000.

Cone, James. *God of the Oppressed*. Maryknoll, NY: Orbis Books, 1975.

Douglas, Kelly Brown. *Stand Your Ground: Black Bodies and the Justice of God*. Kindle ed. Maryknoll, NY: Orbis Books, 2015.

Gafney, Wilda C. *Womanist Midrash: A Reintroduction to the Women of the Torah and the Throne*. Louisville: Westminster John Knox Press, 2017.

Johnson, James Weldon. "Lift Every Voice and Sing." In *African American Heritage Hymnal*. Chicago: GIA Publications, 2001.

Lawrence, Lauress Wilkins. "Where Have All the Women Gone? A Feminist Reading of Obadiah." *Bible Today* 57/3 (May–June 2019): 143–49.

Thompson, Lisa L. *Ingenuity: Preaching as an Outsider*. Nashville: Abingdon, 2018.

Whitfield, James M. "America." In *African American Poetry: 250 Years of Struggle and Song*, ed. Keith Young, 36–40. New York: Library of America, 2020. Originally published in 1853. Also available at poets.org/poem/america-3. Public domain.

THE STRANGER: IMMIGRATION AND SOCIAL JUSTICE

CYNTHIA F. ADCOCK

INTRODUCTION

Migration is central to the human story, to our story. Since the dawn of time, humans have spread across the globe in search of food, water, and land. Some of us did so by choice, but others migrated to escape violence, natural disaster, and famine. Despite the route taken, our indomitable human spirit yearned for more than mere survival. Thus, we also migrated in search of peace, freedom, and plenty. We migrated for a better life for ourselves, our family, and our community.

What is your migration story? Perhaps as a child you migrated with your family from one city to another, one state to another, or even one country to another. When I was a child, my mother and I migrated several times. Our hometown was Rome, Georgia, where she and I were both born, twenty years apart. Twice we migrated to Florida, thinking both times that the relocation was for the best and for good. But when times became hard, we migrated back to live with family in Rome. The security of family can be both an emotional and financial motivator for migration.

What about your ancestors' migration? How did you come to be born *where* you were born? Familial migration stories are sometimes passed down from generation to generation. Others are forgotten with time. With the advent of Ancestry.com and other similar products, more of us are learning when and how our ancestors arrived in America. I recently discovered I came to be born in rural Georgia because ancestors crossed the

Atlantic from Europe in the 1600s and then continued to migrate inland. At that time, there was no regulation of immigration to America. Indeed, Europeans were encouraged to come to America through land grants and apprenticeship programs.

In 2020, there were an estimated 272 million international migrants, i.e., people living in a country other than where they were born, triple the number from fifty years ago. Though just 3.5 percent of the world's population, this number already surpasses some prior projections for 2050. Some of these people migrated for work. The poorest among them migrated despite extreme danger. From 2014–2018, more than 30,900 people died trying to reach a country of refuge. Charlotte Edmond points out that "The Mediterranean Sea remains the deadliest route, claiming the lives of nearly 18,000 people in that time. Since 2014, over 1,800 deaths have been recorded along the border between the United States and Mexico."[1]

In the United States, immigrants may qualify for permanent residency, or a "green card," by being family members of current US residents, recipients of employment visas, refugees and asylum seekers, or winners of a visa lottery.[2] For the past twenty years or so, our government has granted an average of about one million green cards per year. Recently, however, in the wake of numerous domestic crises, some Americans have loudly called for limiting immigration. Politicians have responded with restrictive policies. For example, in 2020, our government cut the number of refugees qualified for green cards to only 18,000. In 2016, the number was 85,000.[3]

How should people of faith in America respond to the desire and the need for human migration?

THE THEOLOGY OF MIGRATION

Migration stories are central to the theology of the three Abrahamic religions—Judaism, Christianity, and Islam. They share one of the oldest migration stories, that of Abraham, who was called by God to migrate: "Now the LORD said to Abram, 'Go from your country and your kindred and your father's house to the land that I will show you. I will make of you

---

1. Edmond, "Global migration, by the numbers," weforum.org/agenda/2020/01/iom-global-migration-report-international-migrants-2020/.

2. Wormald, "Religious Affiliation of U.S. Immigrants," pewforum.org/2013/05/17/the-religious-affiliation-of-us-immigrants/.

3. National Immigration Forum, "Factsheet: US Refugee Resettlement," immigrationforum.org/article/fact-sheet-u-s-refugee-resettlement/.

a great nation, and I will bless you, and make your name great, so that you will be a blessing'" (Gen 12:1-2). Abraham migrated to some seventeen locations from Ur to Heron to Canaan to Egypt and back to Heron, and his migration gave birth to the Jewish people.[4] Yet the greatest migration story of Judaism is that of Moses, who brought the Jewish people out of Egypt where they had been enslaved for hundreds of years. They wandered for forty years before arriving in the promised land of Canaan. The story is told in the aptly named book of the Old Testament: Exodus.

Christianity reveres Abraham and Moses, but its great migration story is of a descendant of Abraham named Joseph. Joseph fled with his wife Mary and their newborn son, Jesus, to Egypt.

> An angel of the Lord appeared to Joseph in a dream and said, "Get up, take the child and his mother, and flee to Egypt, and remain there until I tell you; for Herod is about to search for the child, to destroy him." Then Joseph got up, took the child and his mother by night, and went to Egypt, and remained there until the death of Herod. (Matt 2:13-15)

Egypt was a place of refuge because it was outside the jurisdiction of Herod.[5] When Herod died, God called Joseph to migrate back to Israel.

> When Herod died, an angel of the Lord suddenly appeared in a dream to Joseph in Egypt and said, "Get up, take the child and his mother, and go to the land of Israel, for those who were seeking the child's life are dead." Then Joseph got up, took the child and his mother, and went to the land of Israel. (Matt 2:19-21)

Islam honors the prophets of the Old and New Testaments and adds its great migration story of Muhammad, another descendant of Abraham, from Mecca to Medina. According to Qur'an 8:30, with commentary,

> Remember when those who disbelieved (in God) plotted (at the meeting of the chiefs in the idol worshipper council in Mecca Makkah) against you (Prophet Muhammad, about whether) to restrain you or to kill you or to evict you (from Mecca Makkah), they made (their) plans but God

---

4. "Map of the Journeys of Abraham," *Bible History*, bible-history.com/maps/6-abrahams-journeys.html.

5. Martin, "Were Jesus, Mary and Joseph Refugees? Yes," *America: The Jesuit Review*, December 27, 2017, citing Daniel J. Harrington, *Sacra Pagina: The Gospel of Matthew*, 1991, americamagazine.org/faith/2017/12/27/were-jesus-mary-and-joseph-refugees-yes.

also planned (by commanding you Prophet Muhammad to leave Mecca Makkah) and God is the best of planners.[6]

Known as The Hijra,[7] Muhammad's migration teaches, like the other great migration stories, that God leads the faithful to a place where God's will can be more perfectly fulfilled.

THE CALL FOR EMPATHY

There can be no coincidence the Abrahamic religions place migration stories at the center of their theology *and* repeatedly exhort believers to welcome and to care for the stranger, the migrant from another land. Scripture from these religions calls on believers to remember the great migrations, which are celebrated annually with holidays such as Passover and Christmas, and to act with empathy for new migrants. There are over twenty-two Bible verses exhorting God's people to care for the stranger.[8] The Qur'an similarly requires care of the wayfarer (*ibn-al-sabil*), the stranger far from home who cannot return.[9] Relevant passages include the following:

Old Testament
You shall also love the stranger, for you were strangers in the land of Egypt. (Deut 10:19)

The alien who resides with you shall be to you as the citizen among you; you shall love the alien as yourself, for you were aliens in the land of Egypt: I am the LORD your God. (Lev 19:34)

"Cursed be anyone who deprives the alien, the orphan, and the widow of justice." (Deut 27:19)

When they were few in number, of little account, and strangers in the land, wandering from nation to nation, from one kingdom to another people,

---

6. Voron, "Quran chapter 8, Why did Prophet Muhammad flee Mecca?" *Islam and the Quran*, mobile.sites.google.com/site/islamandthequran/quran-chapter-8-surah-8.

7. Syed, "The Significance of the Hijrah (622 CE)," historyofislam.com/contents/the-age-of-faith/the-significance-of-the-hijrah.

8. "22 Bible Verses on Welcoming Immigrants," *Sojourners*, Sojo.net/22-bible-verses-welcoming-immigrants.

9. Saritoprak, "An Islamic Approach to Migration and Refugees," 522.

he allowed no one to oppress them; he rebuked kings on their account, saying, "Do not touch my anointed ones; do my prophets no harm." (1 Chr 16:19-22)

I was eyes to the blind, and feet to the lame. I was a father to the needy, and I championed the cause of the stranger. (Job 29:15-16)

The LORD watches over the strangers; he upholds the orphan and the widow, but the way of the wicked he brings to ruin. (Ps 146:9)

For if you truly amend your ways and your doings, if you truly act justly one with another, if you do not oppress the alien, the orphan, and the widow, or shed innocent blood in this place . . . I will dwell with you in this place, in the land that I gave of old to your ancestors forever and ever. (Jer 7:5-7)

You shall allot it as an inheritance for yourselves and for the aliens who reside among you and have begotten children among you. They shall be to you as citizens of Israel; with you they shall be allotted an inheritance among the tribes of Israel. (Ezra 47:22)

New Testament
"You have heard that it was said, 'You shall love your neighbor and hate your enemy.' But I say to you, Love your enemies and pray for those who persecute you." (Matt 5:43-44)

". . . for I was hungry and you gave me food, I was thirsty and you gave me something to drink, I was a stranger and you welcomed me." (Matt 25:35)

Contribute to the needs of the saints; extend hospitality to strangers. (Rom 12:13)

There is neither Jew nor Greek . . . for you are all one in Christ Jesus. (Gal 3:28)

Let mutual love continue. Do not neglect to show hospitality to strangers, for by doing that some have entertained angels without knowing it. (Heb 13:1-2)

Beloved, you do faithfully whatever you do for the friends, even though they are strangers to you; they have testified to your love before the church. You do well to send them on in a manner worthy of God; for they began their journey for the sake of Christ, accepting no support from nonbelievers. Therefore, we ought to support such people, so that they may become coworkers with the truth. (3 John 1:5-8)

The Qur'an
Righteousness is not that you turn your faces toward the east or the west, but [true] righteousness is [in] one who believes in Allah, the Last Day, the angels, the Book, and the prophets and gives wealth, in spite of love for it, to relatives, orphans, the needy, the wayfarers . . . . (2:177)

They ask you of what they should give in charity. Tell them: "What you can spare of your wealth as should benefit the parents, the relatives, the orphans, the needy, the wayfarers, for God is not unaware of the good deeds that you do." (2:215)

Worship Allah and associate nothing with Him, and to parents do good, and to relatives, orphans, the needy, the near neighbor, the neighbor farther away, the companion at your side, the wayfarer . . . . (4:36)

Whatever booty God gives to His Apostle from the people of the cities, is for God and His Apostle, the near relations, the orphans, the needy and wayfarers, so that it does not concentrate in the hands of those who are rich among you. (59:7)

FROM EMPATHY TO SOCIAL JUSTICE

Reeling from the vast human toll of World War II, world leaders came together to imagine how to prevent such atrocities from ever happening again. From this effort was born the Universal Declaration of Human Right (UDHR), which "sets out, for the first time, fundamental human rights to be universally protected." It requires that all countries recognize "the inherent dignity and . . . the equal and inalienable rights of all members of the human family" for this "is the foundation of freedom, justice and peace in the world . . . ."[10]

---

10. UN General Assembly, *Universal Declaration of Human Rights* (Paris, 1948), preamble, par. 1.

Immigration was a pressing issue at the time, as millions of refugees from Germany and Eastern Europe needed a place to resettle. In that context, the United Nations sought to balance the sovereign right of countries to manage their borders with the inherent right of the individual to life and dignity. Thus, the UDHR does not recognize an unconditional right to migrate to another country. However, Article 14 provides that "Everyone has the right to seek and to enjoy in other countries asylum from persecution."

Fast-forward seventy years, and the question of what to do with poor international migrants is no less pressing. Only the color of their skin has changed. Fewer come from Europe these days, and in the United States, resistance to immigration has grown. Politicians have responded with draconian immigration policies. As one commentator aptly described in 2019,

> Our government is forcibly returning people who claim asylum to "safe third countries" (that aren't very safe) that those migrants have journeyed through to get to the United States . . . jailing persons who have come here claiming asylum until their claims are processed, . . . continuing to separate children from their parents, sometimes deporting parents without their children or deporting children without their parents; . . . [and] raiding businesses and rounding up everyone who doesn't have legal work authorization, and sometimes those that do.
>
> Our government is targeting people who are trying to get legal documentation through U.S. Citizenship and Immigration Services. Our government is cutting the numbers of work visas it offers each year. Our government is making it more difficult for family members and spouses of U.S. residents and citizens to join their family member in the U.S.[11]

What should be the response of people of faith to questions of social justice?

The Catholic Church, with its long history and worldwide reach, has long taken positions on the treatment of migrants. The United States Conference of Bishops identifies three basic principles of Catholic social teaching on immigration:

---

11. Choate, "Commentary: Jesus Was a Migrant," *Witness for Justice*, United Church of Christ, December 19, 2019, ucc.org/commentary_jesus_was_a_migrant.

(1) People have the right to migrate to sustain their lives and the lives of their families.
(2) A country has the right to regulate its borders and to control immigration.
(3) A country must regulate its borders with justice and mercy.

Accordingly, the Catholic Church recognizes that

> every person has basic human rights and is entitled to have basic human needs met—food, shelter, clothing, education, and health care. Undocumented persons are particularly vulnerable to exploitation by employers, and they are not able to complain because of the fear of discovery and deportation. Current immigration policy that criminalizes the mere attempt to immigrate and imprisons immigrants who have committed no crime or who have already served a just sentence for a crime is immoral.[12]

Protestant denominations have taken similar positions. Recently, on the local level, my home church, Myers Park Baptist Church in Charlotte, North Carolina, embarked on a year-long process of "Awakening Shalom." The goal was "to create a deep understanding and compassion for the world's most marginalized individuals [through] a critical examination of structural, historical, sociological, and theological obstacles to the establishment of equity, wholeness, and fulfillment of all people."[13]

The year of study and reflection consisted of a number of speakers and a facilitated process of deliberative dialogue on immigration reform. Participants in the dialogue

> discussed three options for reform: shoring up our existing system while also providing an acceptable way for the millions of undocumented immigrants currently living here to earn the right to citizenship; tighter control of the border, tougher law enforcement, and stricter limits on immigration quotas; and offering a range of flexible measures such as annual adjustments to quotas that put a priority on our economic needs. At the end of our deliberations most of those in the room (at least the

---

12. Betz, "Catholic Social Teaching on Immigration and the Movement of Peoples," *United States Conference of Catholic Bishops*, usccb.org/issues-and-action/human-life-and-dignity/immigration/catholic-teaching-on-immigration-and-the-movement-of-peoples.

13. Williamson, "Awakening to Immigrant Injustice," Myers Park Baptist Church, myersparkbaptist.org/awakening-to-immigrant-injustice/.

more vocal) landed on option 3: flexible measures promoting economic prosperity.[14]

The year culminated in a sacred pilgrimage for interested congregants. About twenty church members followed the route many undocumented immigrants detained in North Carolina must travel to the federal detention center in Georgia. Pastor Ben Boswell reported to the congregation afterwards: "[O]ur pilgrims heard stories that sounded more like nightmares of how the justice system plays out for America's immigrants. Staggering statistics and consistent tales of inhumane treatment left them all feeling that they must bear witness to what they have seen and heard."[15]

At the end of the process, my church adopted a statement on immigration. In this statement, Myers Park Baptist Church professes that because we are a "people on a journey—and of a faith shaped by people in exile—we are called to love those who are also journeying as God has loved us." The statement calls out the sins of our nation's immigration policies and commits to "engage in education and advocacy, support immigration reform, help provide a more humane and empathetic way to stand alongside all immigrants with love, affirmation, resources, and support."[16]

CONCLUSION

We all are the product of human migration. Through stories from afar in time and place and from near, we know the fear and hope that comes with migration. Our great migration stories remind us never to forget the depth of the experiences of our ancestors, and they call us to take care of those who migrate today. The question for us is how to respond.

---

14. Myers Park Baptist Church, "Deliberative Dialogue: Immigration Reform," *Awakening Immigrant Injustice* (blog), December 10, 2017, awakeningshalom.com/immigrant-injustice.

15. Cadena, "Awakening to injustice: a church goes on a pilgrimage to follow immigrants' journey from undocumented to detained," *Baptist News Global*, October 31, 2018, baptistnews.com/article/awakening-to-injustice-a-church-goes-on-a-pilgrimage-to-follow-immigrants-journey-from-undocumented-to-detained/#.YDUooNWSk2w.

16. Myers Park Baptist Church, "Statement on Immigration," *Our Statements*, approved October 2020, myersparkbaptist.org/statements/.

PUB THEOLOGY

INTRODUCTION: THE STRANGER—IMMIGRATION AND SOCIAL JUSTICE

- Abraham migrated to some seventeen locations from Ur to Heron to Canaan to Egypt and back to Heron, and his migration gave birth to the Jewish people. "Now the LORD said to Abram, 'Go from your country and your kindred and your father's house to the land that I will show you. I will make of you a great nation, and I will bless you, and make your name great, so that you will be a blessing'" (Gen 12:1-2).
- Moses led the Jewish people out of Egypt, where they had been enslaved for hundreds of years. "You shall also love the stranger, for you were strangers in the land of Egypt" (Deut 10:19).
- Joseph fled with his wife Mary and their newborn son, Jesus, to Egypt to escape the deadly fury of King Herod, "for I was hungry and you gave me food, I was thirsty and you gave me something to drink, I was a stranger and you welcomed me" (Matt 25:35).
- Muhammad fled for his life from Mecca to Medina. "Whatever booty God gives to His Apostle from the people of the cities, is for God and His Apostle, the near relations, the orphans, the needy and wayfarers, so that it does not concentrate in the hands of those who are rich among you" (Qur'an 59:7).

These are the US Conference of Catholic Bishops' Principles of Social Justice on immigration:
(1) People have the right to migrate to sustain their lives and the lives of their families.
(2) A country has the right to regulate its borders and to control immigration.
(3) A country must regulate its borders with justice and mercy.

ICEBREAKER

Where are you from (whatever that means to you)?

JUMPING-OFF POINTS

- What is your migration story? What is the story of your ancestors' migration?
- What does it mean to say that America is built on the backs of immigrants?

- What is the connection between Christian-Judeo-Muslim values and social justice for immigrants?
- What is our responsibility to immigrants as Americans given our history and our values?
- What can we do to care for immigrants?

BIBLIOGRAPHY

"22 Bible Verses on Welcoming Immigrants." *Sojourners.* sojo.net/22-bible-verses-welcoming-immigrants.

Betz, Thomas. "Catholic Social Teaching on Immigration and the Movement of Peoples." *United States Conference of Catholic Bishops.* usccb.org/issues-and-action/human-life-and-dignity/immigration/catholic-teaching-on-immigration-and-the-movement-of-peoples.

Cadena, Laura. "Awakening to injustice: a church goes on a pilgrimage to follow immigrants' journey from undocumented to detained." *Baptist News Global.* October 31, 2018. baptistnews.com/article/awakening-to-injustice-a-church-goes-on-a-pilgrimage-to-follow-immigrants-journey-from-undocumented-to-detained/#.YDUooNWSk2w

Choate, Rebekah. "Commentary: Jesus Was a Migrant." *Witness for Justice.* United Church of Christ. December 19, 2019. ucc.org/commentary_jesus_was_a_migrant.

"Map of the Journeys of Abraham," *Bible History,* bible-history.com/maps/6-abrahams-journeys.html.

Martin, James. "Were Jesus, Mary and Joseph Refugees? Yes." *America: The Jesuit Review.* December 27, 2017. Citing Daniel J. Harrington, *Sacra Pagina: The Gospel of Matthew,* 1991. americamagazine.org/faith/2017/12/27/were-jesus-mary-and-joseph-refugees-yes.

Myers Park Baptist Church, "Deliberative Dialogue: Immigration Reform," *Awakening Immigrant Injustice* (blog). December 10, 2017. awakeningshalom.com/immigrant-injustice

Myers Park Baptist Church. "Statement on Immigration." *Our Statements.* Approved October 2020. myersparkbaptist.org/statements/.

Saritoprak, Zeki. "An Islamic Approach to Migration and Refugees." *CrossCurrents* 67/3 (2017): 522–31. jstor.org/stable/26605829.

Syed, Ibrahim B. "The Significance of the Hijrah (622 CE)." *History of Islam: An Encyclopedia of Islamic History.* historyofislam.com/contents/the-age-of-faith/the-significance-of-the-hijrah.

UN General Assembly. *Universal Declaration of Human Rights* (Paris, 1948).

Voron, Sam. "Quran chapter 8, Why did Prophet Muhammad flee Mecca?" *Islam and the Quran.* mobile.sites.google.com/site/islamandthequran/quran-chapter-8-surah-8.

Williamson, Chrissy Tatum. "Awakening to Immigrant Injustice." Myers Park Baptist Church. myersparkbaptist.org/awakening-to-immigrant-injustice/.

Wormald, Benjamin. "The Religious Affiliation of U.S. Immigrants: Majority Christian, Rising Share of Other Faiths." *Pew Research Center.* May 17, 2013. pewforum.org/2013/05/17/the-religious-affiliation-of-us-immigrants/.

MEETING 16

MARGINALIZED PEOPLE

BARBARA B. LUCAS

Feeding the Poor at a Sacrifice

In the first centuries
of Christianity
the hungry were fed
at a personal sacrifice,
the naked were clothed
at a personal sacrifice,
the homeless were sheltered
at personal sacrifice.
And because the poor
were fed, clothed and sheltered
at a personal sacrifice,
the pagans used to say
about the Christians
"See how they love each other."
In our own day
the poor are no longer
fed, clothed and sheltered
at a personal sacrifice,
but at the expense
of the taxpayers.
And because the poor
are no longer
fed, clothed and sheltered
the pagans say about the Christians
"See how they pass the buck."[1]

---

1. Maurin, "Feeding the Poor at a Sacrifice," in *Easy Essays*, easyessays.org/feeding-the-poor/.

INTRODUCTION

Marginalize provides a striking case of how thoroughly the figurative use of a word can take over the literal one. The original (and now obsolete) meaning of this word, "to write notes in the margin of," is analogous to the still-familiar noun *marginalia* "marginal notes or embellishments." A *margin* is, of course, the blank space surrounding the text in a book. Just prior to 1970, *marginalize* took on the sense that is most commonly encountered today, "to relegate to an unimportant or powerless position" (that is, to the metaphorical margins of society). This use of the word can be found as far back as 1968; an article in the *Los Angeles Times* from June 20th of that year reports, "[T]he Negro was kept aside, *marginalized*, thus composing in its large majority the chronically poor." In its newer sense, *marginalize* has assumed a much more prominent place in the vocabulary than it once had.[2]

For the purpose of this discussion, we will consider "marginalized people" as those who have some type of scarcity in their lives, be it respect, love, money, education, adequate housing, etc., and who, because of their scarcity, are pushed to the outside margins of society or excluded from some part of society to which they would like to belong.

I will periodically share some of my own experiences with marginalized people. I worked with many types of disadvantaged people for several years when I directed a counseling organization created by three churches in Charlotte, North Carolina. My hope is that you will become more aware and perhaps more empathetic to the marginalized as your group explores this topic.

MARGINALIZED GROUPS

Individuals who are marginalized typically fit into a group of people who are marginalized for the same reason. Each individual in the group is different from the "norm" in the mainstream culture of their society. They are often left out, disrespected, abused, denied privileges, generally hurt, and made to feel unwanted and powerless to change their lives for the better. Lack of respect is most often an attendant problem, as is lack of opportunity. Consequently, they lose ambition, often turn to drugs, sometimes become

---

2. "Marginalized Writing vs. Marginalized People" section of merriam-webster.com/dictionary/marginalize," *Merriam-Webster.com*.

criminals, and sometimes perform violent acts in an effort to relieve their frustrations.

The treatment of marginalized groups is frequently discussed in neighborhood gatherings, political organizations, churches, and state, local, and national governments. To date, however, little has been accomplished to better the status of many of these groups to the point that they feel acceptance in society. It is true that specific individuals within a marginalized group can move out of marginalization and achieve acceptance. However, this requires strong desire, strength, and effort.

While some individuals who are significantly different from society's accepted standards may not be categorized to fit into a particular group, a great many disadvantaged people do fit into groups. Predominant groups within most societies include people of color, the mentally and physically disabled, poor people of any color, gay and queer people, the uneducated, the unskilled, the unhoused, the elderly, and many others who do not fit particular, generally accepted societal norms.

One thinks of White people in the USA and other developed countries as having "White privilege." However, if a White person is put in a different society, the White privilege can become a source for marginalization. I was born to American parents living in a Spanish country. As a White Caucasian Protestant and very privileged young girl, I was marginalized by the Spanish neighborhood children because of my skin tone, my Caucasian race, and my religion. My privilege disappeared because I was different from the accepted norms of that country. Consequently, the children in the neighborhood mistreated and abused me. On one afternoon, I was placed in a circle and switched with sticks. I was forced to do things that scared me, such as climbing and then jumping down from a tall tree. The neighborhood children often made fun of me, and I was always the last chosen for any team. I was marginalized because of my differences and never really belonged to the neighborhood children's group even though I played with them. My differences kept me on the periphery of the group.

The Bible clearly defines the bad consequences of mistreating people and the good that results from helping the afflicted:

- Proverbs 14:31 (NRSV): Those who oppress the poor insult their Maker, but those who are kind to the needy honor him.
- Psalm 41:1-2: Happy are those who consider the poor; the LORD delivers them in the day of trouble. The LORD protects them and keeps them

alive; they are called happy in the land. You do not give them up to the will of their enemies.
- Matthew 25:35: "for I was hungry and you gave me food, I was thirsty and you gave me something to drink, I was a stranger and you welcomed me."
- Luke 14:13: "But when you give a banquet, invite the poor, the crippled, the lame, and the blind."

In his poem "Feeding the Poor at a Sacrifice," Peter Maurin points to the significant differences in how poor people were fed, clothed, and sheltered in the first centuries through personal sacrifice. Today, the care of the poor and the disadvantaged is primarily a government job with the help of some nonprofit organizations and some churches. In most cases today, taxes are the resource for helping marginalized people. The primary funding of assistance for marginalized people is through state and federal taxes given to various government agencies and nonprofit organizations. Welfare for single mothers, food stamps for the hungry, benefits for the unemployed, special education assistance for the mentally and physically disabled, transportation assistance, housing assistance for the homeless, medical benefits for the mentally and physically disabled, and social security income for the disabled are prime examples.

Some marginalized groups are missing from the list of assistance programs originating from tax dollars: people of color and people of different sexual orientations. These people are not generally eligible for societal benefits unless they belong to one of the marginalized groups named above or have similar problems.

In addition to using taxes for programs to assist marginalized people, the government encourages taxpayers to contribute to churches and nonprofit organizations that help meet of the needs delineated by one or more of the marginalized groups. Prior to the nineteenth century, few formal charitable organizations existed to assist people in need. In the first few decades of the twentieth century, several volunteer organizations were founded.

The Red Cross and the Salvation Army are possibly the two largest nonprofit organizations dedicated to assisting disadvantaged people in the United States. The Red Cross assists in disaster recovery and organizes the collection of donated blood for emergencies and hospitals. The Salvation Army feeds, shelters, rehabilitates, and helps disaster survivors and many others. Many smaller local nonprofit organizations also serve needs of specific marginalized groups. Most organized nonprofit groups, both large and small, provide opportunities for people to volunteer to help the group.

These smaller nonprofit organizations are often created by churches within the community. For example, a nonprofit organization was created by three churches in Charlotte, North Carolina, in the early 1970s to counsel and assist people moving into the Federal Government Subsidized Housing Properties (HUD). I was appointed director of the organization. The purpose of the nonprofit was to help new homeowners and tenants understand their responsibilities of owning or renting a home, paying their monthly mortgage or rent on time, and maintaining the home, keeping it in good condition. The church's intention was to furnish the seed money to get the organization started, and it was expected that the organization would then pursue government grants to continue its work.

Because the organization was independent and nonprofit, it was able to get local government grants to continue its work. It soon became apparent to me that the HUD homes were primarily occupied by people who were poor and lacked education. They needed much more than instruction on the responsibility of home ownership. They were primarily working poor people who needed budgeting skills and instruction on how to find and use community programs such as food stamps, unemployment, and social security to assist them in their daily lives.

While there are many types of disadvantaged and marginalized people struggling to live in today's world, this chapter will focus on just three groups: elder citizens, the uneducated, and the unhoused, often referred to as street people.

ELDER CITIZENS

Older people are often marginalized because their thoughts and ideas are considered "old-fashioned" by a society that has moved on to different and perhaps more advanced ways of thinking and doing. If children were part of the elder person's family group, they have moved from the home and adopted their own ways of living their lives. Often, the children live far from their parents and may see them only once or twice a year. Many children feel love, duty, and/or obligation to their parents, but they often consider themselves too busy to spend time with them and do not value their parents' opinions. Some elderly citizens are more fortunate—if they have enough monetary resources, they can live in one of the many Continuing Care Retirement Homes.

Many elderly people are subject to mild cognitive impairment while others are plagued with some form of dementia and are cut off from their families and the world as they knew it. There are three major forms of dementia: Alzheimer's, Lewy body, and vascular. A recent and comprehensive study on aging, demographics, and memory (ADAMS)[3] showed that the prevalence of dementia increases significantly with age. Five percent of people ages 71 to 79, 24.2 percent of people 80 to 89, and 37.4 percent of those 90 years or older were estimated to have some type of dementia. The ADAMS investigators found fewer years of education and the presence of at least one APOE e4 allele, a genetic risk factor for Alzheimer's dementia (AD), to be strong predictors of AD and other dementias.

THE UNEDUCATED

According to the World Literacy Foundation, 750 million people can't read a single word, and more than 2 billion people struggle to read and write a sentence. Illiteracy is a global tragedy. We often think of illiteracy as not being able to read or write, but what does that mean on a deeper level? It's a much bigger and more complex issue than one might think, and it's important to understand the devastating impacts of illiteracy. Imagine for a moment not being able to read a simple sign or fill out an employment form. For individuals and families across the world, illiteracy remains a real problem that hinders social and economic development.[4]

People who are illiterate have little or no education and may struggle to function effectively in society. They also are vulnerable to unscrupulous people who take advantage of their lack of education. Our counseling agency staff knew a woman who was paying five dollars per week for three years for a black-and-white nineteen-inch TV. A man showed up at her public housing door every week to collect his money. In today's industrialized society, these people are at a significant disadvantage. They are often unable to obtain a driver's license since they cannot read well enough to pass the written test; these obstacles may limit their employment opportunities to unskilled or semiskilled labor.

---

3. Heeringa et al., "Aging, Demographics, and Memory Study [ADAMS]," *Lancet*, February 2015, at thelancet.com/journals/lancet/issue/vol385no9967/PIIS0140-6736(15)X6126-5.

4. Lupus, "How do low literacy levels impact on the community?" *Linkedin*, June 16, 2019, WLF Youth Ambassador 2019, linkedin.com/pulse/how-do-low-literacy-levels-impact-community-tara-lupus.

Semiliterate people are fortunate if they can learn a skill that can become a trade. Some basic reading and arithmetic abilities will enable them to read and understand some written instruction. They are sometimes able to achieve either a high school diploma or a GED designation. Trades require specialized skills that can be achieved through on-the-job training, apprenticeships, and trade schools. Examples of trade jobs that currently lead to acceptance and adequate income include plumbers, carpenters, mechanics, chefs, and landscapers.

Someone who wishes to become literate or even semiliterate must have a desire to learn, pass to the next grade, or improve themselves. In other words, they must understand what is required and be motivated to do whatever is necessary to meet the requirement; they also need the luxuries of time, transportation, and perhaps childcare that such improvement requires.

THE UNHOUSED

The term "street people" was first recorded in 1965. This term refers to unhoused people living on the streets of large cities. People experiencing homelessness are perhaps the most vulnerable of any society. They may have lost stable jobs and homes, been diagnosed with physical or mental illness, or never achieved the sort of stability most people take for granted. Unable to be self-sufficient, some unhoused people rely on government, church, and nonprofit support. In some climates, unhoused people use tents, bed rolls, and pit fires for their as shelter. In certain circumstances, such as cold weather, they may seek a shelter of some kind. Navigating the bureaucracy of government assistance is especially difficult for anyone with mental or physical illness or disability or without transportation or the skills to ascertain what help is even available. And some people resist help.

While circumstances can vary, many people experience homelessness because they cannot find affordable housing. Consider these statistics:[5]

- In January 2014, there were 578,424 people experiencing homelessness on any given night in the United States. Of that number, 216,261 were people in families, and 362,163 were individuals.
- About 15 percent of the homeless population are considered "chronically homeless," and about 9 percent of unhoused people are veterans.

---

5. US Department of Housing and Urban Development, *The 2014 Annual Homeless Assessment Report (AHAR) to Congress.*

These numbers come from point-in-time counts, which are conducted, community by community, on a single night in January every other year.[6] The Department of Housing and Urban Development (HUD) requires communities to submit this data every other year to qualify for federal homeless assistance funds. Many communities conduct counts more regularly.

Even though many people do seek shelter, there are many others who choose not to go to a shelter. Their reasons are many and different, including pride, rules, and fear of the unknown. There currently exist several nonprofit agencies that construct and rent relatively affordable housing in large cities. An example is the nonprofit Home Again Foundation.[7] The homes are for single persons and families whose income is 60 percent or below of the median income of the community.

IS THERE A SOLUTION?

How can we help more people feel accepted in our society? Is it possible that society could show more respect for marginalized people? If so, how? Can churches, synagogues, and other religious organizations better serve their communities and all the people in them? Jesus said, "The poor you will always have with you, but you will not always have me" (Matt 26:11). Should we accept that there will always be segments of society who "just don't fit"? If not, why?

PUB THEOLOGY

INTRODUCTION

In its original meaning, the word *marginalize* meant to write notes in the margins of a document. Just prior to 1970, the word *marginalize* took on a much broader meaning; today, it means "to relegate to an unimportant or powerless position." Our discussion will focus on the marginalization of people and groups of people in today's society. We will discuss how it is applied to people who have a scarcity in their lives. My hope is that you will become more aware and perhaps more empathetic to the marginalized people you encounter.

---

6. Ibid.

7. Laurin Lindstrom, "Energy-efficient affordable cottages welcome residents 'home again' in Charlotte," *Charlotte Observer*, February 24, 2021.

ICEBREAKER

What is one of your favorite places? It can be anywhere…your home, the mountains, a beach, another country, or any place where you feel most comfortable, most yourself, most joyful, most at peace, etc.

JUMPING-OFF POINTS

- Do you associate with any people that you would define as marginalized?
  a. If yes, would you consider any of them friends?
  b. Can you define what makes them marginalized in your eyes?
- Do you volunteer with any of the nonprofits that help the underprivileged?
  a. If yes, do you work with individuals or groups?
  b. Do you and/or your associates believe your assistance is helpful?
- Do you think subsidized housing will help solve the homeless housing problem?
- How can we more effectively help groups of people who are marginalized?

BIBLIOGRAPHY

Heeringa, S. G., et al. "Aging, Demographics, and Memory Study [ADAMS]." *Lancet* 385/9967 (February 2015): 499.

Holmes, David. Interview with Richard Suzman, November 5, 2014.

Lindstrom, Laurin. "Energy-efficient affordable cottages welcome residents 'home again' in Charlotte." *Charlotte Observer*. February 24, 2021.

Lupus, Tara. "How do low literacy levels impact on the community?" *Linkedin*. June 16, 2019. WLF Youth Ambassador 2019. linkedin.com/pulse/how-do-low-literacy-levels-impact-community-tara-lupus.

Maurin, Peter. "Feeding the Poor at a Sacrifice." *Easy Essays*. easyessays.org/feeding-the-poor/.

"Point-In-Time (PIT) Count Version 1.0 and 2.0." Homeless Data Exchange (HDX). January 2014.

Thuault, Sebastien. "Reflections on Aging Research from within the National Institute on Aging." *Nature Aging* 1/14–18 (2021).

US Department of Housing and Urban Development Office of Community Planning and Development. *The 2014 Annual Homeless*

Assessment Report (AHAR) to Congress. October 2014. huduser.gov/portal/sites/default/files/pdf/2014-AHAR-Part-1.pdf

"Why Some Homeless Choose the Streets over Shelters." NPR. December 6, 2012. (Heard on *Talk of the Nation.*) npr.org/2012/12/06/166666265/why-some-homeless-choose-the-streets-over-shelters.

ABOUT THE CONTRIBUTORS

Cynthia F. Adcock is a lawyer, writer, adult educator, and social entrepreneur. She earned a BA in psychology and religion from Carson-Newman College, an MDiv from Southern Baptist Theological Seminary, and a JD and a master of public policy from Duke University. She spent most of her career representing inmates on death row. She is committed to social justice in all its iterations and most specifically to restorative justice, to the power of storytelling, and to the importance of community.

Rev. Dr. W. Benjamin Boswell (he/him) is the senior minister of Myers Park Baptist Church in Charlotte, North Carolina, where he serves at the intersection of strategic leadership, spiritual formation, and social justice. Dr. Boswell is also a former infantry officer in the US Army National Guard, a graduate of Marion Military Institute (AA), Campbell University (BA), Duke Divinity School (MDiv), and Saint Paul's School of Theology (DMin). Dr. Boswell is a preacher, author, and sought-after public speaker who has received numerous awards and honors for his work as a pastor and human rights advocate. In 2021, he was awarded the prestigious Martin Luther King Jr. Medallion by the city of Charlotte, which is the highest honor given to a person who upholds the legacy of Dr. King by promoting racial equality, social justice, and community service. Dr. Boswell also serves on the board of Restorative Justice CLT and facilitates an anti-racism training course he developed called "What Does It Mean to Be White?"

Deborah Moore Clark is an ordained minister who worships with the Myers Park Baptist Church, Charlotte, North Carolina, where she is active in church music ministry as a chorister, soloist, and frequent liturgist in worship. She has twice chaired the church's ministry of music and worship and three task forces charged with examining and augmenting worship practices. In 2018, Deborah led the task force charged with writing the church's current theology of worship. Deborah earned a master of church music degree from The Southern Baptist Theological Seminary (1983) and a master of liberal studies degree in expository writing and communication (1998). Vocationally, Deborah is a retired church music minister but remains active as a writer in several genres: worship, church music ministry, horticulture, and civic issues. She is the author of numerous published articles and one book, *O Come, Let Us Bow Down and Worship*, published by Smyth & Helwys in 2003.

Nancy Culp was raised on sword drills and Training Union in the Southern Baptist tradition. She went on to earn a master of religious education degree from Southwestern Baptist Theological Seminary and a master of organizational leadership from Gonzaga University. After many years living with the challenge of reconciling God, church, and being gay, Nancy connected with Myers Park Baptist Church and has served as chair of ministry of faith formation, deacon, leader of "Rumbling with the Word" Bible group, and a devoted enthusiast of pub theology. With over thirty years working in the world of elder care, she currently serves as parish administrator for St. Martin's Episcopal Church in Charlotte, North Carolina. Nancy thrives on trees, books, growing vegetables, deep questions, and conversations about God. She has been described as unconcerned with the surface of things and has lived a fulfilling life as a lesbian since 1984.

Rev. J. Andrew Daugherty is the senior pastor of Pine Street Church of Boulder, Colorado. He holds degrees in religion and theology from Belmont University and Wake Forest University Divinity School. He is most recently the co-author of *Hebrews*, a homiletical commentary. He has authored numerous articles and columns nationwide for such publications as *Huffington Post*, *Baptist News Global*, and *Boulder Daily Camera*. He is the co-host of *Hyphenated Life* podcast based in Boulder. He lives in the Denver-Boulder area with his two children, Addison and Aidan.

Susan Furr, PhD, is a professor in the Department of Counseling at the University of North Carolina at Charlotte. She is a licensed psychologist who worked in the Counseling Center at UNC Charlotte and now teaches in the Department of Counseling. Her areas of teaching interest include grief and loss counseling, crisis intervention, and group counseling with a focus on psychoeducational groups. Research interests include grief issues in substance abuse counseling, college student development, and issues around the development of counselors-in-training, particularly in the area of gatekeeping. She has held several positions in the North Carolina Counseling Association, including president. She is co-editor of the book Grief Work in Addictions Counseling and has published articles in areas such as suicide in college students, gatekeeping issues in counseling, and grief issues in addiction.

Everett C. Goodwin was most recently the senior minister of the Scarsdale Community Baptist Church in Scarsdale, New York. Prior to that, he was the senior minister of the First Baptist Church of the City of Washington, DC, and earlier he served as pastor of churches in Rhode Island and Connecticut. During 2013–2015, Dr. Goodwin was the interim senior minister of the Myers Park Baptist Church in Charlotte, North Carolina. He earned degrees at the University of Chicago (BA), Andover Newton Theological School (MDiv), and Brown University (PhD). Everett is the author of several books about Baptists and Baptist practices and has served in several leadership capacities in the ABC/USA, including several terms on the boards of the American Baptist Historical Society and the Baptist World Alliance and on boards of several of community service and ecumenical organizations. Since 2013, Everett has served as adjunct professor at the Wesley Theological Seminary in Washington, DC.

Reverend Dr. Bill J. Leonard is professor of divinity emeritus at the School of Divinity, Wake Forest University, where he was the founding dean. He holds degrees from Texas Wesleyan University, Southwestern Baptist Theological Seminary, and Boston University. He is the author or editor of twenty-five books, including *A Sense of the Heart: Christian Religious Experience in the U.S.* and *The Homebrewed Christianity Guide to Church History: Flaming Heretics and Heavy Drinkers*. He and his family are members of First Baptist Church, Highland Avenue in Winston-Salem, the oldest African American-founded Baptist congregation in the city (1879).

Barbara B. Lucas was born in Puerto Rico of American parents and moved to the United States as a young girl. She married Tom Lucas and moved to Charlotte over fifty years ago, where they raised their two children. Barbara served as director of a nonprofit counseling agency where she worked with marginalized people with many different types of problems. She and Tom love to travel and see how other societies are organized and work with their disadvantaged citizens. Barbara retired in 2011 and lives in an independent retirement home with Tom.

Mia M. McClain is an artist, pastor, and king cake lover. She currently serves as the associate minister of faith formation and community outreach at Myers Park Baptist Church in Charlotte, North Carolina. Originally from New Orleans, Mia went on to obtain a bachelor of fine arts in musical theatre from Syracuse University, a master of arts in art and public policy from New York University—Tisch School of the Arts, and a master of divinity with concentration in psychology, religion, and homiletics from Union Theological Seminary in the City of New York. A licensed Baptist minister and ordained in the United Church of Christ, Mia works to interrogate ideas of Blackness at the intersection of spirituality and performance in cultures founded in the African diaspora.

Ted Phillips has led a pub theology group in Charlotte, North Carolina, for seven years. The group meets about fifteen times per year, and he has led and facilitated more than one hundred topical discussions. Ted received his BA in psychology and religion from Carson Newman University, and a MEd in counselor education from the University of Virginia. Ted has served in a variety of church roles including as a deacon, member of the Theology of Worship Re-imagining team, member of the chancel choir and Motet Singers. He has presented on a variety of topics and has published an article "Burnout: Threat to our Greatest Resource." His hobbies include traveling, singing, landscaping, gardening, and developing his backyard into a Japanese garden that includes a Torri gate.

The Rev. Cody J. Sanders, PhD, is pastor to Old Cambridge Baptist Church in Cambridge, Massachusetts, where he also serves as American Baptist chaplain to Harvard University and adviser for LGBTQ+ Affairs in the Office of Religious, Spiritual, & Ethical Life at MIT. His books include *Christianity, LGBTQ Suicide, and the Souls of Queer Folk*; *A Brief Guide to Ministry with LGBTQIA Youth*; *Trouble the Waters: A Christian Resource for the Work of Racial Justice*, edited with Michael Ray Mathews and Marie Onwubuariri; *Microaggressions in Ministry: Confronting the Hidden Violence of Everyday Church*, with Angela Yarber; and *Queer Lessons for Churches on the Straight and Narrow*, which has been translated into Swahili and Japanese.

Rev. Dr. John E. Saunders Jr. has been a minister of education in two churches. He has served as congregational development director for two Baptist associations and as the director of missions for two Baptist associations. He has been married to his wife, Sally, for forty-two years, and they have two children and three grandchildren. Dr. Saunders is a graduate of Mars Hill College (BA) and the Southern Baptist Theological Seminary (MRE and EdD). He has taught at Boyce Bible School of the Southern Baptist Theological Seminary, Campbell University Divinity School, and the John Leland Center for Theological Studies. John and Sally currently reside in Salem, Virginia.

Charles (Chaz) Seale has worked with nonprofit organizations both domestically and around the world. Among Chaz's nonprofit endeavors were the founding of a national Alzheimer's support organization, state-wide children's mentorship programs, children's sports entities, and programs for at-risk youth and gang rehabilitation. He was guest lecturer in eleven Vietnam universities for seven years and served as chair or vice-chair for twenty-six years for endPoverty.org, an international Christian microenterprise organization. He is deeply involved with Myers Park Baptist Church, pub theology, and affordable housing with Mayfield Memorial Church. Chaz has worked within senior management for several of the country's most respected companies and has led a wide variety of smaller entrepreneurial companies. He is currently CEO of Billie Jean King's Eye Coach.

Margaret (Peggy) Anne Seale retired as a registered nurse to devote her life to her family, dedicate time to nonprofit work, work with her husband in children's organizations, and participate throughout her adult life in formal Bible study. Peggy has worked on the USC Norris Cancer Hospital Auxiliary's Board (Los Angeles), at the San Diego Children's Hospital Auxiliary, in hospice work, in Assistance League, in Women at the Well, and in volunteer positions for various churches. Her dedication to her Charlotte church, Myers Park Baptist, has allowed her to lead several ministries and participate wherever she's needed. She has been a participating member of pub theology groups for ten years.

H. Stephen Shoemaker received his MDiv from Union Theological Seminary in New York City and his PhD from the Southern Baptist Theological Seminary, Louisville, Kentucky. Among the churches he has served are Crescent Hill Baptist Church, Louisville, Kentucky; Broadway Baptist Church,

Ft. Worth, Texas; and Myers Park Baptist Church, Charlotte, North Carolina. He is now pastor of Grace Baptist Church, Statesville, North Carolina. He has written eight books, the most recent being *Seekers, Saints and Sinners* (2019), and has published numerous articles and sermons.

Rev. Dr. Oliver M. Thomas, a native of North Carolina, earned a bachelor of arts in political science from North Carolina Agricultural and Technical State University, a master of divinity from Wake Forest University School of Divinity, and a doctor of philosophy in educational studies with a concentration in cultural foundations from the University of North Carolina at Greensboro. Oliver is an ordained Baptist minister associated with American Baptist Churches USA; National Baptist Convention, USA, Inc.; and General Baptist State Convention of North Carolina, Inc. He has served Baptist and non-Baptist congregations as an associate pastor for young adult ministry, director of social justice ministries, and interim pastor. Simultaneously, he has taught high school, undergraduate, and graduate students. His primary research interest is exploring the intersection of Black liberation theology, critical pedagogy, and participatory democracy with a focus on educating student-citizens to critically engage their ecclesial, local, national, and global community as agents of social change.

www.ingramcontent.com/pod-product-compliance
Lightning Source LLC
Chambersburg PA
CBHW051641230426
43669CB00013B/2395